D1479146

MARX, TOCQUEVILLE, AND RACE IN AMERICA

MARX, TOCQUEVILLE, AND RACE IN AMERICA

The "Absolute Democracy" or "Defiled Republic"

August H. Nimtz, Jr.

LEXINGTON BOOKS
Lanham • Boulder • New York • Toronto • Oxford

LEXINGTON BOOKS
Published in the United States of America
by Lexington Books
An imprint of The Rowman & Littlefield Publishing Group, Inc.
4501 Forbes Boulevard, Suite 200, Lanham, Maryland 20706

PO Box 317
Oxford
OX2 9RU, UK

British Library Cataloguing in Publication Information Available

Library of Congress Cataloging-in-Publication Data

Nimtz, August H.
    Marx, Tocqueville, and race in America : the "absolute democracy" or
"defined republic" / August H. Nimtz, Jr.
        p. cm.
Includes bibliographical references and index.
    ISBN 0-7391-0677-5 (alk. paper) — ISBN 0-7391-0678-3 (pbk. : alk.
paper)
    1. Slavery—Political aspects—United States—History—19th century.
2. United States—Race relations—Political aspects. 3. United
States—Politics and government—1783–1865. 4. United States—Politics
and government—1861–1865. 5. Reconstruction. 6. Democracy—United
States—History—19th century. 7. Marx, Karl, 1818–1883—Political and
social views. 8. Engels, Friedrich, 1820–1895—Political and social
views. 9. Tocqueville, Alexis de, 1805–1859—Political and social
views. I. Title.
    E449.N76 2003
        320.973'01—dc21   2003009952

Printed in the United States of America

⊚™ The paper used in this publication meets the minimum requirements of
American National Standard for Information Sciences—Permanence of Paper
for Printed Library Materials, ANSI/NISO Z39.48–1992.

Contents

Preface

"Absolute Democracy" or "Defiled Republic"?
Marx, Tocqueville, and Race in America

Just when Republican Senator Trent Lott thought it was safe to publicly celebrate the "good old days" of Jim Crow, political reality rudely interrupted his nostalgic yearnings. Fresh from the gains his party made in the November 2002 elections he no doubt thought he had license to wax fondly about the bygone era of official racial segregation. The 100th birthday party for fellow Senator Strom Thurmond, Jim Crow's 1948 presidential standard bearer, seemed to be the perfect occasion. Lott was, after all, the most prominent product of the party's so-called "southern strategy." This was the line the Republican Party adopted in the 1960s to woo southern whites away from the Democrats with the not-too-subtle message that a White House and Congress in its hands would be sympathetic to their "way of life." The strategy seems to have worked given the increasing number of elected Republican officials in the South. But the Mississippi politician mistook successes in the electoral arena for the basic facts of American political life and his "faux pas" cost him dearly, his Senate Majority Leader post.

A few days after Lott's demise a *New York Times* article tried to put the affair in perspective. Racial segregation it correctly argued was not unique to the South. The North had, in fact, a long history of such practices. As evidence, the article cited the observation of Alexis de Tocqueville during his travels to the United States in 1831 and 1832: " 'The prejudice of race appears to be stronger in the states that have abolished slavery than those where it still exists.'"[1] What the French traveler suggests is that

vii

the oppression that Blacks faced in the North was unrelated to the peculiar institution in the South and that it made no difference to them where they lived; both parts of the country were equally repressive. Neither suggestion could be further from the truth.

Most problematic with Tocqueville's observation is the context from which it is taken, the last chapter of the first volume of his almost revered *Democracy in America*. Only there did he discuss the situation of Blacks in America. Tocqueville began with the bold assertion that the United States is an "absolute and immense democracy." As for the realities of the "Negroes," such "topics," Tocqueville continued, "are collaterally connected with my subject without forming a part of it; they are American without being democratic, and to portray democracy has been my principle aim."[2] Yet at that very moment, 1835, the year in which the book was published, the slave owners were consolidating their rule both regionally and nationally. For Tocqueville, racial oppression and chattel slavery were marginal concerns in his account of the U.S. political system. But the Lott affair revealed, if anything, just how central race is in a real understanding of America's political reality. To assume, then, as the editors of the *New York Times* evidently do, that Tocqueville can be employed to bring clarity to the politics of race in the United States is naive at best.

For Karl Marx, on the other hand, chattel slavery in the United States and what he called the "branding" of Blacks— their racial subordination—were key in understanding economic and political developments not only in America but worldwide. Shortly after arriving at his new communist worldview in 1844, the young Marx declared that Britain's industrial preeminence, specifically, its textile industry, was largely the product of slave labor, that is, cotton production in America's South. In the United States itself, he held—unlike Tocqueville—that the democratic quest had been hampered by the presence of the peculiar institution. This is just what his letter to Abraham Lincoln in 1864 emphasized. Addressing the president on behalf of the newly formed International Working Men's Association (the First International), Marx congratulated him on his reelection and the progress he was making in the

Civil War against the slave owners. Until the war, he wrote, "the working men, the true political power of the North, allowed [Negro] slavery to defile their own republic" and, thus, "were unable to attain the true freedom of labour."[3] Real democracy in America, Marx argued—what the editors of the *New York Times* could never acknowledge—required freedom for all working people.

America in the middle of the nineteenth century—the "absolute democracy" or the "defiled republic"? My basic argument is that Marx and his partner Frederick Engels had a far more accurate, and, thus, insightful, reading of democracy in the United States than Tocqueville because they understood that the overthrow of slavery and racial oppression were central to its realization. For Tocqueville, these were at best tangential issues having little to do with his portrait of American democracy.

I also intend to show how the grasp of "really existing" democracy in the United States by Marx and Engels played a crucial role in the conclusions they reached on the road to becoming communists. For Marx, Tocqueville's reading of the United States, I argue, served as a major foil for his political development. Marx and Engels were more accurate because—my second argument—of their method, what they called the "materialist conception of history." Rather than treating them as "mores" and customs, as Tocqueville did, slavery and racial oppression were fundamentally grounded in material reality—the exploitation of labor. Most importantly, the method employed by Marx and Engels informed their efforts to advance the democratic struggle in the United States, actions which, I hope to demonstrate, were not inconsequential. As communists, Marx and Engels recognized that theoretical and political insights were useful only if acted upon. They profoundly understood that they had to actively put into practice what they wrote and to learn from practice what to write—a modus operandi that today's progressives would do well to emulate. Finally, their superior reading, I also argue, allowed them to more accurately anticipate the course of American democracy, even up to the present. The two very different perspectives of Marx and Tocqueville are at the heart of the debates about race and democracy in America today, as I posit in the conclusion.

I begin in chapter 1 with Marx's appreciation of the American reality and compare and contrast it to what Tocqueville had to say. It is here that I make the case for my claim that Marx's reading of the accounts of Tocqueville and others about the United States was crucial in his route to communism. If America was the best that liberal democracy had to offer, then clearly, more was required to realize what the young Marx called "true" or "real" democracy. Hence, I challenge the oft-made claim that "Marx never integrated America into his account of the world-historical future of capitalism."[4]

In chapter 2, I show how Marx and Engels's class-analytic perspective informed their efforts to bring about "real democracy" and contrast their practice to that of Tocqueville. The specific focus is on the activities they and their co-thinkers in the United States carried out leading up to the Civil War to assist the struggle against slavery. Chapter 3 details the practice of the "Marx party," as it came to be known, during the war on both sides of the Atlantic. This is the period when Marx was clearest and most explicit about the necessity of ending racism against Blacks, or as he called it, the "branding" process, in order for "labor to emancipate itself"—the prerequisite for "real democracy."

Chapters 2 and 3 highlight perhaps the most striking difference between the Marx-Engels team and Tocqueville. While the latter may be better known for his writings about the American democratic experience, Marx and Engels did more to make democracy a living reality.[5] In chapter 4 I look at the period after the Civil War known as Reconstruction, the most democratic opening in U.S. history prior to the outcome of the civil rights movement of the twentieth century—and Marx and Engels's response to it. I then turn to the overthrow of Reconstruction and their response to this landmark defeat. I end the chapter by discussing the relevancy of their perspective on the subsequent course of developments in the aftermath of this historic triumph of reaction over the democratic quest. In the conclusion, I assess the Marx-Engels perspective in relation to that of Tocqueville in the context of the Second Reconstruction—politics in the United States today—and speculate on the likelihood of a solution to the supposedly insoluble "race question."

Throughout the book, but especially in the first two chapters, I hope to demonstrate that the claims of the Marx-Engels team, rather than those of Tocqueville, are more in accord with the findings of current scholarship about sociopolitical developments in America not only before, but after the Civil War. I do so because the accurate representation of social reality was the premise upon which Marx and Engels operated. Tocqueville, it appears, functioned in a similar fashion. It's not enough, in other words, to subject the writings of all three to the time-worn method of textual analysis. The best that modern research has to offer on the events and processes about which they wrote must be employed for a full assessment of their work. This book is, thus, a conscious effort to rescue not only Marx and Engels, but Tocqueville as well, from the clutches of those who labor primarily in the realm of "texts." An appendix is included in order to critique in detail a recent work that claims to put in doubt Marx and Engels's democratic credentials in their intervention in U.S. working-class politics after the Civil War. In the process, I excavate their views on the "woman question."

I have argued elsewhere that Marx and Engels's perspective and politics can only be fully comprehended in time.[6] No two political theorists and activists were as conscious of and driven by the "lessons of history" as they were. Tocqueville also subscribed, in some ways, to a "lessons of history" approach though less consciously and less systematically than Marx and Engels. This explains the chronological organization of the book. For the most part, I therefore resist the temptation to skip ahead or anticipate later findings and opinions of all the protagonists. In those occasional instances where I do so, such claims are my own, and neither rest on nor are refuted by such references. This also assures a fair comparison of Marx and Engels to Tocqueville, especially since the former outlived him by respectively twenty-four and thirty-six years and had the advantage of hindsight. The actual comparison is therefore limited to chapters 1 and 2, that is, the period before the Civil War when all three protagonists were alive.

An underlying assumption here is that Marx and Engels constituted a partnership with the same perspective. While there may have been nuanced differences between them on various questions—among the issues examined here, one proved in fact to be of significance—it is clear that in politics, the area that was most important for them, they spoke with one voice.

Finally, a comment regarding usage. I employ "Black" in referring to Americans of historical African origin but use "white" in designating Americans who trace their origins to Europe. The capitalization of the former, unlike the latter, is a recognition of the national character of Blacks, especially in the aftermath of the overthrow of Reconstruction—which I discuss in chapter 4. I recognize, of course, that social labels may not always accurately describe current realities. This is especially true for group identities, which are always moving targets. In the conclusion, I raise this possibility for what is sometimes today called "the Black community."

A number of people provided valuable contributions and suggestions in the writing of this book. It began as a conference paper and at that stage the comments of Bruce Baum and Laura Janara were especially helpful. Subsequent feedback from my political science colleagues at the University of Minnesota was largely responsible for my decision to turn the paper into a book-length manuscript. The questions that Lisa Disch raised were particularly useful in helping me to think through my argument. Paul Soper, Bill Scheuerman, Jeff Lomonaco, and Jorge Rivas also made comments that helped in the transition. I am still indebted to Mary Dietz's reading of a chapter from an earlier manuscript in which I compared the practice of Marx and Tocqueville during the revolutions of 1848.

More than anyone, it was David Roediger who made it possible for the manuscript to become this book. His enthusiastic review, which included many thoughtful comments and suggestions, is forever appreciated. I also want to thank the anonymous reviewer who, though more critical of my argument, thought the project should find its way into Lexington's list.

No one pushed me more to think about the political content of the book as much as Jon Hillson, with whom I've collaborated politically for almost three decades. As well, his most thorough editing of the manuscript was invaluable. If the book reads well, it's largely due to Jon's careful eye and editor's pen. The political conclusions reached in chapter 4 also benefited from discussions with

Chris Nisan. Finally, I thank the students who gave me substantive and editorial feedback in the final stages. The graduate students in the American Politics seminar taught by my colleague Jamie Druckman, spring 2003, posed stimulating questions. The undergraduate students in my Politics of Race, Class and Ethnicity course, also, spring 2003, and my teaching assistant, Eric Boyer, took seriously my request that they go over the manuscript with a fine-tooth comb. Notwithstanding all of this assistance, including that of Serena Krombach and her staff at Lexington, I am of course responsible for what finally appears in print.

Notes

1. Peter Applebome, "What Did We Just Learn?" *New York Times* 2002, December 22.
2. Alexis de Tocqueville, *Democracy in America*, Vol. 1 (New York: Vintage Books, 1945), p. 343. This is the edition edited by Phillips Bradley and the one cited here.
3. Karl Marx, "To Abraham Lincoln, President of the United States," Karl Marx and Frederick Engels, *Collected Works*, Vol. 20 (New York: International Publishers, 1985), p. 20. Hereafter, citations from the *Collected Works* will be designated by the volume as **20**, for example, and then the page(s).
4. Gopal Balakrishnan, "The Oracle of Post-Democracy," *New Left Review*, no. 13, Second Series (January–February 2002), p. 154. This is Balakrishnan's reading of Sheldon Wolin, *Tocqueville between Two Worlds: The Making of a Political and Theoretical Life* (Princeton, N.J.: Princeton University Press, 2001).
5. Mark Reinhardt's *The Art of Being Free: Taking Liberties with Tocqueville, Marx, and Arendt* (Ithaca: Cornell University Press, 1997) appears at first glance to resemble this project. Specifically, he subjects *Democracy in America* and a few texts of Marx, "On the Jewish Question," *The Communist Manifesto*, and the *Eighteenth Brumaire of Louis Bonaparte*, to what he calls "textual exercises." But nothing better illustrates the limitations of textual analysis for understanding Marx than Reinhardt's claim that his historical materialist method drove his "evasion of politics." This is a variant of an old and tired marxological fable that this book hopes finally to put to rest.
6. August H. Nimtz, Jr., *Marx and Engels: Their Contribution to the Democratic Breakthrough* (Albany: State University Press of New York, 2000).

1

Democracy in America
Two Perspectives

To understand Karl Marx and Frederick Engels's reading of the United States it would be useful to begin with an overview of their communist project, its origins and evolution—one which has often been misrepresented, particularly its democratic component. Like many German Rhinelanders of their generation—those who came of age politically in the aftermath of the French Revolution of 1789—they sought an answer to the most pressing political question of the day: how could Prussian authoritarianism be replaced by democratic rule and who or what segment of society would lead such a transformation? For the young Marx, working as a cub reporter in 1842 for the liberal daily *Rheinische Zeitung* (Rhineland Magazine), and frequently at odds with government censors, there were more specific questions. Why would a government deny its citizens such basic liberties as freedom of the press and free speech? Why are peasants and the poorer layers of society routinely disadvantaged in the political process? Why are the wealthy privileged?

Marx saw the need to return to Hegel, the intellectual mentor of his generation, who had drawn on the insights of the liberal economists James Steuart and Adam Smith to produce the best that Western thought had to offer on political theory and political economy. Standing on Hegel's shoulders, Marx soon recognized the inadequacies of this towering intellect, especially his disdain for "true democracy." It was precisely the quest to realize "true democracy—the sovereignty of the people," that motivated Marx to begin his lifelong inquiry into political economy.[1]

1

His inquiries pointed to the emergence and role of private property in social evolution, a development that reached its logical conclusions with the rise of the capitalist mode of production in the second half of the eighteenth century. Along with the alienation of individuals from one another, or the erosion of community, came the commodification of all of society including most of all human labor. Private ownership of the means of production, uniquely associated with capitalism, generated increasing inequality. The simultaneously unprecedented increase of wealth *and* poverty appeared as one of the most striking aspects of the new system of production for those who survived its arrival. The inequalities of previous class societies, those based on private property, began to pale in comparison.

Marx concluded as early as 1843 that as long as social inequality—class society—persisted, real democracy, the "sovereignty of the people," was impossible. His position was not unique. As C. B. Macpherson persuasively argues, almost all Western visions of democracy before the nineteenth century assumed a "classless or a one-class society, not merely a political mechanism to fit such a society."[2] Unlike other socialists and self-styled communists, Marx argued that the fight for social justice could not be successfully pursued unless it was linked to the struggle for democratic rights. Thus, the prerequisite for the socialist revolution was the democratic revolution—the conquest of political democracy, which provided the best terrain on which the oppressed could prepare itself for taking power and self-rule. As Hal Draper correctly notes, "Marx was the first socialist figure to come to an acceptance of the socialist idea *through* the battle for the consistent extension of democratic control from below. . . . [H]e was the first to fuse the struggle for consistent political democracy with the struggle for a socialist transformation."[3] Many years later, Engels acknowledged that it was the Chartists, the working-class fighters for democratic rule in England in the second quarter of the nineteenth century, who taught them about the importance of the political struggle.[4]

Based on his newly arrived at claim that the proletariat constituted the only class that had both the capacity and interest to realize the "sovereignty of the people"—to which his aforementioned letter to Lincoln alluded—Marx, now in partnership with Engels, provided the small communist tendency of the broader socialist movement for the first time an explicit program that clarified its relationship to the democratic struggle. Drawing on Engels's draft for the *Manifesto of the Communist Party*, Marx incorporated the essence of this position in its second section, "Proletarians and Communists": "the immediate aim of the Communists is the same as that of other proletarian parties: formation of the proletariat into a class, overthrow of the bourgeois supremacy, conquest of political power by the proletariat." The goal of this struggle, is as stated later in that section, "to win the battle of democracy."[5] For communists, the most "advanced" or "extreme wing," as they described it, of the "democratic party," the fight for political democracy is an essential task.

It must be stressed that in moving from radical democracy to communism Marx and Engels did not abandon the demand for the former. Marx polemicized in 1847 that, like the Chartists in Britain, the German proletariat, "can and must accept the *bourgeois revolution* as a precondition for the *workers' revolution*. However, they cannot for a moment accept it as their *ultimate goal*."[6] Clarity on this essential point distinguished communists from other democrats. As they stated repeatedly, political democracy was the best means for socialist transformation and, thus, had to be fought for and defended. When a critic charged in 1892 that Marx and Engels ignored forms of democratic governance, Engels retorted: "Marx and I, for forty years, repeated ad nauseam that for us the democratic republic is the only political form in which the struggle between the working class and the capitalist class can first be universalised and then culminate in the decisive victory of the proletariat."[7] The task now is to see more concretely how the two, particularly Marx, arrived at their conclusions about the relationship between democracy and communism.

The Lessons of the "Most Progressive Nation"

To reach such conclusions, Marx's new method required that he draw on, as he liked to call it, the "real movement of history." He emphasized, above all, the actual course of the democratization process in various settings and times. For him, the reality of the United States, "the most progressive nation," as he sometimes called it, provided the best example.[8] It was also, as he described in his notebooks some fifteen years later, a "country where bourgeois society did not develop on the foundation of the feudal system, but developed rather from itself . . . where the state, in contrast to all earlier national formations, was from the beginning subordinate to bourgeois society, to its production, and never could make the pretense of being an end-in-itself."[9] Though lacking a feudal base, what was so revealing for Marx was the fact that class inequality was quickly emerging there in the absence of a tradition of class inequality—a claim supported by modern scholarship to be discussed later. This offered crucial evidence for his thesis about the consequences of private ownership of the means of production.

What was the specific evidence about the U.S. reality that the young Marx drew upon to reach his communist conclusions? As the "most progressive nation" in the world, it was especially useful in his method of inquiry—the study of a "pure" case. "Naturalists seek by experiment to reproduce a natural phenomenon in its purest conditions. You do not need to make any experiments. You find the natural phenomenon of freedom of the press in *North America* in its purest, most natural form."[10] A year later in his critique of Hegel he addressed the issue of elections and suffrage. Though he made no explicit reference to the United States there is no doubt he had the United States in mind—then the country with the most democratic elections. But for Marx, it was a question "of the *extension* and greatest possible *generalisation* of *election*, both of the right to *vote* and the right to *be elected*."[11] To what degree the United States conformed to such a standard is an issue to be discussed shortly.

Marx's first sustained discussion of the U.S. political reality came at the end of 1843 in his two articles, "On the Jewish Question." Again, it must be emphasized that this was written during Marx's pre-communist years, or perhaps more accurately, en route to his communist "world view."[12] Some of his discussion about civil society and the state carried with them much of the "phraseology" of German philosophy. He admitted as much two years later in *The German Ideology*, the work that first presented his and Engel's historical materialist perspective.[13] Arguably the key text of this period, the central claim of the "Jewish Question"—notwithstanding its title—is that political liberation, or what would later be called liberal or bourgeois democracy, however much an advance for humanity, should not be mistaken for human emancipation.[14] To substantiate his argument, Marx drew on the reality of what was until then the two most advanced developments in political democracy, revolutionary France and the United States. As the *German Ideology* explained, "one has to 'leave philosophy aside'. . . one has to leap out of it and devote oneself like an ordinary man to the study of actuality, for which there exists also an enormous amount of literary material, unknown, of course, to the philosophers."[15] The U.S. "actuality" would provide the most insights.

Firstly, as he argued, it was in the United States that the "political state exists in its completely developed form . . . in its purity" because "the state ceases to adopt a *theological* attitude towards religion."[16] Yet, in that most "developed" state form religion was pervasive in society—"pre-eminently the country of religiosity." The "existence of religion is the existence of a defect"—because it promoted narrowness and sectarianism, alienating humans from one another, an earlier conclusion that Marx and the Left Hegelians had reached.[17] Thus, the U.S. case revealed that even in the most developed state such a "defect" could exist. The problem, then, was to be sought in the nature of the secular state, in its limitations and its own narrowness. This necessitated an interrogation not of religion but the state itself. The question in particular was why the secular state is not only inadequate for the achievement of but an obstacle to "human emancipation," or, as Marx explained, "the relation of political emancipation to human emancipation."[18]

It's worth noting that in his critique of religion Marx was actually arguing for freedom of religion—in this case, for Jews—especially since he wrote this shortly before his often misrepresented comment about religion being "the *opium* of the people." It makes clear that his critique wasn't part of a campaign to ban religion. Rather, it expressed his concern to know why such de-fective thinking persisted. The answer, he argued, and the moti-vation of his lifelong political economy project, was to be found in civil society, the basis of the secular state.

Secondly, Marx looked at the limitations of political emanci-pation in another arena—private property. Indeed, as revealed by laws in various U.S. states, the state might free itself of private property by banishing property qualifications in voting. But such a measure did not abolish private property, it "even pre-supposes it." The basis for the state's claims of universality, which comes with the banishment of property qualifications, rest on the existence of private property. The particularity of pri-vate property was, in other words, a necessary given for the uni-versality of the secular state. The state, therefore, "allows private property, education, occupation, to *act* in *their* way. . . . to exert the influence of their *special* nature. Far from abolishing these *real* distinctions, the state only exists on the presupposition of their existence."[19] As long as inequalities in wealth—as well as educa-tion and occupation—persisted, Marx noted, there would be in-equalities in access to the electoral process including the "right to be elected"—a reality of U.S. politics that obviously has deep roots. Again, the U.S. case revealed that "political emancipation is not human emancipation."

Thirdly, as the "most progressive nation" the United States, along with France, was where "the rights of man" existed in "their authentic form." But these rights were those of the citizen on the one hand and the individualistic man of civil society on the other. They did not, however, lead to real liberation as long as they were treated as uncritiqued givens. They rested on the erro-neous assumption that human fulfillment was based "not on the association of man with man, but on the separation of man from man" and the related claim that individualistic or "egoistic" man was the actual basis for society.

Real "human emancipation" could only be accomplished by rejoining individual and political man in every arena in daily life—citizen and man—merging his individual and social being as the realization of his real "species-being."[20] Marx set himself the task of trying to understand how the reintegration of the social and political being of humans could be accomplished. His critique of private property, the material basis of civil society's individualistic character, would soon lead him to a critique of capitalism and a program for its overthrow—the necessary step for human or, in later terms, social emancipation.

Finally, the United States revealed how "*money* has become a world power" even within the world of Christianity. Anticipating the even more blatant commodification of religion in today's America, Marx stated "in North America. . . . the *preaching of the Gospel* itself and the Christian ministry have become articles of trade, and the bankrupt trader deals in the Gospel just as the Gospel preacher who has become rich goes in for business deals."[21] Marx was describing one manifestation of what later historians called the "market revolution" of Jacksonian America—about which more will be said later.

While critical of the "most progressive nation," Marx made clear that "political emancipation is. . . . a big step forward," though not the "final form of human emancipation in general."[22] His acknowledgment of what had been achieved in North America—a necessary step on the road to real emancipation—was indeed sincere. If citizenship was limited because it represented only political emancipation, it's acquisition was not to be dismissed. In the *German Ideology*, again written within two years of the "Jewish Question" thus expressing the views of the communist Marx and Engels, they were clearly supportive of this advance. "The workers attach so much importance to citizenship, i.e., to *active citizenship*, that where they *have* it, for instance in America, they 'make good use' of it, and where they do not have it, they strive to obtain it. Compare the proceedings of the North American workers at innumerable meetings, the whole history of English Chartism, and of French communism and reformism," the two wrote.[23]

Later, when onetime ally Ferdinand Lassalle told Marx in 1862 that the "Yankees have no 'ideas'. . . . 'The freedom of the individual' is merely a 'negative idea,' etc.," he dismissed Lassalle's comment as "antiquated, mouldering, speculative rubbish."[24] The theoretical and therefore, political import of the U.S. case for Marx was that it revealed the best that "really existing" democracy had to offer. It was just such a conclusion that drove Marx to look beyond "political emancipation"—to reach communist conclusions.

Where did Marx obtain his evidence about the United States? How valid was it? He drew on three sources in the "Jewish Question" articles, one of which was Tocqueville's *Democracy in America*, published eight years earlier. Other than employing the latter to substantiate his point about the United States being "pre-eminently the country of religiosity," Marx did not make any other explicit reference to Tocqueville. He was informed by the writings of Tocqueville's travel companion to North America, Gustave de Beaumont (1802–1866) and secondarily Thomas Hamilton (1789–1842), an English writer.

Though Beaumont's work, *Marie or, Slavery in the United States* was a novel published in 1835, the same year as his companion's book—about a romance between a young Frenchman and mulatto woman doomed by the racial prejudices of the era— it contained highly informative appendices and notes about Blacks, Indians, women, religion, and other subjects. His data about religious life was the basis for Marx's observations about its role and character in U.S. society. In reference to the overall theme of his book—racism in the United States—Beaumont addressed in the foreword why his book might give the reader "different impressions" of the United States than Tocqueville's work. "The true reason is this: M. de Tocqueville has described the institutions; I myself have tried to sketch the customs. Now, in the United States, political life is far finer, and more equitably shared, than civil life [*la vie civile*, in original]. While men may find small enjoyment in family life there and few pleasures in society, citizens enjoy in the world of politics a multitude of rights."[25] This is revealing in that it suggests that Tocqueville, like Marx, also employed the civil-political society distinction. This might help explain why Tocqueville treated the reality of Blacks, Indians—and women also—as peripheral to his analysis of democracy. The apparent assumption that the U.S. political community could be explained without an examination of civil society or, more specifically, slavery—and vice versa—was exactly what Marx argued and fought against.

It might be argued that Beaumont's comment refers only to the first volume of *Democracy in America* and not to the second, published five years later, where the author addressed "customs" and "mores"—themes that properly belong to civil society. There is some merit to the retort but what Tocqueville does present is a very incomplete description of civil society. (Neither is it always clear, unlike the first volume, if Tocqueville is referring to U.S. or European realities.) Political economy, regarded then by many as the central component of civil society, is most undeveloped—an issue to be addressed later. Whatever the case, the reality of slavery, Blacks, Indians, and women is even more tangential to his concerns in the second volume.

Thomas Hamilton's two-volume travelogue, *Men and Manners in America*, was published two years before *Democracy in America* and *Marie*. Beaumont drew on it in his discussion of U.S. religious life.[26] Although the only explicit reference to Hamilton in the "Jewish Question" concerns electoral laws and the pervasiveness and commodification of religion, Marx's extant notebooks indicate that he keenly read Hamilton—in all likelihood the first detailed account of the United States he had encountered.[27] There is much to suggest that it was Hamilton's reading of the United States that Marx prioritized for his assessment of the country and, by implication—if my argument about the impact of the U.S. reality on him is correct—played a decisive role in the communist conclusions he would later draw.[28] Again, the focus here is the pre-communist Marx who had not yet concluded that the proletariat was the truly revolutionary class. Precisely because he doesn't understand this phase in Marx's development, let alone his overall project, Seymour Lipset gratuitously claims that Marx, on the basis of the latter's reading of Hamilton, thought that socialism was on the U.S. political agenda as early as 1829.[29]

The focus here is only on what Marx noted and excerpted from Hamilton's work and what were some of the central claims Hamilton made about U.S. society. Aside from the above-mentioned references to Hamilton that Marx made, his notebooks excerpted other matters from the book. Among them were the details of Virginia's electoral laws, specifically, the fairly high property qualifications for who could vote and be elected—evidence for Marx about the limitations of the suffrage in what Hamilton called "the most democratic state in the Union."[30] Marx cited a discussion on public schools in New England including the interesting observation by Hamilton that their purpose was so that "every man. . . . shall qualify. . . . for a useful member of the State. No member of society can be considered as an isolated and abstract being, living for his own pleasure, and labouring for his own advantage."[31] Could this have been an inspiration for Marx's major argument about the desirability of rejoining egoistical and political man?

Lastly, there are the very important excerpts from Hamilton regarding class inequality and conflict in New York City and the activities of what was apparently the recently formed Working-men's Party, the first working-class party anywhere. These realities seemed to have escaped Tocqueville's observant eyes during his visit to the city at almost the same time, several months before Hamilton, in May 1831. Hamilton's observations were exactly the evidence that Marx could rely on to make his case about the limitations of "political emancipation."

The last point speaks to a central difference between Hamilton's entire book and *Democracy in America*, its greater attention to both the class and racial inequalities in the United States—while recognizing at the same time what had been gained in the way of political democracy. It's useful to note that his visit and book were prompted by the many claims being made in the newly reformed parliament in London about the wonders of U.S. democracy. While Tocqueville sought to see what Europe—France in particular—could learn from the U.S. experience, Hamilton came with a certain degree of skepticism about the United States as a model.

As for the class issue, Hamilton noted that it was the "Workies," as he called the Workingmen's Party—a tendency he was clearly leery of probably because they were in the forefront of the democratic impulse—that demanded "equal and universal education."

> It is false, they say, to maintain that there is at present no privileged order, no practical aristocracy, in a country where distinctions of education are permitted. . . . There does exist then—they argue—an aristocracy of. . . . knowledge, education and refine-

ment, which is inconsistent with the true democratic principle of absolute equality. . . . There are others who go still further, and boldly advocate the introduction of an AGRARIAN LAW, and a periodical division of property. These unquestionably constitute the *extreme gauche* of the Worky Parliament.[32]

Marx's above-cited comment about how the "state allows private property, education, occupation, to *act in their* way . . . to exert the influence of their *special* nature" may indeed have been inspired by the "Worky" program. It should be noted again that Marx wrote this before he had concluded that the proletariat would be the class to achieve the realization of real democracy and, thus, human emancipation. Thus, it may well be the case that the conclusions he would draw within a year and a half of writing the "Jewish Question" were profoundly influenced by what he learned from Hamilton. The latter had more to say not only about the Workies but other aspects of class inequality and tensions in the United States, along with the prospects for class struggle. Again, this is in sharp contrast to Tocqueville's account, which says virtually nothing about the growing workers' movement in the country.

The other major theme in Hamilton's account is its attention to racial inequality and the impact of slavery. Throughout both volumes he depicts the horrors of the institution and how it fostered racism beyond the slaveholding states. He rejected the views of the slave owners, with whom he discussed the issue, who claimed that they too favored abolition but were "slaveholders by compulsion alone." Hamilton dismissed their excuses. The abolition they wanted was "of a peculiar kind, which must be at once cheap and profitable . . . [to] enrich his master." The real reason slavery was maintained was that its end would "put a stop to the cultivation both of sugar and rice in the United States, and the compulsion of which the planters speak is the compulsion of money."[33] It was the "pecuniary interests" of the planters that explained its continuance. For Hamilton, material interests drove the "peculiar institution."

More than anything, Hamilton viewed slavery as an affront to the democratic claims of the country, a "national disgrace." He was especially appalled by what he saw in the nation's capital.

Washington the seat of government of a free people, is disgraced by slavery. . . . While the orators in Congress are rounding periods about liberty in one part of the city, proclaiming, *alto voce*, that all men are equal, and that "resistance to tyrants is obedience to God," the auctioneer is exposing human flesh to sale in another! [One day in Washington he remembered when] the members of this enlightened and August body [the Senate] were driven to the Capitol by slave coachmen, who were at that very moment waiting to convey them back, when the *rights of man* had been sufficiently disserted on for the day. . . . [T]hat slavery should exist in the district of Columbia, that even the footprint of a slave should be suffered to contaminate the soil peculiarly consecrated to Freedom, that the very shrine of the Goddess should be polluted by the presence of chains and fetters, is perhaps the most extraordinary and monstrous anomaly to which human inconsistency—a prolific mother—has given birth.[34]

The reality of Washington helped to explain what he also took note of—the disproportionate influence of the slavocracy in the national government. As for the future of the peculiar institution: "To suppose that slavery can long continue in this country when other nations shall have freed themselves from the foulest stain which has ever polluted their humanity, is to contemplate a period when the United States will become a nuisance upon earth, and an object of hatred and derision to the whole world." And in anticipation of the Civil War, Hamilton proclaimed: "My own conviction is, that slavery in this country can only be eradicated by some great and terrible convulsion. The sword is evidently suspended; it will fall at last."[35] In no uncertain terms slavery for Hamilton had indeed made the United States into a "defiled republic"—what Marx would later note in his letter to Lincoln—and undermined any claims for it as a model of democracy. As will be seen shortly, this was clearly not the portrait that Tocqueville had painted.

Though none of this found its way into Marx's extant notebooks it's unlikely that it didn't influence his reading of U.S. democracy. For example, when he argued in the "Jewish Question" that even if the state was free of religious affiliation, religion could still have a hold on its citizens—the tendency to encourage narrowness and separation—it's likely that he had Hamilton's narrative in mind, particularly, his account (see below) of racial segregation in Protestant denominations.[36] Whatever the case, Hamilton's book, in combination with Beaumont's *Marie*, introduced Marx to the reality of race and slavery in the United States and doubtlessly was influential in his argument about the limits of political emancipation.[37]

Tocqueville's America

Although the only explicit reference Marx made to *Democracy in America* concerns the country's religiosity, it's instructive at this stage of my analysis, before turning to the communist Marx, to look more closely at Tocqueville. To start, how did the evidence from Hamilton and Beaumont that Marx employed in the "Jewish Question" and excerpted in his notebooks compare to what Tocqueville had to offer? Secondly, how did Tocqueville's account compare to what Hamilton had to say on the social inequality, race, and slavery issues discussed above? And finally, how did Tocqueville's conclusions about U.S. democracy compare to those of Marx?

Regarding the United States as "pre-eminently the country of religiosity," Tocqueville, as already noted, was one of Marx's sources for this characterization. "On my arrival in the United States the religious aspect of the country was the first thing that struck my attention," he stated. But what is most notable about Tocqueville's account is the relative lack of concrete evidence about U.S. religious life. His tendency instead was to make broad generalizations without supporting evidence. About the United States, for example, and no doubt betraying his admitted pro-Catholic sympathies, "they,"—the Catholics—"constitute the most republican and the most democratic class in the United States."[38] Or, in regard to Christians in general, "They are not hostile to anyone in the world. . . . they love their contemporaries while they condemn their weaknesses and lament their errors."[39]

To appreciate the reality of religion in the United States, Marx turned to Beaumont and Hamilton. The picture they presented was more complex than Tocqueville's portrait and revealed that all was not as brotherly as he suggested. Hamilton was critical, for example, of the racial practices of Protestants. "No white Protestant would kneel at the same altar with a black one. He asserts his superiority everywhere, and the very hue of his religion is affected by the colour of his skin."[40]

Beaumont cited Hamilton's observation, possibly because it praised, he wrote, the Catholic Church for including "worshipers of all colours and classes" in their services—the basis, perhaps, for Tocqueville's claim about Catholicism's democratic and republican credentials. Beaumont also provided details on Christian sectarianism, particularly *"l'hostilité des protestants contre les catholiques; la seconde est l'hostilité de toutes les sectes chrétiennes contre les unitaires."*[41] As a product and victim of Germany's long history of religious sectarianism, all of this no doubt struck a responsive chord with Marx. Religious sectarianism and the racial practices of Protestants to him were evidence of the "defect" of religion—again, the separation of humans from one another.

That Marx saw the need to cite Tocqueville only once doesn't mean, however, that he dismissed his account. On the contrary, a case can be made that Tocqueville's observations about U.S. religiosity played a key role in the conclusions Marx drew about the limits of its democracy. The major theme in Tocqueville's discussion on religion was how, in distinction to Europe, the separation of church and state actually increased the influence of Christianity. "In the United States religion exercises but little influence upon the laws and upon the details of public opinion; but it directs the customs of the community, and, by regulating domestic life, it regulates the state," Tocqueville wrote.[42] He believed the influence of Christianity was one of the "causes to maintain democracy" in the United States.

The reality that Tocqueville described in the United States led Marx to draw very different conclusions. To understand why it must be noted that in his prior writings, especially his critique of Hegel, Marx had argued that the problem in Germany, that of how to realize democracy, had to take into account the reality of civil society—humans in their social relations outside the state, such as the religious sphere. Tocqueville's insight about the consequences of the separation of church and state in the United States may indeed have been the basis for what Marx noted in *The Holy Family*, his first collaborative work with Engels and written about a year after the "Jewish Question": "religion develops in its *practical* universality only where there is no *privileged* religion (cf. the North American States)."

Marx continued, "in the developed modern state . . . the dissolution of *religion* by the abolition of the *state church*, to this proclamation of their civil death corresponds their most vigorous life, which henceforth obeys its own laws undisturbed and develops to its full scope."[43] Both statements are clearly consistent with Tocqueville's explanation for the flourishing of religion in the United States.[44]

Secondly, while Tocqueville saw the non-Christian as suffering from an "aberration of intellect,"[45] for Marx, it was the religious believer who was afflicted with a "defect." If Tocqueville thought that Christianity's regulation of "domestic life" sustained democracy because it regulated the state, Marx most certainly did not, as he argued in opposition to Hegel. Not only was religion a form of defective thinking, but—in anticipation of some feminist critiques of liberal democracy—"domestic" or "family life" for Marx meant the world of "patriarchal laws" which therefore made it "unfit . . . where it was a question of the *political* [i.e. democratic] state, of *citizenship*.[46]

In effect then, Tocqueville provided Marx with just the kind of evidence he needed to support his thesis about the limitations of a state-centered theory of democracy. If in the most democratic country in existence religious influence could not only persist but actually increase, then indeed political emancipation wasn't sufficient for human emancipation. Tocqueville's evidence and insight, therefore, allowed Marx to ground his thesis in a way he had not been able to until then—for Marx, a necessary step on the road to a communist perspective. What this suggests, then—perhaps a moment in the development of nineteenth century political thought not appreciated until now—is that Tocqueville served as an important foil for Marx's political development.

With regard to suffrage and related issues of private property and education, Tocqueville claimed that "universal suffrage has been adopted in all the states of the Union." Furthermore, it was "the most powerful of the causes that tend to mitigate the violence of political associations in the United States."[47] Another factor that helped to still the passions of the masses was that "in America there are no paupers. As everyone has property of his own to defend, everyone recognizes the principle upon which he holds it."[48] Regarding education, Tocqueville noted that access to formal education was very limited and varied from one part of the country to the other, the least available in the South and West. The "learned," he offered, are very "few." Yet, he "was surprised to find so much distinguished talent among the citizens and so little among the heads of government."[49] The most educated, evidently, were not privileged when it came to the political arena. For Tocqueville, an inveterate elitist, this was not admirable. " 'When the right of suffrage is *universal*, and when the deputies are paid by the state, it's singular how low and how far wrong the people can go,' he had noted in his diary."[50] An example of such an outcome was the election of Davy Crockett to the House of Representatives in 1828 from Memphis. If Crockett, probably the most popular figure in the country after Andrew Jackson, was a real hero for those wary of the increasingly elitist character of rule in the country, he was, for Tocqueville, someone " 'who has had no education, can read with difficulty, has no property, no fixed residence, but passes his life hunting, selling his game to live, and dwelling continuously in the woods. His competitor, a man of wealth and talent, failed.'" Tocqueville's diary account leaves little doubt about for whom he would have voted and his real opinion of universal suffrage.

As noted before, Hamilton's account made clear that contrary to Tocqueville's assertion, universal suffrage was not a norm; property qualifications were very much in force. His comments on education, however, were virtually in agreement with those of Tocqueville. These included the above-mentioned point about the low correlation between levels of education and occupation of political office. Most divergent were their treatments of the issue of class and social inequality. Tocqueville did not deny the existence of social inequality in the United States. With manufacturing came, he stated, "rich men," although "the class of rich men does not exist. . . .[they don't act as a] definite class."[51] But as is so often the case in Tocqueville's second volume—where he addressed such questions—it's not always clear if he referred specifically to the United States. Whatever the case he clearly feared that the acquisitive nature of U.S. society, especially that associated with the growing industrial revolution, would aggravate social inequality.[52] This was something Marx expected, "the effects of private property" acting "in their way."

At the same time, Tocqueville found that in the United States, "fortunes are scanty and insecure" and the "equality of conditions . . . prevents any [member of the community] from having resources of great extent."[53] His chapter in the second volume, "Influence of Democracy on Wages," is oftentimes insightful—it even mentions "the constant struggle for wages . . . between these two classes," i.e., "the workman" and "employer"[54]—but is not necessarily informed by the U.S. reality.

Thus, absent from Tocqueville's descriptions, especially in contrast to Hamilton, was the specificity of class conflict in the U.S. context. His overall tendency was to focus on the factors that mitigated its possible eruption. And since slavery, the most unambiguous expression of class inequality, was peripheral to his analysis of democracy, his forebodings about it centered at best on racial, not class conflict. In effect, Tocqueville didn't inform his reader about the class conflicts already underway in the United States, let alone prepare them to understand how those conflicts would actually advance the democratic struggle.

Tocqueville's cursory attention to the class question reflects a larger problem—the absence of any sustained discussion on the U.S. political economy, particularly industrial development. It's clear from his diary, notes, and travel schedule that he simply had little or no interest in the matter, not only in the United States but also in England, which he visited a few years later. "Beaumont also felt at a loss in trying to orient his friend [Tocqueville] where it was a 'question of political economy.'"[55]

This is in sharp contrast to his countrymen, Michel Chevalier, who traveled to the United States a couple of years later, for the same amount of time, and wrote extensively on the economic changes underway in the country. That the latter was a follower of the utopian socialist Claude Saint-Simon (1760–1825) was no doubt determinant. That Tocqueville, on the other hand, was largely ignorant of political economy of any variety was also determinant—in ways to be discussed later. Suffice it to note here the earlier observation, based on a comment by Beaumont, that political economy for Tocqueville appears to have been in the sphere of civil society and therefore, like race and gender, tangential to the concerns of *Democracy in America*. To the extent that he interested himself with economic matters in and beyond the book he came close to being a land determinist, believing that "[e]ssential political and psychological relationships in a society depended on the existing pattern of landholding."[56] The contrast with Marx, who would soon conclude that socioeconomic relations were central, couldn't be starker.

Although Tocqueville relegated the Black experience to the periphery, it's important to look at what he did have to say.[57] First, his views on Blacks can only be described as racist: "we are almost inclined to look upon him as a being intermediate between man and the brutes," Tocqueville claimed.[58] He betrayed, as well, an essentialist opinion of race relations: "wherever the whites have been the most powerful, they have held the blacks in degradation or in slavery; wherever the Negroes have been strongest, they have destroyed the whites: this has been the only balance that has ever taken place between the two races."[59] It's possible to dismiss such opinions on the grounds that they were representative of the times, which is partially true; it's not as if Hamilton was that much more progressive. However, there were others in France who proceeded Tocqueville who had far more enlightened ideas, specifically, Abbé Grégoire, the author of the well-known antiracist tract, *De la littérature des Nègres, ou, Recherches sur leurs facultés intellectuelles* (1810). In this polemic, he criticized Thomas Jefferson's thesis of Black racial inferiority. Tocqueville had to be familiar with Grégoire's views.[60]

As for his spin on slavery, Tocqueville is certainly more tentative than Hamilton. It's true that he considered that the free states were more "populous and prosperous" than the slave states. Neither did he defend the institution—"God forbid that I should seek to justify the principle of Negro slavery."[61] But in devoting as much time as he does to explaining why it would be almost impossible to get rid of the "peculiar institution" he comes close to being its apologist.[62] Perhaps this explains why his narrative, in comparison to Hamilton's, gives little or no sense of the horrors of servitude for the slaves themselves. Tocqueville noted that while the laws in the South were atrocious for slaves, the slavocracy, in fact, has "not . . . augmented the hardships of slavery; on the contrary, they have bettered the physical condition of the slaves."[63] His description of sugar-cane cultivation in Louisiana is strikingly at variance with Hamilton's. Tocqueville was impressed by how "exceedingly lucrative" it was for the slave owners—why it would be difficult to abolish—whereas Hamilton, upon visiting such a plantation, was struck by how it "was only carried on at an appalling sacrifice of life" for the slaves.[64] In providing a richly informed description of the depths of racial prejudice in the North—again, no doubt based on Beaumont's research—Tocqueville suggests that things were actually worse there for Blacks than in southern bondage.

Given the tone of his treatment, it's no surprise that, unlike Hamilton, there is no sense of outrage in Tocqueville's account about slavery. While he had no hesitation in asserting that Jefferson was "the most powerful advocate democracy has ever had," Hamilton saw Jefferson, the slave owner, as the embodiment of the "national disgrace."[65] It becomes obvious why *Democracy in America*, as well as Beaumont's *Marie*, "appear to have excited no hostility toward [the authors] . . . in the South. They caused no indignation among slaveholders."[66] Or, it's "no wonder that despite [Beaumont and Tocqueville's] condemnation of the principles and practices of slavery . . . their works on America furnished ample material for the spokesmen of the anti-abolitionists in France."[67] Neither is it surprising that a leading Black abolitionist "accused Tocqueville's writing of aiding 'the perpetuation of American slavery.'"[68]

With regard to slavery's future and that of the union, Tocqueville made a most telling comment about his methodology: "Slavery has not created interests in the South contrary to those in the North. . . . Slavery, then, does not attack the American Union directly in its interests, but indirectly in its manners."[69] The differences between the North and the South, in other words, were not to be sought in matters of political economy, as Hamilton suggested, but rather in "manners" and "habits"—theoretical premises about which more will be said shortly. If Tocqueville didn't anticipate a war between the states to be fought over the slave question, he was nevertheless pessimistic about the future of race relations in the country. Given the situation in the North, "I do not believe that the white and black races will ever live in any country upon an equal footing."[70] Hence, he predicted an all-out race war or the recolonization of Blacks back to Africa as the only outcomes to the conflict. Yet, in spite of his hedging, he was clearly opposed to slavery, but in typical Tocquevillian fashion he seemed more fearful of what it would take to bring it to an end—a lot of bloodshed. He doubted that such a price was worth the effort because "if liberty be . . . given . . . to the Negroes . . . they will before long abuse it."[71]

In contrast to Hamilton, Tocqueville failed to foresee the Civil War and its significance for the advancement of democracy. His foreboding about the coming carnage was sustained but clearly not in the way he thought. Because of his assumption about democracy's supposed fulfillment in the United States, it could never occur to him that war would be necessary to make real democracy a living reality. Thus, the absence of any discussion in his *Democracy in America* of the seven-year war that brought the democracy he so admired into existence. Since slavery, for him, was a collateral issue, he could only be pessimistic about what it would take to end it. Any struggle to abolish it would be a detraction from the democratic impulse rather than an advance for it. These, we'll see, were just the opposite of the conclusions drawn by Marx and Engels.

What most significantly distinguished Marx from Tocqueville—at this stage in the analysis—was the former's conviction that the vanguard example of the democratic movement was still very much a work in progress. Tocqueville's portrait, including his claim that the United States was the "absolute democracy," supplemented by those of Beaumont and Hamilton, revealed to Marx what remained to be done. The criteria he employed in reading Tocqueville, based largely on his critique of Hegel, allowed him to be more sober. Rooted on terra firma—the reality of the United States—Marx was now in a position to undertake the requisite inquiry to learn what it would take to realize real democracy, the "sovereignty of the people."

The most politically liberated society had taught that as long as private property—the fundamental underpinning of civil society—was in place then human emancipation, the rejoining of the social and political, was not possible. If there was now clarity on the diagnosis of the problem, then a prescription for its solution was in sight. This was the next stage in Marx's quest.

Only as a result of his political economy research in the next two years leading to what he and his new partner called their "materialist conception of history," would he be able to say in no uncertain terms that the overthrow of slavery was the necessary condition for full political emancipation—and thus, eventually, human emancipation—not only in the United States but in Europe as well. Again, the conclusions Marx reached in 1843 about the limitations of the U.S. polity, based in part on his reading of Tocqueville, were a necessary step in the position he would soon take on the peculiar institution.[72]

The Judgement of Recent Scholarship: A Balance Sheet

How has Tocqueville's portrait of U.S. democracy stood up to the test of modern scholarship? What about the conclusions that Marx reached? To be clear, the comparison at this time is their differing assessments of Jacksonian America, the period which informed *Democracy in America*, as well as the texts of Beaumont and Hamilton. This was the historical moment, based on these texts, that informed the young Marx en route to communism in making his earliest claims about the United States.[73] In subsequent chapters, especially 2 and 3 and the appendix, I will subject Marx and Engel's views about developments leading up to and after the Civil War to the same kind of scrutiny.

Perhaps what testifies best—for the purposes of this book—to Marx and Engels's accomplishments in the next two years is that their historical materialist perspective, and not Tocqueville's analysis, served as the framework for what is now considered to be the definitive account of the period, Charles Sellers's *The Market Revolution: Jacksonian America, 1815–1846*, published in 1991. Sellers notes at the outset that his study is informed by "the most powerful conceptual tools for understanding America's central transformation," namely, the perspectives of Marx and Engels.[74] The central theme of his work is that the Jacksonian period can best be understood as one engulfed in a gigantic class struggle between what he calls, on one side, the "developmentalist capitalist" forces and, on the other, the array of "patriarchal republicans." The former constituted those who were prepared to employ and expand an activist state to put in place the requisite institutions and infrastructure to promote a capitalist mode of production. The latter embodied the Jeffersonian ideal of the small, rural, white male property owner.

A particular strength of Sellers's work, and more relevant for present purposes, is that it treats the religious ferment underway in the country that Tocqueville and Beaumont reported on as a key component of the anti-developmentalist coalition in all of its contradictory manifestations. As Sellers demonstrates, there was a deep reactionary side to the second "Awakening," one that exhibited the kind of defective thinking that Marx associated with religion. Sellers shows how all of this was reflected in the political realignments of party politics. With Jackson as its titular leader, the coalition sought to put a halt to the market revolution engineered by the "developmentalists." At stake was not just the country's heart and soul but its very direction: would it become a full-fledged and, later, advanced capitalist country with all that implied for class formation, or the agrarian republic in the image of Jefferson. The outcome, of course, was victory for the developmentalists. But as Sellers, pointedly concludes, on the eve of the Civil War, "market revolution made slavery the great contradiction of the liberal American republic."[75]

The portrait that Sellers paints is quite different than that of Tocqueville. It isn't the case that the latter necessarily misrepresented reality but provided a description that was totally incomplete. With his almost exclusive focus on what Beaumont described as the political "institutions," Tocqueville offers at best a snapshot—full of errors—that lacks a sense of the big ferment underway that Sellers describes or the seismic forces that drove the "great contradiction." What Tocqueville presents are political institutions, minus the driving force of the politics of civil society. Little wonder that much of modern political science analysis finds Tocqueville so attractive.[76]

In contrast, there is the even more incomplete evaluation by Marx—again, on the road to communist conclusions—but one whose outlines anticipates Sellers. Though the historical materialist assumptions of his analysis—particularly, the tensions and conflicts between different modes of production—would take Marx and Engels two more years to formulate, the attention that Sellers gives to the religious tumult underway in Jacksonian America is exactly what Marx honed in on while reading Tocqueville, Beaumont, and Hamilton. He already grasped, unlike Tocqueville, that religiosity, religious conflict and sectarianism reflected more fundamental aspects of civil society that political institutions alone couldn't explain. It was indeed this realization that led him to an examination of, as he would later explain, the "anatomy of civil society," that is, political economy. Two years later, the "new world outlook" of historical materialism would emerge.

Bruce Levine's *Half Slave and Half Free: The Roots of Civil War*, published in 1992, a year after Sellers's book, covers similar terrain but fleshes out the details of the "great contradiction" that the latter concludes with. As the title indicates, Levine's masterly synthesis of extant research argues that the Civil War was the result of "two antagonistic systems of social organization." Consistent with Marx's historical materialist perspective, he demonstrates convincingly that the "distinctive ways in which North and South organized their labor systems left their mark on all aspects of regional life—including family, gender, and leisure patterns and both religious and secular life. Such cultural changes, in turn, deeply influenced political life."[77]

Tocqueville, it may be recalled, didn't view the differences between the North and South in their political economies but rather in "manners" and "habits." The latter, for Tocqueville, appear to have an independent existence. For Levine they are the product of the two very different systems of production.

More recently, Anthony Gronowicz's *Race and Class Politics in New York City before the Civil War* verifies at the local level many of the developments that Sellers and Levine describe nationally, but with the added emphasis on race. Gronowicz proves that previous research on the period, especially, Sean Wilentz's classic study, *Chants Democratic*,[78]—that tried to explain the class struggle without taking into account race and racial slavery—was woefully inadequate. While Tocqueville also slighted the effects and dynamics of chattel bondage in his account—that he spent time in New York during his visit is noteworthy—for Gronowicz they are central in understanding the city's politics in the Jacksonian era.

The limitations of the workers's movement prior to the Civil War on the race and slavery questions, what Gronowicz focuses on and what Sellers in part means by the "contradictions" of the anti-developmentalist coalition—"patriarchy, racism, and fee-simple property"[79]—is exactly what Marx alluded to in his 1864 letter to Lincoln. More completely, he wrote: "While the working men, the true political power of the North, allowed slavery to defile their own republic; while before the Negro, mastered and sold without his concurrence, they boasted it the highest prerogative of the white-skinned labourer to sell himself and choose his own master; they were unable to attain the true freedom of labour or to support their European brethren in their struggle for emancipation." Or, as he put it in *Capital* three years later: "In the United States of America, every independent movement of the workers was paralysed so long as slavery disfigured a part of the Republic." As long as the movement of free labor, therefore, failed to fight for the liberation of bonded labor but rather "boasted" of what David Roediger calls the "wages of whiteness," its own struggle against the "developmentalists" could never succeed. The details of Gronowicz's work will be examined in chapter 3.

As for the many specific claims in *Democracy in America*, there exists a fairly extensive body of literature that severely questions

Tocqueville's portrait. Edward Pessen's book, *Riches, Class, and Power before the Civil War*, remains the most detailed and exacting challenge. Its purpose was "to determine the extent to which" the claim that Jacksonian America was an "era of the common man," whose "chief architect . . . was Alexis de Tocqueville," is actually "borne out by the evidence."[80]

Pessen subjected key claims in Tocqueville's work to empirical data. Regarding Tocqueville's assertion that the "equality of condition" in the United States prevented any of its citizens "from having resources of great extent," he concluded: "The notion that antebellum America lacked substantial fortunes is not borne out by the evidence, primarily, as will be noted, because of its faulty assumption concerning the alleged distribution of 'resources to all members of the community.'"[81] The data also questioned Tocqueville's most basic claim about "the general equality of condition among the people." Facts "establish that increasing inequality rather than equality was a central theme of American life during the 'era of the common man.'"[82] As to the claim that the wealthy were not involved in the country's governance, the data suggested otherwise: "the more affluent classes and 'those who carried on the business of the country' had a great deal of influence over the government of the nation's cities during the second quarter of the nineteenth century. . . . [to the contrary] the rich appear to have been a true 'governing class.' Despite his possession of the suffrage, the common man had little influence, let alone power, in the nation's cities during the era named in his honor."[83] In general, the young Marx would not have been surprised at Pessen's findings given the position he had reached earlier about the "effects of private property . . . to act in their way."

As for the suffrage question, Alexander Keyssar purports to contest in his recent work the supposed finding—whose "most well-known early celebrant" was Tocqueville—that "the history of suffrage," at least in the United States, "is the history of gradual, inevitable reform, and progress." He presents overwhelming evidence that this was simply not the case. Tocqueville's specific claim that "universal suffrage has been adopted in all the states of the Union" was patently false, not only for women, non-slave Blacks, migrants, the poor, and felons but also for significant numbers of working-class white males at the time of *Democracy in America*'s publication in 1835. While it is true that the latter acquired, on average, more access to the vote before their cohorts in Europe did, Keyssar shows convincingly that they did so prior to becoming members of the working class as small farmers or petty artisans. The "critical fact," he concludes, is "that the reforms of the antebellum era were not designed or intended to enfranchise a large, industrial, and partially foreign-born working class."[84]

Levine also disputes Tocqueville's mantra about the equality of condition in the non-slave owning areas of the United States. He begins chapter 2 with a quote from Tocqueville to this effect and then systematically presents evidence to the contrary. The particular focus is on increasing disparities in wealth and ownership of property from the inception of the republic to the Civil War. Levine presents data and opinions about U.S. social reality during the period of Tocqueville's visit that convincingly challenge his claim. He concludes with the bleak assessment made by Philip Hone in 1847: "Our good city of New York has already arrived at the state of society to be found in the large cities of Europe; overburdened with population, and where the two extremes of costly luxury and living, expensive establishments, and improvident waste are presented in daily and hourly contrast with squalid misery and hopeless destitution."[85] Tocqueville's description of the city in 1831 would not have prepared its readers for such an evolution.

Various retrospectives were made on the enduring value of the first volume of *Democracy in America* on the sesquicentennial anniversary of its publication. In 1985, a number of these were collected in *Reconsidering Tocqueville's Democracy in America*, edited by Abraham Eisenstadt. The volume brings together a number of distinguished scholars from various disciplines who subject Tocqueville to a critical review. To varying degrees they raise serious questions about his classic as an accurate portrayal of the reality he claimed to have described—criticisms that are elaborated on in the aforementioned works.

The most recent, and perhaps most well-known, challenge to Tocqueville's overall reading of the United States is the monumental effort of Rogers Smith's *Civic Ideals: Conflicting Visions of Citizenship in U.S. History*. Smith argues that the main problem with the Tocquevillian interpretation is that it focused only on the "political life" of the United States, which appeared "remarkably egalitarian in comparison to Europe."[86] Such an interpretation tends to ignore the "array of fixed, ascriptive hierarchies" throughout the history of the country—especially, the subordination of women, Native Americans, and Blacks—the painstaking details of which is the substance of his tome. The title of chapter eight, "High Noon of the White Republic: The Age of Jackson, 1829–1856," leaves little to the imagination. Smith describes—in great detail—how the country that Tocqueville visited in 1831–1832 was in the process of creating a democratic republic that excluded nonwhites. "If ever an era fit [an] account in which racist, nativist, and patriarchal views structured American political development and conflicts as fully as liberal republican ones, this is it."[87]

Smith's critique, nevertheless, is fundamentally within Tocqueville's own framework. Like the latter, his is the "political cause of liberal democracy."[88] What he faults Tocqueville and his modern day followers for is ignoring the existence of the "White Republic" for most of the country's history and failure for not advocating a more inclusive liberal democracy. The young Marx would have argued, on the other hand, that even if the ascriptive hierarchies had been dismantled, the liberal democratic polity would still have been inadequate for the task of human emancipation.[89] Given his affinities with Tocqueville, it's no accident that as comprehensive as Smith's case is it is devoid of what Marx considered crucial, the undemocratic impact of private property on the political process—in other words, the class question. I will critically revisit Smith's thesis in the conclusion.

Finally, there is Michael Goldfield's recent book, *The Color of Politics: Race and the Mainsprings of American Politics*, an inquiry also informed by Marx and Engels's perspective.[90] His main interest is the historical interaction between race and color in the United States. In the process he draws on a number of their observations, some of which have been quoted earlier. Much of what Goldfield has to say will be addressed in subsequent chapters. Suffice it to note here that with facts and figures he is able to show convincingly that there was in the United States in the decades leading up to the Civil War—the Jacksonian era, and contrary to what Tocqueville suggested—a national ruling class profoundly tied to wealth, whose economic base was slavery.

In sum, then, modern and current scholarship challenges, successfully in my readings, the portrait Tocqueville painted of Jacksonian America and sustains the incipient class analytic perspective of the young Marx. As a last piece of evidence for this claim, a case can be made that Marx offered a convincing explanation why Tocqueville's interpretation of the era misses the mark. To do so requires an appeal to Marx the communist, who was now armed with his historical materialist framework.

In a letter to Joseph Weydemeyer in New York in 1852, Marx observed: "in the United States bourgeois society is still too far immature for the class struggle to be made perceptible and comprehensible."[91] He was referring, specifically, to the preeminent economist in the United States, Henry Carey, and the limitations of his analysis, but his comment could just as well have applied, and even more justifiably, to Tocqueville, whose work was based on observations made two decades earlier.[92] There was a striking similarity between their views. Both saw class conflict as relevant only in the European setting and certainly not in the United States, which lacked a feudal legacy. If, as Marx suggests, that it was difficult to see the class struggle in 1852, then for Tocqueville in 1831, before the "developmentalist coalition" had consolidated its rule, it was even harder.

Marx's observation is valid but it begs other questions; why was Hamilton able to be sensitive to the incipient class struggle in the United States and Tocqueville not? To employ the mature Marx again and his own experience, which he himself acknowledged, it was not until he went to the homeland of Hamilton in 1845—the site of the most advanced capitalist country, Britain—that he fully appreciated the industrial revolution then well underway. It was no accident that it was Engels, who had spent two years in Manchester, in the entrails of the industrial revolution, who led Marx to study political economy.

Tocqueville, owing to his class and national origins—the relatively underdeveloped character of France vis-à-vis Britain—had too many feet in the past to be fully cognizant of what was underway in the United States. Hamilton was located in a framework of the most advanced developments. As noted earlier, Tocqueville had difficulty interesting himself in political economy. Even in his first trip to England in 1833 his "interest . . . was in castles and landed estates rather than its factories and railroads."[93]

Neither did Tocqueville's intellectual ancestry prepare him to grasp what was unfolding. Marx believed that his contributions were based on the pioneering work of intellectual giants like David Ricardo, Adam Smith, and James Steuart, as well as Hegel, none of whom Tocqueville, as far as can be determined, had been exposed. To the extent that Tocqueville was informed by a theoretical presupposition, it was—as he stated in the introduction to his work: "The gradual development of the principle of equality is, therefore a providential fact"—a claim that he repeated in prefaces to subsequent editions of his book.[94] Divine intervention, in the final analysis, was the explanation for what he claimed to have found in the United States. In a letter to John Stuart Mill in 1836, he described himself as a " 'new kind of liberal,' seeking to base a stable civic culture not upon a materialistic individualism but upon a socially integrating religion."[95] What this revealed, as Seymour Drescher correctly argues, is that Tocqueville lacked a "systematic theory of social change."[96] For Marx, the appeal to religion as a foundation for a philosophical, methodological, or political perspective was exactly the kind of defective thinking that he criticized in Hegel and to which he sought an alternative. That Christianity for Tocqueville was the only valid religion—Islam and Hinduism certainly weren't— was further evidence for Marx of the paucity of thought that religion fostered, expressing itself in all forms of sectarianism.[97]

Having said this, I am fully aware of Tocqueville's subsequent travels to Britain and the impact it had on him. But this raises another interesting question. Why didn't he address in introductions to later editions of *Democracy in America* any reflections on new ideas or changes under way in the United States, which he no doubt followed? Marx and Engels often used prefaces and introductions to new editions of their works to revisit claims based on new developments or new data. That Tocqueville did utilize the occasion of the twelfth edition of his work in 1848, in the aftermath of the revolutionary upheavals in France and elsewhere in Europe, to acknowledge the "sudden and momentous . . . events'" revealed that he could indeed be conscious of the times in which each edition appeared. Not only did he *not* recognize the need to rethink anything about his analysis but he advocated even stronger for the United States as a model for Europe.

What the preceding suggests is that in addition to the inadequacies and defects of his framework, there was another dimension of Tocqueville that figured significantly in the image he drew of the United States—his own political core, his most basic political instincts. Like Marx and Engels, Tocqueville, too, was the product of the French Revolution, perhaps even more so than Marx and Engels.

But just as Stalinism in the aftermath of the Bolshevik revolution left for some doubts about the desirability of revolutionary overturns, the Terror in France had performed the same function for many in the aftermath of its Revolution. Tocqueville, owing to his class origins, was a victim of the Revolution and a prime example of such sentiment. The guillotine had taken its toll on his own family. Thus, his particular spin on the United States—the realization of democracy without a revolutionary struggle—that has many latter-day adherents. While the drive toward equality was, as he argued, inexorable, his story of the United States showed that it could be forged without revolutionary intervention by the masses.

As Europe erupted in revolution in 1848, beginning in France in February, he urged the European readers of the latest edition of his book to look to the United States as the embodiment of democratic governance. "The institutions of America . . . ought to be a subject of study for republican France. It is not force alone, but good laws that give stability to a new government. After the combatants comes the legislator; the one has pulled down, the other builds up," he wrote. And in recognition of the revolutionary situation he had to face—for a truncated time hopefully—"each has his office."[98] The belief that the legislative arena and not the streets was the center of politics is what Marx and Engels soon came to call—on the basis of practical experience with individuals who held views similar to those of Tocqueville—"parliamentary cretinism."

Nothing better captures Tocqueville than this admission in a self-reflective moment sometime between 1839 and 1841:

> 'My mind is attracted by democratic institutions but I am instinctively aristocratic because I despise and fear mobs. At the most fundamental level, I passionately love freedom, legality, respect for rights, but not democracy. I hate demagoguery, the disordered action of the masses, their violent and unenlightened intervention in public affairs. . . . I belong neither to the revolutionary nor the conservative party. But, when all is said and done, I incline towards the latter rather than the former because I differ from the conservatives over means rather than ends, while I differ from the revolutionaries over both means and ends.'[99]

This suggests that Tocqueville was not incapable of seeing what Marx and Engels anticipated and later explained, and is now verified by current scholarship—U.S. class formation and conflict in the making. His second volume, published in 1840 five years after the first tome, clearly saw the possibility for such a messy reality since it was already underway in Europe. But the political conclusions he would have had to draw—the need for a revolutionary mass movement to prevent Sellers's "developmentalists" and all that Tocqueville despised about them from establishing their hegemony—went against his political grain. The Revolution and the Terror had cast too long a shadow over him. Tocqueville's disposition reminds one of the individual that Frederick Douglass had in mind in his oft-quoted speech on the eve of the Civil War: "Those who profess to favor freedom, and yet deprecate agitation, are men who want crops without plowing up the ground." Perhaps it was his fundamental dislike for the plow of mass struggle that led Tocqueville to overstate the size of the harvest that he so desired, without sweat, blood, and all that accompanies the "disordered action of the masses."

Marx and Engels's political core was just the opposite of Tocqueville's. They reveled in the fight. They were heartened whenever the oppressed anywhere went into motion against their oppressors. Sheldon Wolin, in his new book on Tocqueville, is right to say that in contrast to the latter, "Marx thought of politics as a form of combat." But the remainder of the comparison is invidious. To posit that "Tocqueville might be the last influential theorist who can be said to have truly cared about political life" and that "[f]ew of his contemporaries did," is dead wrong.[100]

There was nothing in Marx's life, nor that of Engels, to suggest that either "truly cared about political life" any less than Tocqueville. But what he and his partner understood and the latter could not fathom was that "caring" wasn't enough. Combat is at the heart of class politics—on either side of the barricades. The question is whether one is willing to put in the requisite time, energy, and sacrifice to join the battle. History revealed that Tocqueville was not so disposed while Marx and Engels were, and single-mindedly so. The excerpt from Douglass's aforementioned speech could easily have been authored by either of them. Exactly because they sincerely believed, like Douglass, that "If there is no struggle there is no progress," they understood in their bones what it would take to bring about real democracy in the United States—the subject to which we now turn.

Notes

1. For details on Marx's political evolution at this stage see my *Marx and Engels: Their Contribution to the Democratic Breakthrough* (Albany: SUNY Press, 2000), chapter 1.

2. C. B. Macpherson, *The Life and Times of Liberal Democracy* (Oxford: Oxford University Press, 1977), p. 10.

3. Hal Draper, *Karl Marx's Theory of Revolution*, Vol I. (New York: Monthly Review Press, 1977), p. 59.

4. **27**, p. 405.

5. **6**, pp. 498, 504. In the catechismic style of his draft, Engels wrote, in reply to the question, "What will be the course of this [proletarian]

revolution?": "In the first place it will inaugurate a *democratic constitution* and thereby, directly or indirectly, the political rule of the proletariat" (**6**, p. 350).

Hal Draper, *The Annotated Communist Manifesto* (Berkeley: Center for Socialist History, 1984), pp. 175–77, makes a convincing case that unlike Engels in his draft, Marx was deliberately vague in his usage of "democracy" here and in other passages in the *Manifesto*, mainly because he was not as clear as his partner on the role of the democratic struggle in the transition to socialism. Within a year, however, he had clearly embraced Engels's position.

    6. **6**, p. 333.

    7. **27**, p. 271.

    8. **38**, p. 102.

    9. Karl Marx, *Grundrisse* (Middlesex, England: Penguin Books, 1973), p. 884 (hereafter, *Grundrisse*).

    10. **1**, p.167. Marx wrote this in 1842. Note the similarity to what he said twenty-five years later in the preface to *Capital* about his reason for beginning the inquiry with the analysis of the commodity: "in the analysis of economic forms neither microscopes nor chemical reagents are of assistance. The power of abstraction must replace both. But for bourgeois society, the commodity-form . . . is the economic cell-form," or, later, "its elementary form." *Capital*, Vol I. (New York: Penguin, 1977), pp. 90, 125. The commodity, in other words, as the "pure case" for understanding of capitalism.

    11. **3**, p. 120.

    12. This crucial fact about Marx's writings in this period is exactly what Seymour Lipset ignores or doesn't understand in his clumsy effort to challenge Marx's understanding of the U.S. reality. See his "Why No Socialism in the United States?" *Radicalism in the Contemporary Age*, eds. Seweryn Bialer and Sophia Sluzar (Boulder, Colo.: Westview Press, 1977). More about Lipset's legerdemain later.

    13. For a most informative discussion on Marx's usage of "civil society" see Jan Rehmann, " 'Abolition' of Civil Society?: Remarks on a Widespread Misunderstanding in the Interpretation of 'Civil Society,' " *Socialism and Democracy* 13, no. 2 (fall–winter 1999).

    14. Draper's discussion of the articles and their context is first rate as well as his appendix, "Marx and the Economic-Jew Stereotype," which convincingly disputes the anti-Semitic charge often directed at the work (*Karl Marx's Theory of Revolution*, Vol. 1, respectively, chapter 5 and pp. 591–608). Gary Teeple's reading of the two articles in *Marx's Critique of Politics: 1842–1847* (Toronto: University of Toronto Press, 1984), pp. 100–108 is also useful, especially if read together with Draper. For a

more recent reading that also does justice to Marx's argument, see Y. Peled, "From Theology to Sociology: Bruno Bauer and Karl Marx on the Question of Jewish Emancipation," *History of Political Thought* 13, no.3 (fall 1992) 463–85.

15. **5**, p. 236.

16. **3**, p. 150.

17. The replies of evolutionary biologist David Sloan Wilson to a reporter's questions about his study of religion would have probably resonated with the young Marx and the Left Hegelians. While religion may have promoted what he calls a "guarded egalitarianism" and "willingness of people to cooperate with others," it could also be divisive. "Religions and other social organizations may preach kindness and cooperation within the group, but they often say nothing about those outside the group, and may even promote brutality toward those beyond the brotherhood of the [bee] hive. That has been the dark side [Marx's "defect"] of religion" (*New York Times*, 24 December 2002).

18. Ibid., p. 151.

19. Ibid., p. 153.

20. Ibid., pp. 162–68.

21. Ibid., p. 171. Commenting on the brief spurt in religiosity in the United States in the aftermath of September 11, 2001, Robert Wuthnow, director of the Center for the Study of Religion at Princeton University, made a comment that Marx would have understood all too well: " 'We are in some ways a very religious country, especially compared to Western Europe,' Mr. Wuthnow said. 'But we're of two minds, and the other mind is that we are pretty secular. We are very much a country of consumers and shoppers, and we're quite materialistic. And as long as we can kind of paste together a sense of control through our ordinary work and our ordinary purchases, we're pretty happy to do that' "(*New York Times*, 26 November 2001, p. B6). Marx later remarked on the U.S.–Western Europe difference; see below, pp. 12–13.

22. **Ibid.**, p. 155.

23. **5**, p. 217. It's possible that Marx relied on Thomas Hamilton's observations, cited below, about the Workingmen's Party in New York in making this point.

24. **41**, p. 390.

25. Gustave de Beaumont, *Marie or, Slavery in the United States* (Baltimore: The Johns Hopkins Press, 1999), p. 7.

26. Thomas Hamilton, *Men and Manners in America*, 2 volumes (Edinburgh: William Blackwood, 1833). Unfortunately, the 1999 edition of *Marie* doesn't include the appendix on religious groups that refers to

Hamilton's book. For the reference, see *Marie ou L'esclavage aux États-Unis,* 5th ed. (Paris: Charles Gosselin, 1842), p. 271.

27. Karl Marx and Frederick Engels, *Gesamtausgabe,* Abt. 4, Bd. 2 (Berlin: Dietz Verlag, 1981), pp. 266–75. Hamilton's characterization of the money-grabbing New Englander—"The whole race of Yankee pedlars . . . resemble the Jews"—may have been the basis for Marx's central argument in the second article about the Judaization of the Christian world. See Hamilton, Vol. 1, pp. 229–30.

28. Maximilien Rubel, "Notes on Marx's Conception of Democracy," *New Politics,* 1, no. 2 (winter 1962): 83–85, also argues that Hamilton exercised a decisive influence on Marx. His treatment, however, is far more suggestive and less systematic than what is presented here. Lewis Feuer, "The North American Origin of Marx's Socialism," *Western Political Quarterly,* 16, no. 1 (March 1963): 53–67, makes a similar argument but with particular focus on Hamilton's treatment of the Workingmen's Party of New York and in greater detail. A close reading of both Rubel and Feuer reveals that my argument differs significantly from their reading of Marx's reading of the United States.

29. Lipset, pp. 35–36.

30. Hamilton, Vol. 1, p. 217.

31. Marx and Engels, *Gesamtausgabe,* Abt. 4, Bd. 2, pp. 268–69. For the comparable pages in Hamilton, see Vol. 1, pp. 221–22.

32. Hamilton, Vol. 1, pp. 299–301. For details on the party in New York at the time see Anthony Gronowicz, *Race and Class Politics in New York City before the Civil War* (Boston: Northeastern University Press, 1998), chapter 3.

33. Hamilton, Vol. 2, pp. 226–27.

34. Ibid., pp. 142–43. Hamilton also denounced Thomas Jefferson for hypocrisy: "Continually puling about liberty, equality, and the degrading curse of slavery," he not only fathered children by his slaves but later, according to Hamilton, sold them into slavery—a charge that has greater credence given the recent DNA findings about his descendants. See Vol. 1, pp. 324–25.

35. Ibid., pp. 225, 227.

36. Ibid., p. 210.

37. There are other interesting issues addressed by Hamilton worth noting but are not necessarily germane to the topic at hand. One, for example, was the protective tariffs' policy of the U.S. government, which Hamilton opposed. It's possible that this was not only Marx's introduction to the topic but one from a perspective, i.e., against protectionism,

that would figure significantly in his political economy writings. It should be made clear that no claim is being made here that Marx necessarily agreed with all of Hamilton's views.

38. Tocqueville, Vol 1, p. 311.

39. Ibid., p. 324.

40. Hamilton, Vol. 2, p. 210.

41. Beaumont (1842 edition), pp. 272–75. Again, unfortunately the recent English edition of *Marie* does not include the appendix, *Sur le Mouvement Religieux aux État-Unis.*

42. Tocqueville, Vol. 1, pp. 314–15.

43. **4**, pp. 116–17.

44. If Marx was indeed informed by Tocqueville's insight, it reveals—especially in the context of his larger argument in which these statements originate—the difference between the feudal and the modern state, Marx went much further to explain the fundamental differences between both states, i.e., beyond just how they related to religion.

45. Ibid., p. 321.

46. "Contribution to the Critique of Hegel's Philosophy of Law," **3**, p. 94. Tocqueville's claim must have seemed contradictory to Marx given his assertion that other components of U.S. civil society such as slavery and the treatment of Indians were "collateral" to an explanation of democracy. His other assertion, that the Catholic Church was a paragon of democracy, must have appeared ludicrous to Marx in view of his critique of the Church (p. 51).

Marx's critique of "patriarchal laws" anticipates Rheinhardt's critique of Tocqueville's defense of "America's gendered hierarchy"(Mark Reinhardt, *The Art of Being Free: Taking Liberties with Tocqueville, Marx and Arendt* [Ithaca: Cornell University Press, 1997], p. 69).

47. Tocqueville, Vol. 1, pp. 206, 204.

48. Ibid., p. 254.

49. Ibid., pp. 327, 207.

50. George Wilson Pierson, *Tocqueville in America* (Baltimore: Johns Hopkins University Press, 1996), p. 608.

51. Alexis de Tocqueville, *Democracy in America*, Vol. 2 (New York: Vintage Books, 1945), p. 170.

52. I owe this insight about Tocqueville to Laura Janara, specifically, chapter 4 of her dissertation, "After the Mother: Authority, Autonomy and Passion in Tocqueville's *Democracy in America*," University of Minnesota, 1998.

53. Tocqueville, Vol. 2, pp. 250, 258.

54. Ibid., p. 199. Tocqueville makes another interesting observation in explaining why the modern state tends to grow in power: "the manu-

facturing classes [workers] require more regulation, superintendence, and restraint than the other classes of society, and it is natural that the powers of government should increase in the same proportion as those classes." Ibid., 327. Here, he makes clear that he is only referring to Europe though the implications for the United States in his thinking can only be speculated on.

55. Seymour Drescher, *Dilemmas of Democracy: Tocqueville and Modernization* (Pittsburgh: University of Pittsburgh Press, 1968), p. 54n.

56. Ibid., p. 56.

57. Though it would be instructive to look at Tocqueville's views on American Indians, given the almost complete absence of anything comparable in Marx I have confined this discussion to the situation of Blacks in his analysis. For a thoughtful critique of his views on Indians, see William E. Connolly, "Tocqueville, Territory and Violence," *Theory, Culture & Society*, 11 (1994): 19–40.

58. Alexis de Tocqueville, *Democracy in America*, Vol. 1 (New York: Vintage Books, 1945), p. 372. Regarding Marx and Engels's views on Blacks, see, p. 25 n.85.

59. Ibid., p. 373.

60. Tocqueville was active in France's abolitionist circles (more about this in chapter 2), a milieu that was influenced by Grégoire's book. For the new English edition, see Henri Grégoire, *An Enquiry Concerning the Intellectual and Moral Facilities, and Literature of Negroes* (New York: M. E. Sharpe, 1997).

61. Tocqueville, Vol. 1, p. 394.

62. For a somewhat similar assessment, see Peter Augustine Lawler, "Tocqueville on Slavery, Ancient and Modern," in *Comparative Issues in Slavery*, ed. Paul Finkelman (New York: Garland Publishing, Inc., 1989).

63. Ibid., p. 395.

64. Ibid., p. 378n; Hamilton, Vol. 2, p. 229.

65. Tocqueville, Vol. 1, p. 280.

66. Drescher, *Dilemmas of Democracy*, p. 184n.

67. Ibid., p. 177.

68. Reinhardt, p. 64. In the section of his book from which this comes, Reinhardt makes a case similar to the one presented here. Tocqueville's "evasion of the politics of actively confronting slavery is more than a refusal to invent easy and fanciful solutions to complex and stubborn problems; it amounts, despite his moral distress and the acuity of his analyses, to the subversion of his condemnations, to a backhanded legitimation of this condition" (p. 66).

69. Tocqueville, Vol. 1, p. 412.

70. Ibid., p. 389.

71. Ibid., p. 397. This is a curious comment. Was he referring to the Haitian Republic or, perhaps, the Nat Turner rebellion in 1831, the year of his visit, to which he made no explicit reference anywhere?

72. The argument here is anticipated to some degree in Maximilien Rubel, "Marx and American Democracy," in *Marx and the Western World*, ed. Nicholas Lobkowicz (London: University of Notre Dame Press, 1967), and Robert Weiner, "Karl Marx's Vision of America: A Bibliographical and Bibliographical Sketch," *The Review of Politics* 42, no. 4 (October 1980). However, a close reading of both articles reveals that in the former the thesis is not really proven to the degree it is here while in the latter the significance of Marx's reading of Tocqueville is not fully appreciated.

73. It's likely that other materials also informed him but the extant record only reveals these sources.

74. Charles Sellers, *The Market Revolution: Jacksonian America, 1815–1846* (New York: Oxford University Press, 1991), p. 6n.

75. Ibid., p. 396.

76. This is not to imply in any manner that Marx and Engels, in their move toward political economy, ignored political institutions. To the contrary. Any close and honest read of the young Marx would reveal not only sincere interest in but detailed attention to the state and its various institutions. For a useful summary of the evidence for this claim, see Teeple, chapter 5.

77. Bruce Levine, *Half Slave and Half Free: The Roots of the Civil War* (New York: Hill and Wang, 1992), pp. 14–15.

78. Sean Wilentz, *Chants Democratic: New York City and the Rise of the American Working Class, 1788–1850* (New York: Oxford University Press, 1984).

79. Sellers, p. 6.

80. Edward Pessen, *Riches, Class, and Power before the Civil War* (Lexington, Mass.: D. C. Heath, 1973), p. 1. See also Pessen's debate with a Tocqueville partisan on some of these questions in *Revue Tocqueville* (1981–1982).

81. Ibid., p. 26.

82. Ibid., p. 43.

83. Ibid., pp. 298–89.

84. Alexander Keyssar, *The Right to Vote: The Contested History of Democracy in the United States* (New York: Basic Books, 2000), pp. xvii, 76.

85. Levine, p. 70.

86. Rogers M. Smith, *Civic Ideals: Conflicting Visions of Citizenship in U.S. History* (New Haven: Yale University Press, 1997), p. 17.

87. Ibid., p. 199.

88. Ibid, p. 472.

89. This was exactly what he understood about the oppression that Jews faced in Germany in both the political and civil spheres; he was resolute, it should be quickly added, in defending religious and political freedom for Jews. For details, see Draper, *Karl Marx's Theory*, Vol. 1, pp. 110–13.

90. Michael Goldfield, *The Color of Politics: Race and the Mainspring of American Politics* (New York: The New Press, 1997).

91. **39**, p. 62.

92. See Eric Foner's "New Introductory Essay" in his *Free Soil, Free Labor, Free Men: The Ideology of the Republican Party before the Civil War* (New York: Oxford University Press, 1995), p. xxi.

93. Drescher, p. 54.

94. Tocqueville, Vol. 1, pp. xi, 6.

95. Jack Hayward, *After the French Revolution: Six Critics of Democracy and Nationalism* (New York: New York University Press, 1991), p. 149.

96. Drescher, p. 278.

97. For a critical assessment of Tocqueville's religious views, see Michael Levin, *The Spectre of Democracy: The Rise of Modern Democracy As Seen by Its Critics* (New York: New York University Press, 1992), pp. 115–18.

98. Tocqueville, Vol. 1, p. ix.

99. Tocqueville, *Mon Instinct, mes opinions,*" quoted in Antoine Rédier, *Comme disait M. de Toqueville* (Paris, 1925), p. 48; quoted in Hayward, p. 149. See also André Jardin, *Tocqueville: A Biography* (New York: Farrar, Straus, Giroux, 1988), p. 305, for a more abbreviated version of this statement. To understand in a broader sense what Tocqueville meant see Roger Boesche, *The Strange Liberalism of Alexis de Tocqueville* (Ithaca: Cornell University Press, 1987), and Alan S. Kahan, *Aristocratic Liberalism: The Social and Political Thought of Jacob Burckhardt, John Stuart Mill, and Alexis de Tocqueville* (New York: Oxford University Press, 1992).

100. Sheldon S. Wolin, *Tocqueville between Two Worlds: The Making of a Political and Theoretical Life* (Princeton, N.J. Princeton University Press, 2001), p. 5.

2

Toward the "General Conflagration"
Theory and Practice

Even before Marx and Engels arrived at their historical materialist perspective, they agreed that "ideas cannot carry out anything at all. In order to carry out ideas men are needed who can exert practical force." As immortalized in Marx's *Theses on Feuerbach* (1845), revolutionary practice was the means by which not only the oppressed were educated but also the "educator . . . [to] be educated." The "educator" had to engage in the same revolutionary activities as the proletariat and other oppressed layers and for the same reasons. To avoid doing so, Marx held, would mean to "divide society into two parts, one of which is superior to society." This third thesis, along with the more famous eleventh—"the philosophers have only *interpreted* the world in various ways; the point is to *change* it"—would forever inform their politics. In no instance was such a perspective more evident than in the activities of Marx and Engels and their co-thinkers in the years preceding and during the U. S. Civil War. But for such revolutionary practice to be efficacious revolutionary theory was required.

The "New World View"

Marx and Engels's "materialist conception of history" posited that the capitalist mode of production was an unprecedented advance for humanity. First presented in *The German Ideology* in

1845–1846, it argued that with capitalism's arrival—in the last quarter of the eighteenth century—the material prerequisites for human emancipation were in place for the first time. As long as the system of production allowed for only a limited surplus for social needs—based on the legacy of prior modes of production—enough for some but not all to enjoy, then inequality was the invariable outcome. When and where social equality existed it did so on the basis of generalized poverty or an absence of a social surplus. Capitalism created the possibility of an unlimited surplus—a first in human history.

Most importantly, it brought into existence the requisite human material, the proletariat, the first oppressed layer that had both the interest *and* capability in bringing about "real democracy." Only with the abolishment of social inequality, that is, class society, could "real democracy" be realized. This posed the need to overthrow the most developed expression of class society, capitalism. An advance over prior modes of production due to its increasingly social character—eventually encompassing the entire globe—capitalism was, at bottom and ultimately, incompatible with the private ownership of the means of production upon which it rested. This explosive contradiction could only be resolved in humanity's favor by abolishing the latter. And, unlike any previous economic systems, capitalism forged its own grave diggers—the proletariat.

Marx and Engels did not intend that their "new world view"—what they also called "scientific communism"—to be used as a crystal ball. In the final analysis, the validity of the materialist conception of history depended on its ability to accurately represent what Marx and Engels called "the real movement of history." In terms of the subject before us, this refers to the actual course of the democratic movement. In the context of a world in which precapitalist socioeconomic formations dominated, or in particular settings in which this was true, real democrats, especially its most radical wing, the communists, were obligated to ally with the bourgeoisie in opposition to retrograde modes of production like feudalism and slavery. The *Manifesto of the Communist Party* concluded that "as soon as" the bourgeoisie fought to institute liberal democracy, communists stood side by side with them.[1] The institution of the political program of the bourgeoisie (liberal democracy) was required for the working class to advance its own interests. They should, thus, fight for and defend it. Yet, by the middle of the nineteenth century, the real movement had revealed that the bourgeoisie no longer had an interest in fulfilling its historic mission, leading the charge for political or liberal democracy.[2] Tocqueville had a role in this default.

In the European context, at least, the workers movement would have to take the lead in the struggle to institute political democracy—the "battle for democracy"—by forming its own political party, in which communists would simply be the most active and conscious members. An alliance with peasants and other petit bourgeois forces would also be necessary. But workers should never equate political democracy with what the young Marx termed "human emancipation." The latter would require a social revolution, one that took political democracy as its starting point.

In a general sense, Tocqueville, like Marx and Engels, felt that the course of history was headed toward liberal democratic outcomes and social equality. Unlike the latter, however, he saw no difference between such outcomes. Even so, on the question of action to advance either goal, Tocqueville was more comfortable as a passive observer while Marx and Engels functioned as militant protagonists. As already suggested above and in chapter 1, Tocqueville's practice raises severe questions about his democratic credentials—again, an issue to be revisited. Also, unlike them, he had no theoretical explanation for this claim about history's direction other than to describe it as "a providential fact" that "constantly eludes all human interference."[3] The egalitarian quest for Tocqueville was inevitable and ordained. It required neither program nor actors. Precisely because the democratic goal and the end of class society was *not*, for Marx and Engels, a foregone conclusion, consciousness, in the form of program and practice, was essential to the realization of such ends—what communists like themselves sought to bring to the process.

One of the most challenging issues for Marx and Engels with their new perspective was what stance to take on precapitalist societies subjected to the imperialist policies of capitalist states, be they liberal democratic or not. Should such policies be supported by the workers movement and its communist leadership and, if so, under what circumstances? At least three cases put their historical materialist framework to the test: Algeria, India, and Mexico. For present purposes, Algeria and India are most instructive. The case of Mexico will be assessed in the next chapter. Because both the Marx-Engels team and Tocqueville addressed the Algerian and Indian realities—to varying degrees—a comparison of their positions allows for a more concrete appraisal of their politics and democratic credentials.

When, in 1847, French military forces captured the Algerian nationalist leader, Abd-el-Kader—who had led a fifteen-year-long resistance movement against Paris's efforts to consolidate its imperialistic venture in Africa—Engels reported approvingly on the success of the tricolor. "Upon the whole it is, in our opinion, very fortunate that the Arabian chief has been taken . . . the conquest of Algeria is an important and fortunate fact for the progress of civilisation. . . . And after all, the modern *bourgeois*, with civilisation, industry, order, and at least relative enlightenment following him, is preferable to the feudal lord or to the marauding robber, with the barbarian state of society to which they belong."[4] The newly formulated "materialist conception of history" is clearly what informed Engels's position—views that paralleled those of his partner regarding Mexico, as will be seen later.

Ten years later, however, Engels saw the "barbarians" in a very different light. "From the first occupation of Algeria by the French to the present time, the unhappy country has been the arena of unceasing bloodshed, rapine, and violence. . . . This barbarous system of warfare has been persisted in by the French against all the dictates of humanity, civilization and Christianity . . . [A]ll that can be said of Algeria is that it is a school of war for French generals and soldiers." Beyond just a critique of the horrors of French rule, Engels had by 1857 come to the side of the indigenous Algerians. Their continued resistance to these horrors "proved that the natives had neither lost courage nor contracted affection for their invaders. . . . The tribes still assert their independence and detestation of the French regime."[5]

Although Engels didn't indicate when or why he changed his views, this telling adjustment apparently had to do with his and Marx's more sober view of the bourgeoisie as a result of its betrayal of the liberal democratic revolutions of 1848. The same troops and their general, Louis Cavaignac, who had brutally suppressed the resistance of Abd-el Kader, were employed by Paris to do just that to its own proletariat in June 1848. The real movement had taught that the quest for democracy at home was incompatible with imperialism abroad. The fate of workers and peasants in what would become the Third World of the twentieth century would forever be linked to the same two classes in advanced capitalist countries—and vice versa.

Like Engels, Tocqueville also applauded the capture of Abd-el Kader in 1847.[6] But Tocqueville was more than an observer from afar. As a National Assembly deputy assigned to draw up a report and make recommendations on Algeria that year, he proved to be a leading architect of French imperialism in Africa. It was his report, in fact, that called for an uncompromising war against the Algerian leader. The tone was established at the outset: "We must admit therefore, as a demonstrated truth, that our domination of Africa must be firmly maintained."[7] The report made clear that the indigenous population must be treated as conquered subjects and at no time should the impression be given that they "are our compatriots and our equals."[8] The only nod to democracy that Tocqueville made in the report was his advocacy of liberal democratic rights for the French settlers in Algeria. As André Jardin, Tocqueville's most competent and evenhanded biographer, notes, the "unequal society thus envisaged hardly seemed to conform to that divine plan for equality among men described in the *Democracy* [*in America*]." Tocqueville was motivated, he concludes, by imperialist leanings that had their roots in the feudal absolutist world of Louis XIV. "This aspect of his character has sometimes been overlooked by those who see Tocqueville only as he appears in the *Democracy*."[9] Unlike Engels, there is nothing to suggest that Tocqueville ever changed his views on Algeria. In hindsight, Tocqueville's approach helped inform the historical, moral, ideological, and military continuity with French carnage 120 years later as Paris sought to keep Algeria in its empire, at the cost of one million Algerian dead—when the colony had a population of 14 million.

In the final year of his life, Marx, from February to May 1882, visited Algeria in the hope that the climate there would help restore his health. His correspondence indicates that he too, like Engels, had come to the side of the native population in the face of the European settler population's "barefaced arrogance and presumptuousness vis-à-vis the 'lesser breeds' " and the oppressive nature of colonial rule. He clearly identified with their refusal to be totally broken in spirit by their French oppressors. "Nevertheless, they will go to rack and ruin without a revolutionary movement."[10] Seventy years later the Algerians would heed Marx's advice. The Algeria case reveals, therefore, that the Marx-Engels team and not the author of the *Democracy* proved to be the real democrats, in that their notion of the "demos" was far more ecumenical. It was exactly Tocqueville's more restricted notion of the demos that led him to portray the United States as an "absolute democracy." His stance on Algeria foreshadowed what he would do within a year in France.

Marx's first sustained treatment of India in 1853 struck a similar tone to what Engels first wrote about Algiers in 1848—European imperialism as a necessary evil in the country's social transformation. However "sickening as it must be to human feeling to witness" the consequences of British rule, it had to be admitted that it promoted a "social revolution" in India. And "whatever may have been the crimes of England she was the unconscious tool of history in bringing about that revolution."[11] For sure, Marx, in this period, didn't pull punches about the "crimes" of Britain's ruling class. "The profound hypocrisy and inherent barbarism of bourgeois civilization lies unveiled before our eyes, turning from its home, where it assumes respectable forms, to the colonies, where it goes naked."[12]

But by the time of the Sepoy Mutiny against British rule in 1857–1859, Marx and Engels's support for the anticolonial struggle was unequivocal. For Marx, as he told his comrade, the uprising was "delicious." He elaborated a bit later. "In view of the DRAIN OF MEN and BULLION which she will cost the English, India is now our best ally."[13] In his journalistic writings Marx defended the mutineers against the self-righteous railings of Britain's "civilized" press.

Tocqueville, on the other hand, made no bones about where his sympathies laid in the uprising. Early in the revolt and two years before his death, he wrote to a scion of England's nobility that "[y]our dramas in India have caused genuine emotion within the Tocqueville walls. I have . . . never for an instant doubted your triumph, which is that of Christianity and of civilization." His hope was that the rebellion would spur reforms in Britain's colonial policies. "Only then will you attain the level of your task, which is not only to dominate India, but to civilize it. These two things, indeed, are closely connected."[14] Even when Marx, in 1853, thought, erroneously, the imperial project to be historically progressive he never had any illusions about it's "civilizing mission." Until the end, Tocqueville identified heart and soul with the imperial ruling elite. Nothing in his basic character allowed him to embrace the demos, be it in Europe or elsewhere.

The conclusions that the young Marx and Engels reached about the democratic potential of the proletariat have been substantiated by recent scholarship. In their pathbreaking work, *Capitalist Development and Democracy*, Dietrich Rueschmeyer, John Stephens, and Evelyn Stephens (1992) demonstrated convincingly that the working class was the leading protagonist in the liberal democratic breakthrough at the end of the nineteenth and beginning of the twentieth century. Contrary to the then widely held position that the middle class was the chief agent for this development, they show that the breakthrough occurred when workers in Europe began organizing in alliance with other layers, especially the peasantry, to further their political interests. I argue, however, that there was nothing inevitable about the political organization of workers and the alliances they formed, as Rueschmeyer, Stephens, and Stephens seem to suggest.[15] Rather, conscious programmatic and practical leadership was essential in this process. No two individuals contributed more to this than Marx and Engels. What happened in Europe was very much related to an earlier democratic breakthrough, the overthrow of slavery in the United States—a process that also saw the involvement of Marx and Engels.

Slavery, Free Soil, and the Workers' Movement

The "materialist conception of history" spoke immediately to the reality of the United States. In defense of his and Engels's new method, Marx, in his important article, "Moralising Criticism and Critical Morality," returned once again to the other shore of the Atlantic. If the "Jewish Question" shows how the U.S. example pointed him to scientific communism, this article, written four years later in 1847, registers how far he had come. The best that "really existing" democracy had to offer revealed that "political emancipation is not human emancipation," owing in large part to the "influence of private property." In the second article he could be more specific: "The question of property . . . has . . . a meaning only in *modern bourgeois society*. The more advanced this society is, in other words, the further the bourgeoisie has developed economically in a country and therefore the more state power has assumed a bourgeois character, the more glaringly does the *social* question obtrude itself. . . . Thus, for example, the conflicts of the credit system, speculation, etc., are nowhere more acute than in North America. Nowhere, either, does *social* inequality obtrude itself more harshly than in the eastern states of North America, because nowhere is it less disguised by political inequality."[16]

Exactly because it was the most politically democratic nation, the social inequalities that private property generated in the United States—especially in those parts of the country where market relations were the most developed—made them all the more visible and with all of the political significance therein.[17] To make his case Marx drew on new data about growing social inequality in America. As noted in chapter 1, Marx's finding were in broad accord with modern scholarship.

If political democracy was an advance because it put the social question on the political agenda in an unprecedented way, this didn't mean that every thing about the U.S. political system was progressive. Elsewhere in his article Marx criticized German republicans who took "as a model . . . the American federal system." In "feudally fragmented" Germany, it would be contrary to the interests of "any democratic revolution . . . to put the

'American federal system' in place of the *one* indivisible republic and its levelling centralisation."[18] U.S. federalism, by implication, was not, from the perspective of their method, an advance and not to be emulated for the bourgeois democratic revolution. Though Marx didn't offer a reason at the time why such a retrograde arrangement existed in this "most progressive" of nations, the record is clear that federalism was the outcome of the effort at Philadelphia in 1787 to accommodate the interests of the most retrograde feature of the American social formation—the slave owners.[19] Only with the overthrow of the slavocracy, Marx stated, would "*one* indivisible republic and its levelling centralisation" come into existence in the United States for the first time. Little wonder then that Marx and Engels were unconditional supporters of the antislavery cause.

· Like feudalism, slavery was a precapitalist mode of production that, at one time, had a progressive role in human history. As Marx explained in his 1847 polemic with Proudhon, *The Poverty of Philosophy*, North American slavery had made a particular contribution to social development: "Direct slavery is as much the pivot of bourgeois industry as machinery, credits, etc. Without slavery you have no cotton; without cotton you have no modern industry. It is slavery that gave the colonies their value; it is the colonies that created world trade, and it is world trade that is the precondition of large-scale industry. . . . Without slavery North America, the most progressive of countries, would be transformed into a patriarchal country. Wipe North America off the map of the world, and you will have anarchy—the complete decay of modern commerce and modern civilisation. Cause slavery to disappear and you will have wiped America off the map of nations."[20] Clearly within the framework of his historical materialist perspective, and contrary to Proudhon, Marx argued that the progressive and reactionary aspects of slave production, like all economic categories, could not be separated.

Modern scholarship verifies Marx's claims about the importance of slavery in the U.S. economy and society as a whole. Recent discussions, motivated by the debate about reparations to descendants of slaves, have brought the issue to public consciousness in an unprecedented way. It is now clear to many for the first time that the institution was not peculiarly southern but actually national. Revelations about the links between slavery and major financial institutions, such as Aetna and Hartford Insurance Companies, or centers of learning, such as Yale University, also in Connecticut, testify to this fact. The fact that "cotton exports between 1815 and 1860 accounted for over half the value of all" U.S. domestic exports, as Michael Goldfield notes in his *Color of Politics*, explains the enormous political weight of the slavocracy in national politics.

"Five of the first seven presidents of the Republic, for thirty-two out of the first thirty-six years, forty of its first forty-eight years, fifty of its first sixty-four years was a slaveholder," Goldfield states. "The Speaker of the House for twenty-eight out of the first thirty-five years was a slaveholder. It was an anomaly if the president pro tem of the Senate was not. A majority of cabinet members and Supreme Court justices were slave owners. It was only in 1863 that Salmon P. Chase of Ohio succeeded the slave owner Chief Justice Roger Taney, who had originally been appointed by slaveholder Andrew Jackson. . . . With only a fraction of the population of the North and West by the time of the Civil War (even counting the noncitizen slaves), the South had an overwhelmingly disproportionate influence in national politics."[21] To characterize the United States before the Civil War as a slavocracy is not an exaggeration. But for the author of *Democracy in America*, this reality was tangential to his "subject."

In counterposing his method to that of Proudhon, it could appear that Marx gave a backhanded endorsement to slavery, specifically U.S. slavery, in the same way that Engels, writing at about the same time, applauded French imperialism in Algeria—that is, a necessary evil in societal development. Such a reading, however, would conflate a description of reality with the political conclusions that one draws from such an analysis. This was exactly the problem, Marx argued, with Proudhon's approach. This alternative reading of Marx, one that distinguishes between description and prescription, is given credence in light of his having ridiculed Proudhon six months earlier for trying to find the "golden mean . . . the balance between slavery and liberty."[22]

Marx clearly did not believe such a mean existed. There is no doubt that he sided with liberty. Further evidence for this conclusion comes from Engels, writing at the same time about the differences between slaves and the proletariat. The "latter," in a draft for what would become the *Communist Manifesto*, "stands at a higher stage of development. The slave frees himself by *becoming a proletarian*, abolishing from the totality of property relationships *only* the relationship of *slavery*. The proletarian can free himself only by abolishing *property in general*."[23] The overthrow of slavery, therefore, increased the size of the proletariat, and thus was a step toward human emancipation as a whole, to be achieved by socialist revolution.

Whatever redeeming features slavery might have once had, including its most advanced form in the United States, the emergence of capitalism had rendered it obsolete, an obstacle to human progress and a social system to be opposed. In his notebooks ten years later, Marx defended the appellation of American slave owners as "capitalists" because it "is based on their existence as anomalies within a world market based on free labour."[24] Scientific communism allowed them to see what Tocqueville either was blind to or denied. To employ Sellers's language: "market revolution made slavery the great contradiction of the liberal American republic."[25] Implicit here, also, is the claim that the overthrow of slavery, specifically, its replacement by capitalism, was an advance for human emancipation because it enlarged the ranks of the proletariat, the only oppressed layer in history that had both the material interest in and social capability to uproot the objective basis of class oppression—private property relations. It should also be remembered, as noted in chapter 1, that Marx and Engels's optimism about the proletariat was enriched by the U.S. experience. There, as they pointed out in *The German Ideology*—based most likely on Thomas Hamilton's observations about the Workingmen's Party in New York in 1831—workers had shown that they knew how to "make good use" of citizenship. Events in the United States revealed quite early in its formation—along with England's experience with the Chartists—that workers were indeed capable of organizing themselves politically and in their own interests, undertaking the necessary steps to their taking power and spearheading social revolution.

Except for a comment in *Wage Labour and Capital*, written in 1849, there is virtually nothing in Marx and Engels's early writings that reveal what they thought specifically about Blacks and the issue of "race." But what they said about U.S. slavery is relevant since its chattel bondage was profoundly racial. A comment in *Wage Labour and Capital* recognizes this fact. To illustrate his point that capital constituted a social relationship, Marx wrote: "What is a Negro slave? A man of the black race. The one explanation is as good as the other. A Negro is a Negro. He only becomes a *slave* in certain relations. A cotton-spinning jenny is a machine for spinning cotton. It becomes *capital* only in certain relations. Torn from these relations it is no more capital than *gold* in itself is *money* or sugar the *price* of sugar."[26] Marx was, as it might be called in some academic settings today, deconstructing the concept of "Negro." By the mid-nineteenth century, in Western Europe at least, Black identity had become increasingly synonymous with servitude. This was especially true in the United States where—especially in slave states— with each succeeding decade of the nineteenth century the laws and courts made the condition of "free Blacks" increasingly impossible. Marx therefore challenged the racist conclusions about Blacks that derived from their oppression and exploitation. That in the very next sentence he employed the example of the "cotton jenny" is not coincidental. It's useful to recall here the previously cited passage in the *Poverty of Philosophy*, written two years earlier, about the cotton-slavery nexus. Only with the outbreak of the Civil War in 1861 would Marx and Engels write in a sustained way about race and slavery in the United States.

With their new perspective Marx and Engels sought immediately to link up with Europe's proletariat. In 1846 they launched their first political organization, the Communist Correspondence Committees. This was the vehicle for their first intervention in U.S. politics.

In their newly formed partnership they were especially concerned about German émigrés in the United States who claimed to speak in the name of German communism, among them, the well-known German activist Wilhelm Weitling. One of their first polemics in defense of scientific communism was with a disciple of Weitling, Hermann Kriege, who, through his weekly newspaper in New York, *Der Volks-Tribun,* exercised some influence amongst German workers in the city and elsewhere.[27] David Herreshoff argues persuasively that Kriege's conscious opposition to Marx and Engels's materialist conception of history led to a denial of the class struggle and the proletariat as the revolutionary class.[28] Kriege eventually broke with scientific communism, became an activist in Tammany Hall and the Democratic Party, and an avowed opponent of abolition.

Shortly after his arrival in the United States, Kriege concluded that the agrarian arena offered the best hope for German artisan and working-class immigrants in their new homeland. Agrarian republicanism as a social panacea soon led him to support the Free-Soil reform program. In 1845, he formed his Association der Social-Reformer which employed the language of the National Reform Association, the leading Free-Soil organization led by George Henry Evans, and elevated the right to the land as the most important issue. "The SRA soon boasted between four and six hundred members in New York, and affiliates in Newark, Philadelphia, Boston, Milwaukee, Cincinnati, and St. Louis. . . . The land reform theme also echoed through the broader network of immigrant reform *Vereine,* including labor associations. . . . Turner groups, and Freemen societies."[29] In other words, Kriege's efforts garnered a serious response amongst German American workers.

As had often been the case with Free-Soilers, Kriege and his followers abstained from the struggle against slavery. Because of his influence this meant that for "several years, the German American socialists played no role in the struggle against slavery," Herreshoff notes. Kriege argued that "the slave system was essentially a question of property" and, in anticipation of the arguments of racists in the New York City draft riots in 1863, "if the abolitionist crusade succeeded, it would only increase competition among free workers and depress the white workers without elevating the blacks. 'We feel constrained therefore to oppose abolition with all our might, despite all the importunities of sentimental Philistines, and despite all the political effusions of liberty-intoxicated ladies.'"[30] For Weitling, his mentor, the slavery question was also a "side issue."

Again, like Evans, Kriege eventually concluded that "anti-slavery and land reform were conflicting priorities. Repugnant as chattel slavery was, Kriege would not support emancipation until the conditions of free labor had fundamentally improved. To act otherwise, he argued, would only worsen the already difficult position of the wage earner; the newly emancipated slaves would surely stream northward, drastically increasing job competition there. The New York *Volks-Tribun* had thus announced in 1846 'that we should declare ourselves in favor of the abolitionist movement' only 'if we wished . . . to extend competition among "free workmen" beyond all bounds, and to depress labor itself to the last extremity.' The unfortunate truth, Kriege concluded, was that 'under the conditions prevailing in modern society, we could not improve the lot of our "black brothers" by abolition, but only make infinitely worse thereby the lot of our "white brothers."[31]

One of the key planks of the Free-Soil movement was endorsement of the Wilmot Proviso, a congressional measure which banned not only the extension of slavery to new states but prohibited the migration of free Blacks who might want to farm there. Not only did Free-Soilers actively abstain from the fight against slavery but they saw no place for former slaves in their small, property-based, republican utopia. It is not coincidental that the intellectual father of this democratic vision, Thomas Jefferson, was a slave owner who also saw no future for Blacks in America. For the Free-Soilers, like Jefferson, emerging industrial capital—not the slave system—was the greater evil, what Sellers calls the "contradiction of . . . fee-simple property." Tocqueville's portrait of democratic America bore many similarities to the Jeffersonian Free-Soiler vision, with slavery and Blacks peripherally placed in the picture.

Marx and Engels's critique of Kriege was a collective effort, a communique from the Brussels Correspondence Committee, the leading body of their new political network. Signed by all eight of its members—except for Weitling—the document reproached Kriege for several reasons, not the least of which was his conflation of the political struggle of the proletariat with a religious crusade and sentimental socialism. More germane for present purposes was the accusation that Kriege had adapted to a reformist illusion—that the salvation of workers was through the Free-Soilers program of ownership of 160 acres of land. "We fully recognise," the document said, "that the American national Reformers' movement is historically justified. We know that this movement has set its sights on a goal which, although for the moment it would further the industrialism of modern bourgeois society, nevertheless, as the product of a proletarian movement, as an attack on landed property in general and more particularly in the circumstances obtaining in America, will by its own inner logic inevitably press on to communism."[32]

The newly formulated "materialist conception of history" was clearly on display. Land reform via the Free-Soilers program was a necessary step toward Sellers's "market revolution," i.e., capitalist property relations and eventually capitalist industrialization. More importantly, such a transformation would bring on the proletariat and its line of march. While such a program may have been necessary in the particular circumstances of Jacksonian America, and thus, from a communist perspective could be supported, it was unprincipled to do so uncritically or as an end in and of itself.

The musical-chair character of the market would predictably lead to increasing class stratification amongst farmers in which the majority would be reduced to the status of "farm labourer," that is, working for a few rich "neighbours" and producing for "rapacious speculators"—a reality that has proved to be all too true. "If Kriege," the document continued, "had seen the free-land movement as a first, in certain circumstances necessary, form of the proletarian movement, as a movement which because of the social position of the class from which it emanates must necessarily develop into a communist movement, if he had shown how communist tendencies in America could, to begin with, only emerge in this agrarian form which appear to be a contradiction of all communism, then no objection could have been raised. As things are, however, he declares what is after all a still subordinate form of movement of real specific people to be a matter for mankind *in general*, presents it, against his better knowledge, as the ultimate, supreme goal of all movement in general, and thereby transforms the specific aims of the movement into sheer, extravagant nonsense."[33]

To say to workers, as Kriege did, that the solution to their dilemma was to become property owners was a violation of the real communist program. Such a "solution" was, at best, temporary. To present it as the be-all and end-all of the fledgling labor movement would impede an understanding by workers of their historic task, to struggle for a world transcending private ownership of the means of production. Humanity's emancipation rested on the shoulders of those who were the dispossessed, those who had no investment in private property relations—the modern proletariat. It was exactly this long view of history that would forever ground Marx and Engels's practice in the United States—to mobilize the proletariat and to relentlessly campaign to enable workers to see clearly where their true interests lay.

The Kriege critique, written in April–May 1846, made no mention of slavery or the abolition question. At the time the Brussels committee wrote it—apparently and mostly by Engels—Kriege had not revealed his anti-abolitionist stance.[34] The document noted, in its conclusion, that "hardly has he arrived in New York when [Kriege] sends out circulars to all rich German merchants," such as John Jakob Astor, in order to get their financial support for his schemes. His appeals to German merchant capital accurately anticipated his political course—into their arms. "Though wooed by Whig free labor advocate Horace Greeley, both Kriege and Weitling joined the Democratic Party. They no doubt recognized that sectional labor segmentation benefited New York laborers: engaged as they were in activities associated with the cotton trade, as well as in the manufacture of goods destined for the South. New York workers' tasks complemented and reinforced the slave system."[35] Within a month of the critique's issuance, "Kriege called on the association [SRA] to establish itself as 'the left wing of Tammany Hall' and," as Marx and Engels could have easily predicted, "on July 4 the *Volkstribun* dropped the slogan 'Up with Labor! Down with Capital' from its masthead and declared that the association was no longer communist."[36] To be sure, there is no suggestion in the critique that the demand of the Free-Soilers would necessarily lead to a compromise with the slavocracy. But in the particular reality of New York City and other major East Coast urban cen-

ters, overtures to merchant capital—which it did criticize—
would most likely lead to the Democratic Party and, thus, an alliance with the slavocracy.[37] The abstention of the Free-Soilers
from the abolition struggle facilitated this alliance.

The Free-Soiler position began, after initial empathy, to draw
the wrath of Black abolitionists like Frederick Douglass and
Charles Lenox Remond. "At a meeting of the Pennsylvania Anti-
Slavery Society in 1848, Remond announced that he 'was out of patience' with land reformers who were indifferent to chattel slavery
and argued that only wage slavery mattered. . . . Remond concluded the discussion with the observation that 'the Anti-Slavery
cause was the cause of labour, of man, of freedom, without regard
to colour, and it was the duty of the workingmen to come to *our*
platform, not for us to go to them.'"[38] Marx and Engels, given their
clearly stated position that "wage slavery," however degrading,
was an advance over "chattel slavery"—it brought the essence of
the private property question to the fore unlike any prior form of
class subjugation—would have agreed with Remond.

What this episode reveals is that the German American
working class was as much affected by the Free-Soilers and their
anti-abolitionist stance as were other layers of white workers—
and, in the case of those under the sway of Kriege and Weitling,
in the name of German communism. Marx and Engels's campaign against Kriege had, therefore, long-term if not immediate
significance for abolitionism. To allow his views to have gone
unanswered would have denied those German workers who
looked to communism an opportunity to learn its real program.
For Marx and Engels the overthrow of slavery and other precapitalist forms of exploitation—such as feudalism and its vestiges in Germany—and institution of political democracy was
the necessary precondition for the struggle between capital and
labor. Clarity among workers about their real class interests and
the effective solution to their class oppression, as opposed to the
chimera of free soil, would facilitate, as subsequent events
would demonstrate, clarity on the abolition question.[39]

Marx and Engels's intervention in German American politics should not be interpreted to mean that they saw revolution
on the immediate agenda in the United States, and contrary to

what Seymour Lipset claims.[40] As the most progressive and most middle class of nations, the United States engendered the deepest illusions in the producing classes about their situation. The Free-Soil movement exemplified this reality. In 1851, Engels warned Joseph Weydemeyer, one of their comrades in struggle during the German revolution of 1848–1849, about the danger for revolutionaries in moving to the United States. The ease in being "drawn off into the country" owing to availability of land, and "increase in prosperity" thereby leads workers "to regard bourgeois conditions as the *beau idéal,* etc."[41] Marx followed up with a similar warning: "once over there, who can say that you won't lose yourself in the FAR WEST!"[42] A year later, Marx advised Weydemeyer to be realistic about the prospects for socialist revolution in the land, for some, of milk and honey: "in the United States bourgeois society is still far too immature for the class struggle to be made perceptible and comprehensible."[43] Six years later Marx was of the same opinion when writing in his notebooks about the unprecedented economic advances in the United States: "even the antitheses of bourgeois society itself appear only as vanishing moments."[44]

The evidence makes clear, therefore, that their orientation at this stage was to the class struggle in Europe and not the United States. Marx leaves little doubt about this when he told Weydemeyer before his departure in 1851 that if he had no other recourse it would be better if he settled in New York: "you will at all events find it easier, in case of revolution, to return to Europe from there than we [Engels and I] from here [London]."[45] Again, the Free-Soil movement no doubt taught them that a hereditary proletariat without the possibility of becoming property owners, of being able to escape its class situation, was not yet in place in the United States.

Back in France, Tocqueville, too, had to confront the reality of slavery. As a member of the Chamber of Deputies in 1839–1841 that grappled with the future of the peculiar institution in its colonies, the author of *Democracy in America* was the acknowledged expert on such matters. He played a leading role in deliberations on the slavery issue. Tocqueville had also taken a public role in the country's leading abolitionist body. On behalf of a parliamentary commission, he proposed state-managed emancipation over the course of a number of years—a kind of phased liberty in which wages to the freedmen would be used to indemnify the masters. "By thus interposing the power of the State, Tocqueville hoped to prevent the bloody settling of accounts between the two races that had so struck him in the United States."[46] The proposal, filed in 1839, however, never "reached the floor for debate." It was published as a pamphlet by the Society for the Abolition of Slavery.

François Guizot, the prime minister, appointed a commission headed by the Duc de Broglie to look into the question again. When it presented its report in 1843, Guizot intervened to prevent implementation and, instead, made a few superficial changes "in the colonial regime (the Mackau law of 1845)." Tocqueville wrote a series of articles about the document. After making the case for abolishing slavery in the colonies—mainly as a means for defending French colonial interests—he concluded: "It certainly doesn't follow from this argument that we must throw ourselves blindly into emancipation, nor that it is proper to proceed without taking all precautions necessary to secure benefits from it and to limit its costs and risks."[47] Although Tocqueville criticized Guizot's actions, he "openly . . . spoke in favor of the Mackau law: it retained the principle of arbitration between colonists [masters] and blacks." No doubt one of the reasons for Tocqueville's proposal and his support for the Mackau law was that it recognized and respected the property rights of the slave owners. For the patrician commentator, this was the beginning of wisdom.

By this time Tocqueville, like a number of key individuals in France's abolitionist circles, had begun to increasingly retreat from a stance of immediate slave abolition.[48] Also, as would be the case with his approach to Algeria, he was more concerned with the democratic rights, specifically, property rights, of the colonists than with those of their subjects. In the end, he accurately anticipated that Guizot would simply ignore the watered-down recommendations of the Broglie commission. But, as Lawrence Jennings points out, Tocqueville and the other defenders of the report were unwilling, like other French abolitionists, to

mobilize—as had been done in Britain—public opinion in opposition to slavery.[49] This was completely consistent with the posture Tocqueville adopted in the upheavals of 1848–1851.

The slavery question was finally resolved not by parliamentary action but by the February Revolution of 1848, whose government abolished slavery in the colonies once and for all, the
only progressive measure of the revolution that was not overturned. The original abolition of slavery in France and its
colonies was a product of the 1789 Revolution, during its most
revolutionary phase. This advance was overturned by the counterrevolution of Napoleon, a lesson lost upon Tocqueville whose
incessant fear of the masses in motion drove him to look for a
non-solution to the question in the only arena in which he felt
comfortable—the legislative one. Again, the real movement of
history, in Marx and Engels's terminology—in this case the upheavals of 1848—demonstrated what it would take to abolish
slavery in the United States.

The failure of Tocqueville and his abolitionist cohorts to mobilize mass support in France on behalf of their cause is also consistent with his failure to render any assistance to the abolitionist
cause in the United States. He clearly exercised a degree of influence amongst liberal intellectual circles there that could have been
of some benefit to advancing abolitionism.[50] Neither public nor
private records document any such initiative. Tocqueville died
two years before the Civil War. But to anyone as familiar with the
U.S. reality as he was, the issue of slavery was unambiguously at
the top of the political agenda by at least 1854 with the Nebraska-
Kansas Compromise, if not before. The stance of Marx and Engels
and their cohorts, or "Marx party" as they had begun to be
known, stood in stark contrast to Tocqueville's abstentionism.
While it is true that they prioritized the European revolutionary
process, Marx and Engels saw developments on both sides of the
Atlantic as interconnected. Once it became clear by the early 1850s
that the revolutionary wave in Europe had ebbed, the "party"
gave increasing attention to the United States, seeing it as the
venue where the democratic struggle could be continued. To understand why, it's necessary to look first at their practice in Europe. Comparing it to that of Tocqueville is also instructive.

During the 1848–1849 revolutions, Marx and Engels as communists, and therefore as revolutionary political activists, gave their undivided attention to developments on the European continent. Within the framework of their historical materialist perspective, they viewed the overthrow of the vestiges of feudalism in Europe as an integral element of the movement to end slavery in the United States, the democratic revolution. Marx, as the editor of the *Neue Rheinische Zeitung*, carried news about the abolitionist movement in the United States including a piece that "criticized the work of a recent American anti-slavery convention on the ground that the 'delegates and speakers loosed all sorts of shafts against the planter and his system but took no practical steps toward its abolition.'"[51] Since Marx argued the year before in 1847 in his famous polemic against Joseph Proudhon, *The Poverty of Philosophy*, that "*freedom* and *slavery* constitute an antagonism,"[52] it's not surprising that he wanted his readers to know how the struggle against feudalism's sister institution in the most advanced bourgeois democracy was unfolding.

Marx party members threw themselves into the democratic revolutions of 1848–1849 as thinkers and activists.[53] Marx, in particular, carried out tasks as diverse as editing the most consistent democratic voice in all of Germany during the thirteen-month period, the NRZ—"*Organ of Democracy*" was its subtitle. He headed up the mass democratic organizations in the city of Cologne, helping to forge alliances between workers and peasants in the region. He led the preparatory work for the armed defense of democratic forces in Cologne and the assembling of revolutionary legal defense work for himself and other party members. The events of 1848–1849 were Marx and Engels's baptism of fire in the revolutionary process.

The *Communist Manifesto*, written on the eve of the upheavals, outlined what their overall strategy would be in Germany; "to fight" to bring about the "bourgeois revolution" in order to proceed "immediately" to the "proletarian revolution." Their experiences in the actual movement and the lessons they drew permanently stamped all their subsequent activism, including their efforts in relation to U.S. politics. Marx and Engels established two principles drawn from the combat experience of the revolutions: only the workers, in alliance with the peasantry, could be counted on to push the bourgeois revolution to its conclusion and, second, only through independent, working-class political action could the proletariat liberate itself.

By the end of 1849 the counterrevolution had effectively crushed the revolutionary upheavals everywhere on the continent. The record makes clear that the role Tocqueville played in France was not unimportant.[54] In the parlance of the period, he was a "latter-day republican," someone who became a republican advocate after the revolution broke out in February 1848. He had "opposed *every* concrete proposal made to reform suffrage [that is, to extend it] during the July Monarchy," the regime in power at the time.[55] He was leery about the revolution from the beginning, fearful that the political reforms it instituted would soon lead to social reforms and, thus, infringe on private and capitalist property. His concerns were not unfounded. In April 1848, the new government signed in a decree that resulted in the immediate abolition of slavery in the colonies, effectively without compensation. Tocqueville, it may be recalled, had recommended a phased abolition with compensation to the slave owners.

Tocqueville feared exactly what Marx and Engels fought for in Germany—to enable the bourgeois revolution in France to proceed immediately to a proletarian revolution. When it appeared Tocqueville's worst nightmare was about to erupt in France with the June Revolution, this leading member of the Chamber of Deputies did every thing he could to thwart it. Tocqueville endorsed the Assembly's decision to institute what he termed a "military dictatorship under General Cavaignac"—flush from his recent victory over Algeria's peasants—in order to crush the workers of Paris on the barricades. At one point Tocqueville stooped from his pedestal and went to the streets to help assist in the slaughter in order to forestall the "providential" inevitability of the egalitarian quest.

In the Assembly, in the aftermath of the defeat of the uprising, he led the charge for the adoption of a "conservative policy of order." Later, as a member of the government, Tocqueville enabled the overthrow of the republican government in Rome. This blow helped to set the stage for the coup d'état of Louis

Bonaparte in December 1851, which exhausted the life of the Second Republic. Tocqueville's attempts as a government minister to humor Bonaparte in the months prior to his coup emboldened the future dictator. Tocqueville admitted on the eve of the coup that a new Bonapartist dictatorship was preferable to a new mass revolutionary upsurge. His self-reflection eight years earlier—"I am instinctively aristocratic because I despise and fear mobs"—foreshadowed the concrete actions he would later take. Soon after the coup Tocqueville decided to withdraw from politics and, until his death in 1859, concentrate on research and writing. He preferred to engage in musings about "democracy" in the abstract since the actual, living battle provided openings for the plebian hordes whose yearnings for emancipation were a threat to every aristocratic bone in Tocqueville's body. Thus in 1848–1849, he cast his lot with tyranny and bloody repression against the most limited outline of bourgeois democratic reform.

Preparing for a New Revolution

If Tocqueville no longer had the stomach for politics, that certainly wasn't true for Marx and Engels and other revolutionaries in Germany. They were now forced by defeat and repression to withdraw from the field of battle there and to look for new political opportunities elsewhere. They went into exile in England—this was after Marx had given serious thought to moving to the United States, like many of his fellow fighters—and undertook the next communist task: distill the lessons of 1848 and get them into print and into the hands of revolutionary workers in order to prepare for the next upsurge. Engels explained in the introduction to his *Revolution and Counterrevolution in Germany*, their summary statement on the German events, revolutionaries were obligated in the "interval of rest" between revolutionary upsurges "to study the causes" that led to both the "outbreak [of 1848–1849] . . . and its defeat." Their other balance sheets on the 1848 events included a series of articles that Engels later collected under the title *Class Struggles in France*, Marx's *The Eighteenth Brumaire of Louis Bonaparte*, and Engels's *The Peasant War in Germany*.

The political struggle required that the writings be published and disseminated to the most class-conscious workers. To this end they labored mightily to put out a theoretical journal, the *NRZ Revue*—the venue for the *Class Struggles* articles. Only a few issues ever appeared. The effect of their increasingly depleted resources and the shrinkage of political space as reaction began to set in throughout much of Europe forced them to look to the United States as the best place to get their views into print. When Marx learned in 1851 that Joseph Weydemeyer was moving to New York, he told him that this would be "of service to our party . . . and with the wholesale suppression of newspapers in Germany, it is only over there that we can conduct the struggle in the press."[56] It was in Weydemeyer's journal in 1852, *Die Reform*, the first Marxist periodical in the United States, that *The Eighteenth Brumaire* was published.

Engels's *Revolution and Counterrevolution* first appeared, in serial form (1851–1852) in the influential and antislavery *New York Daily Tribune*, a paper read in Europe as well as the United States. Founded in 1841, it "became the gospel for rural Americans, especially thousands of prairie farmers, many of whom migrated west during the 1840s and 1850s. After New York, *Tribune* readership was greatest in Pennsylvania, Ohio, Illinois, and Indiana—all critical states in national affairs. . . . By 1860 it was the most widely read newspaper in the United States, and perhaps the world, with an estimated one million readers . . . the established leader of America's mass media in the 1850s."[57] Its publisher, Horace Greeley, gave Marx and Engels a venue and audience they had never had before or after. A leading voice of the Whig Party, defender of indigenous capital, Free-Soil advocate and, later, an opponent of slavery, the paper and its publisher saw common cause with Marx and Engels, at least to the extent their ideas were understood. Approximately 528 of their articles were published over a ten-year span, from 1851 to 1862, or about one article a week in either the daily, semiweekly or weekly editions.[58] It was through the *Tribune* that Marx became known to U.S. audiences for the first time. Henry Carey, the first major American economist, came to know and admire Marx through the pages of the paper.

The Carey example reveals that however often Marx and Engels's writings appeared in the *Tribune* they were under no illusion that it served as a "party" paper. For Marx it was primarily a source of very needed income in a difficult financial period and not a means for disseminating his full program. The Marx that Carey knew through the pages of the *Tribune* was no threat to his brand of bourgeois economics. But Marx and Engels could write for it without any qualms about compromising principles. As Marx explained in 1859, "My real business with the *Tribune* consists in writing leaders about anything I choose."[59] The *Tribune* represented the interests of the ascendant industrial bourgeoisie against the slavocracy—with Carey as its chief literary representative.[60] As Marx and Engels had written in the final section of the *Manifesto*, communists in America were prepared to support the program of free soil (though with qualifications, as the critique of Kriege made clear). And in "Germany, as soon as the bourgeoisie acts in a revolutionary way the Communist party fights together with the bourgeoisie against the absolute monarchy, feudal landed property, and the petty-bourgeoisie."[61]

Thus, an alliance with free soilers—aspiring peasants—and an ascendant bourgeoisie against the U.S. version of feudalism—slavery—objectively unfolded as Marx and Engels wrote for the *Tribune*. This was completely in accord with a communist program. To advance the bourgeois revolution was to advance the proletarian revolution. The fact remains, though, that in spite of their access to the paper and other publications in Europe—*Die Presse*, the Viennese liberal daily, and their effort on one occasion to establish a specifically "party press" during this period—they never had a venue that allowed them to carry out the "struggle in the press" in the manner they had with the *NRZ* in 1848–1849.

As an English-language publication it is impossible to know what the *Tribune*'s German American readership was. It is reasonable to assume that Engels's articles on the German Revolutions of 1848–1849, the only in-depth analysis of its kind in print on either side of the Atlantic, attracted an enormous audience within that community. It should also be noted that press censorship instituted in Germany by then meant that the largest number of Germans who read Marx and Engels resided in the

United States. Since the articles were published in Marx's name and in what was then one of the most prestigious papers in America, it is likely that he acquired a degree of credibility within the community theretofore unattained. This could only have grown more for both Marx and Engels as their articles became regular features in the paper over the next decade. By 1859, Marx could report that "[a]mong the said subscribers to the *Tribune* there are a great many Germans. Moreover, the "German-American newspapers . . . reprint stuff from it."[62] He was clearly referring to pieces that he and Engels had written.

The "struggle in the press" was part of the larger goal of party-building work. To that end, two letters from Marx and Engels were waiting Weydemeyer when he arrived in New York in November 1851. One asked him to take the enclosed English translation of the *Manifesto* (Marx had just sent it along with twenty copies of the German version to a contact in the city) and see "if you can publish, distribute and sell it." Marx also requested that Weydemeyer send "20–50 copies for ourselves" to be distributed in England. Another instruction was that Weydemeyer look into the possibility of publishing a "kind of pocket library" of *NRZ* articles since the paper "was not widely distributed in America." The specific pieces he suggested for the collection were a series of articles on the peasantry written by Wilhelm Wolff (the comrade to whom Marx dedicated *Capital*); "The Silesian Milliard," another series that Engels wrote on the Hungarian struggle for self-determination; and his own article about the German events, "The Bourgeoisie and the Counter-Revolution." He also recommended that Weydemeyer reproduce in pamphlet form some of his and Engels's important polemics with German opponents who were now living in the United States. Marx also suggested that in the future the *NRZ Revue* articles should be reprinted. In spite of their best efforts very few of the things they had published in the United States reached workers in Europe. In the United States itself, except for Engels's *Revolution and Counterrevolution*, what was published was confined largely to the German émigré community in whose language it mainly appeared.

Until his death in 1866, Weydemeyer functioned as the de facto head of the Marx party in the United States. Within a few months of his arrival in New York in November 1851 he began to publish *Die Reform* and six months later, along with three other émigrés, founded the first Marxist party in the United States, *Proletarierbund*, Worker's League. All of this was achieved in consultation with Marx and Engels. The significance of both steps became immediately clear: "German New York was the third capital of the German-speaking world. Only Vienna and Berlin had larger German populations than New York City between 1855 and 1880."[63] With the *Bund* as his base he then organized the more inclusive German-speaking labor organization, *Amerikanische Arbeiterbund* or American Labor Union—one of the first efforts to form a labor party in the United States. Following the lessons that Marx and Engels had drawn from the upheavals of 1848–1849, Weydemeyer saw the Union as a vehicle for independent, working-class political action and, therefore, a means for undermining Kriege and Weitling's efforts to lead German workers into the Democratic Party. His efforts during that period made him the "'most prominent German Labour agitator in America.'"[64] The economic crisis of 1854–1855, however, brought all labor organizing to a halt and eventually forced Weydemeyer to leave New York and look for greener pastures to the west, first Milwaukee and then Chicago.

Weydemeyer, through first *Die Reform* and then other newspapers, played a crucial role—again, in consultation with Marx and Engels—in waging an important and largely successful fight inside the German émigré community to counter the pro-slavery influence of the Democratic Party whose fortunes had been promoted by Kriege and Weitling. He also helped lead a mass campaign in New York's German community against the 1854 Kansas-Nebraska Act, which had opened up new territories to the slavocracy.

"Like Marx, Weydemeyer believed that the free labor movement could not develop as long as slavery existed and hampered the growth of industrial capitalism. In articles in the *Turn-Zeitung* and the Illinois *Staats-Zeitung*, Weydemeyer reiterated that the heart of the slavery controversy was the struggle between the industrial and slave economy, and that the success of the former through the abolition of chattel slavery would create new possibilities for the development of free labor. He brushed aside the contention of . . . Kriege and Weitling, that the abolition of wage slavery was the primary issue and the abolition of Negro slavery a 'side issue.' He insisted that wage workers could not advance further in American society until chattel slavery was eliminated, that they must play an important role in hastening its downfall, and that its demise would in turn strengthen their organization for the subsequent fight against capital."[65]

Thus, if Marx and Engels's critique of Kriege six years earlier had not explicitly addressed the slavery question, the Marx party, led by Weydemeyer, left little doubt about their position. Bruce Levine presents convincing evidence that the strongest antislavery sentiment in the German American communities came from its working-class layers rather than its bourgeoisie—evidence that would have hardly surprised Marx and Engels.[66]

Weydemeyer's efforts were not without trial and tribulation. Not only did the legacy of Kriege and Weitling continue to be a challenge but the material reality of the United States itself—the very thing that Marx and Engels had warned Weydemeyer about when he moved to the United States—was an ever present obstacle. "In 1858, Weydemeyer had written to Karl Marx that in America, 'the workers are incipient Bourgeois and feel themselves to be such', so that the prospects for 'proletarian propaganda' were poor."[67] In general, the party had its greatest influence amongst the refugees of the 1848 revolutions—they were the Germans most disposed to embracing their program and looking to them for leadership. It's no accident that a veteran of 1848 and a friend of Weydemeyer, Albert Komp, took the initiative to revive, in the latter's absence, the Marxist movement in New York in 1857. The Communist Club of New York, arguably the "first Marxist organization in the Western Hemisphere," was also unique in being "the only socialist (and labor) organization that invited Blacks to join as equal members. Its constitution required all members to 'recognize the complete equality of all persons—no matter of whatever color or sex.'"[68] Among its recruits was Friedrich Sorge, the individual in the United States with whom Marx and Engels would work most closely following Weydemeyer's death. The club sought Marx's assistance—though the record is not clear how much he actually provided. Fleeting references in correspondence suggest that Marx's political economy work took priority though he was evidently encouraging; even correspondence from Weydemeyer was put on hold for at least a year.[69] From Milwaukee, Weydemeyer was certainly helpful by making contacts for it in other cities and leading to the formation of new clubs in Chicago and Cincinnati.

The New York Club revived the *Arbeiterbund* but it was clear by 1859 that the perspective for independent working-class action for which Weydemeyer had fought when he lived in the city had been replaced with a reformist perspective and leadership in the German working-class movement. This included some veterans of 1848—further evidence for Marx and Engels's warnings to Weydemeyer about the political reality of the United States. In spite of the reformist obstacles the Marx party faced, the "Communist Clubs were in the forefront of the anti-slavery fight." In New York, the club "used its influence in insisting that the anti-slavery struggle had to be recognized as a main task of the working class."[70] Elsewhere, their members played an important role in mobilizing the German American workers in opposition to the peculiar institution, if not always successfully in New York, then in other cities.

Ever on the lookout for a revival of the revolutionary movement, Marx and Engels took to heart two events at the end of 1859. Marx declared—and Engels concurred—"that the most momentous thing happening in the world today is the slave movement—on the one hand, in America, started by the death of Brown, and in Russia, on the other." Marx was referring, of course, to the abortive rebellion of the abolitionist John Brown at Harpers Ferry, Virginia, a few months earlier, which in turn had stimulated at least one slave uprising in its aftermath. As for Russia, its "slaves," i.e., serfs, had also been on the march for emancipation as he had noted the previous year. A year later, in a move to preempt a revolt from below, the czar abolished serfdom. The Russian movement's coincidence with abolitionism in

the United States was of enormous significance. Precisely because they viewed social conflicts from an international perspective, Marx and Engels gave more weight to the simultaneity and
conjuncture of class struggles in various countries than to isolated ones. The fight against slavery and other precapitalist
modes of exploitation was bound inexorably to the democratic
revolution and a necessary step in labor's struggle against capital. The Brown rebellion registered the depths of the impending
crisis within the United States itself. For antislavery fighters it
gave a needed lift to their cause, providing a hero of deeds of the
first order, an abolitionist Jacobin, whose state execution would
inspire still further antislavery protest. The veterans of 1848 responded predictably. In Cincinnati, August Willich, who once
fought with Marx and Engels in the German revolution, "headed
a giant torchlight procession through the streets of Cincinnati to
protest and mourn the execution of John Brown."[71] The mobilization was in tandem with a meeting in the city's German
"Over the Rhine District." A summary of an account of it by the
anonymous and unsympathetic "Spectator" is worth repeating
in full.

> The main floor and galleries of the hall were packed, Spectator
> reported. Some two-thirds of those present were Germans;
> most of the rest were black—"lineal descendants of Ham."
> Black-red-gold banners hung from the gallery, and on the main
> stage were the Stars and Stripes, "with a stalwart nigger as stan-
> dard bearer." The purpose of this singular gathering became
> clear when Spectator turned toward the speaker's platform. It
> was draped in the black crepe of mourning and bore the words,
> "In Memory of John Brown." Among those who spoke was the
> Unitarian minister Moncure Daniel Conway, destined to be-
> come the outstanding advocate of Thomas Paine's ideas and
> the editor of his works. John Brown, Conway asserted on this
> occasion, was "the last apostle and martyr" of "Paine's creed."
> After Conway came Peter A. Clark, the black abolitionist prin-
> cipal of the Western District Colored School. Clark was gratified
> to "address a meeting of the only freedom-loving people of this
> city," the only ones who were prepared "to do justice to his
> race" and "to vindicate the principles of freedom."

But Spectator seemed most shaken by the words of a third speaker—August Willich, leader of the city's *Arbeiterverein* [Worker's Union] and editor of its newspaper. Spectator listened in stunned disbelief as Willich not only mourned Brown and denounced slavery, the Democratic party, and its supporters but also "exhorted his hearers to whet their sabers and nerve their arms for the day of retribution, when Slavery and Democracy would be crushed in a common grave." No less alarming than these speeches was the reaction of the interracial crowd. The fiery words delivered from the podium, Spectator reported indignantly, "received the rapturous applause of the motley gathering." Indeed, he continued, "the fiercer the denunciations of slavery and Democracy, the more uproarious were the wooly-heads and their allies."[72]

Even committed abolitionists like Frederick Douglass were reluctant to go as far as Willich had gone in not only praising Brown but in urging those in attendance to do what would indeed—within two years—have to be done. For defenders of the peculiar institution, Brown's rebellion was greeted with fear and loathing. They correctly realized that their way of life was threatened unlike ever before. The reports of those like the Spectator confirmed their worst fears.

The reactions of both camps to the Brown rebellion quickly found their way into the electoral arena. Most opponents of slavery embraced the Republican Party founded just six years earlier. "The Germans . . . were the most outspoken and energetic antislavery elements in the Republican party."[73] Most Free-Soilers also recognized, in the aftermath of the Nebraska-Kansas Act, that their cause could only be realized if the slavocracy was overthrown. The veterans of 1848—Weydemeyer in particular—actively campaigned to make not only this connection but the deeper point that slavery's overthrow was the necessary condition for the emancipation of the working class. [74] The question for the upcoming 1860 presidential election was who would be the party's standard bearer and on what kind of antislavery program.

With Weydemeyer at the helm, the Marx party played an active role in advancing the antislavery cause at this very crucial moment—specifically, in the nomination and election of Abraham

Lincoln. To do so, however, required a venue that Milwaukee—where Weydemeyer was headquartered—couldn't offer. Thus, he didn't hesitate to accept the invitation of the Chicago *Arbeiterverein* to move there at the beginning of 1860 to edit its newspaper, *Stimme des Volkes*. The Chicago local of the newly formed *Allgemeine Arbeiterbund von Nord-Amerika* (General Worker's League of North America) had not succumbed to the reformist tendencies to which the New York movement had fallen prey. It was willing to take on national responsibilities for the organization, an attitude that was especially appealing to Weydemeyer. Chicago was the site of the upcoming Republican national convention and located in the state of one of its presidential aspirants, Abraham Lincoln. This fact may also have been influential in Weydemeyer's decision to move there. Upon assuming his new duties he immediately contacted Marx for assistance and consultation. Marx responded enthusiastically by appealing to "party" members in Europe to become correspondents for the paper: "as party work it is *very* important. W[eydemeyer] is one of our *best* people."[75]

From Chicago, Weydemeyer worked with another 1848 veteran, Adolph Douai, "to mobilize support among German-American workers for the Republican party" in New York.[76] Douai had already established his well-deserved antislavery credentials, first, as the leading abolitionist voice in Texas—during his stay in San Antonio from 1852 to 1856[77]—and then, later, in Boston where he challenged the reactionary views of the well-known Harvard naturalist, Louis Agassiz. "He attacked Agassiz not only as a reactionary but as a racist, noting that his belief in Negro inferiority—as set forth in his 1850 essay 'The Diversity of the Origin of the Human Race'—helped to provide a rationale for slavery."[78]

On the eve of the Republican national convention in May 1860, Weydemeyer and Douai were delegates to the Deutsches Haus conference in Chicago. The event was organized by German Republican clubs around the country to influence the outcome of the convention. German American Republicans listed a number of priorities: that the convention take a strong antislavery position, that it oppose Know-Nothing "Americanism"—specifically, restrictive naturalization laws, and that it support congressional passage of the Homestead Act—the Free-Soil legislation. All of these positions were reflected in the resolutions of the conference.

Regarding the first item, the conference asked that the founding principles of the Republican Party from the 1856 convention be "applied in a sense most hostile to slavery."[79] While accounts of the conference are sketchy, Weydemeyer was one of its "forceful characters" and he "worked closely together" with Douai to realize its aims.[80] There is some suggestion that Weydemeyer, while actively participating in the conference, didn't see it, as some apparently did—especially those from the east—as an effort to give marching orders to the German American delegates to the Republican convention. To have done so would have meant "usurping the rights of the people" who elected delegates to the latter—an indication that he, a Marx party member, took democratic norms seriously.[81]

The Deutsches Haus delegates "requested" the German American delegates to the Republican convention to make every effort to have the resolutions become part of the party's platform. Though they were only partially successful, in "the end, the Republican National Convention did satisfy many of the Deutsches Haus concerns."[82] If the platform wasn't as "hostile to slavery" as they hoped, it did adopt positions with which they could live. For other concerns—naturalization laws and the homestead legislation—they were more successful. Though the Deutsches Haus meeting tactically decided not to back a particular nominee, its inaction actually improved the chances for Lincoln—an outcome that was apparently not inadvertent. Some German American communities and groups had concluded by the time of Chicago that Lincoln, though not as antislavery as they preferred, was more electable.[83] Weydemeyer's *Stimme des Volkes* "judged the . . . platform 'certainly something short of a radical one, and a little lukewarm,' but one nevertheless 'that in general satisfies the demands we make upon it.' It believed Lincoln was 'the choice of the conservative wing of the Republican Convention' but vowed to support him as the 'lesser of two evils.' Willich's *Cincinnati Republikaner* took the party's preference for Lincoln over an outright radical as 'a stunning blow.' But at least, it noted, Lincoln was free of Know-Nothing taint. . . . 'If Lincoln is not enshrined in the hearts of the people like Frémont [Republican presidential candidate in 1856], he has nonetheless labored among the people all his life—he is truly a self-made man!'"[84] It was in a similar spirit that Frederick Douglass viewed the Lincoln nomination. While Illinois's "favorite son" was not an abolitionist, the "slaveholders know that the day of their power is over when a Republican President is elected. . . . I sincerely hope for the triumph of that party over all the odds and ends of slavery combined against it."[85]

In spite of their reservations about Lincoln, veterans of 1848, and Marx party members in particular, actively campaigned for his election. An ad in Willich's *Republikaner* said, "Close Ranks! For Free Labor, against Slavery. Abraham Lincoln for President! Hannibal Hamlin for Vice President!"[86] As Marx explained to one party member in Europe, "This time there seems good reason to hope that victory . . . will go to the REPUBLICAN PARTY."[87] Weydemeyer moved to New York in August 1860 to collaborate more closely with Douai on the campaign. This proved to be of enormous importance since the clothing industry bosses—Democratic partisans like most of the city's bourgeoisie—carried out a scare campaign to get their tailors to vote for the Democratic-fusion ticket that the slavocracy could live with. A vote for Lincoln, they argued, would lead to secession, an economic crisis, and the lost of their jobs.

Since the German American vote, concentrated in the city, could tip the state's vote in favor of Lincoln, and since the vast majority of the tailors in the city were German, Weydemeyer's presence—and political intervention—was considered essential. Through Douai's paper *New Yorker Demokrat*, the Communist Club, and his own participation in the mass movement, Weydemeyer proved to be an effective campaigner. In the end he was able to undermine the scare tactics of the bosses.[88]

Although Lincoln lost New York City—the influence of it's bourgeoisie and the weight of Irish voters were decisive—Weydemeyer and Douai's efforts were not without reward. The Republican vote in the predominantly German wards increased significantly over that of the 1856 vote. This was of special significance in the wards in Brooklyn where most of the tailors lived—precisely those German workers to whom Weydemeyer had given special attention—that Lincoln actually won a majority of the German American vote.

What happened in New York was part of a national pattern. First, as was true in Brooklyn, "most organized German craftworkers and other radical democratic organizations evidently supported Lincoln in 1860."[89] Second, in those parts of the country where the Republican Party carried with it the taint of nativism, such as New York and other east coast states, Lincoln did less well amongst German Americans. In the Midwest, where, in general, this wasn't the case, Lincoln clearly won their vote. In Illinois and Missouri the German American vote was decisive in Lincoln winning the state. In other cities where there was a Communist Club, Chicago and Cincinnati, Lincoln, respectively, won or was nearly successful, no doubt in part due to the Communist Club campaigners.[90]

It was one thing for the candidate of the Marx party to win the election. It was another matter for him to stand firm on the slavery question. This became most apparent in the wake of Lincoln's victory as the slavocracy began to take the first steps toward secession. As Engels wrote to Marx in early January 1861: "In North America things are. . . . heating up. With the slaves the situation must be pretty awful if the SOUTHERNERS are playing such a risky game. . . . [which] might result in a general conflagration. At all events . . . slavery would appear to be rapidly nearing its end."[91]

While history would prove Engels's prediction to be true, it was far from certain at that moment that the president-elect would stand up to the slave owners. Such uncertainty was clearly the sentiment of the milieu with whom the Marx party worked most closely for Lincoln.

Three days after the election, Douai wrote in his paper that those who campaigned for Lincoln but were not, like himself, Republican Party members, had the "special task to see to it that what has been achieved with our help is not again undone but is built up still more; and if reactionary elements in the Party of Reaction intend to do that, we must form a counter-weight to them and press forward to further gains."[92] Vigilance now was the cardinal

duty, avoiding the assumption that the election had necessarily settled anything. In subsequent issues Douai concluded that the
struggle at hand was, as Engels had noted, for the complete abolition of slavery. He also argued that the "slave has in every condition the right and in certain conditions even the duty to free
himself by every means possible from slavery,"[93] or, as Malcolm X
would teach almost a century later, liberation "by any means necessary." This was clearly a stance far beyond what the president-
elect understood his mandate to be, but one that Engels accurately
predicted he would be compelled to advance.

When Lincoln, on the way to his inauguration in Washington, visited Cincinnati in February 1861, he learned that the
kinds of sentiments Douai expressed in his paper were far from
unique. A delegation of two thousand German American workers greeted him with the following message:

> Sir—We, the German free workingmen of Cincinnati, avail our-
> selves of the opportunity to assure you, our . . . sincere and heart-
> felt regard. You earned our votes as the champion of Free Labor
> and Free Homesteads. [We reject any efforts] to create an impres-
> sion, as if the mass of workingmen were in favor of compromises
> between the interests of free labor, and slave labor, by which the
> victory just won would be turned into a defeat. . . . We Trust, that
> you . . . will uphold the Constitution and the laws against secret
> treachery and avowed treason. If to this end you should be in
> need of men, the German free workingmen, with others, will rise
> as one man at your call, ready to risk their lives in the effort to
> maintain the victory already won by freedom over slavery.[94]

Thus, in no uncertain terms this group of German workers
made clear to Lincoln "what had to be done," an unmistakable
effort to steel him for the widely expected "general conflagration." One of the individuals doubtless present at Lincoln's reception was Willich, who played a leading role in Cincinnati's
German working-class movement and the broader democratic
struggle through his newspaper Republikaner. His politics
"earned him the nickname 'Reddest of the Red.'"[95]

Willich's profile and story is especially revealing. It testifies to the power of an effective theoretical perspective and the

results of making ideas known. Though Willich had fought with Marx and Engels in the German revolutions of 1848–1849 as a member of the Communist League, he broke with them in a bitter fight within the organization in the aftermath of the upheavals. Put simply, he disagreed with Marx and Engels's judgement that the prospects for a new revolutionary upsurge had ended. Willich and his faction argued that revolution was still on the agenda. Reality proved Marx and Engels to have been correct.

Like the other 1,848 veterans, Willich found his way to the United States and eventually settled in Cincinnati in 1858. Though the sequence of events is not entirely clear, what is known is that when Marx published his book *A Contribution to the Critique of Political Economy* in 1859, Willich embraced it and recommended it to his readers. To have done so is significant because it was in the work's famous preface that Marx sketched his historical materialist perspective—"the guiding thread for my studies." It was exactly that perspective that Willich rejected in the split with Marx and Engels in 1851.

Willich's change of mind is evidence that Marx was right to have prioritized what he called the "scientific work" in the preceding decade and to avoid unnecessary political activities, such as the request of the New York Communist Club organizers in 1857 for his active assistance. A few months before the publication of *A Contribution*, Marx left no doubt, in a very belated reply to Weydemeyer, of its purpose. "I hope to win a scientific victory for our party."[96]

Earlier in the decade Marx told Engels that "[w]e must recruit our party entirely anew."[97] Willich's conversion also testifies to Marx's political acumen in waging the "struggle in the press." In 1859, the preface first appeared in the periodical most approximating a "party" organ during this period—the very short-lived *Das Volk*. Two months later he informed Engels that the preface had been "reprinted from the *Volk* and variously commented on by German papers from New England to California."[98] Willich's *Republikaner* was one of those papers. Thus, the combination of theoretical and practical work effectively brought Willich back into the Marx party fold.

Willich's return may have had practical consequences as well. It's possible that with his embrace of Marx's method he began to pursue a line of politics independent of but completely consistent with what Weydemeyer was doing. Like the latter, he offered critical support to the Republican Party "until labor could organize a national party of its own."[99] The earlier Willich, who Marx correctly criticized for seeing the revolutionary process as a matter "of *will*" and taking "power *at once*," would have rejected any support to the Republicans. His perspective had been that of instant communist revolution.[100] By 1859, at least, he viewed as a central priority the overthrow of slavery as a necessary condition for workers taking power—the same *longue durée* vision that informed Weydemeyer's practice. Thus he supported Lincoln in spite of reservations. The changed scenery of the United States helped make it possible for Willich to understand Marx and Engels's historical materialist perspective in a way that revolutionary Europe of 1848–1849 could not—a moment when even the authors of the *Manifesto* thought that socialist revolution was imminent. Marx later acknowledged, on the basis of his record both before and during the Civil War that his criticisms applied only to the earlier Willich. "In the American Civil War Willich demonstrated that he was something more than a weaver of fantastic projects."[101]

Douai's trajectory is likewise noteworthy. Though a veteran of 1848, he, unlike Willich, had not been a Marx party member or part of its milieu. Politically, he had been closer in fact to the sentimental socialists like Kriege against whom Marx and Engels had polemicized. But during his stay in the United States Douai's practice increasingly converged with that of the Marx party, including intimate collaboration with Weydemeyer in New York in behalf of Lincoln's election. At the level of theory, though, Douai wasn't yet a Marxist. His justification for supporting Lincoln is instructive. Like Weydemeyer, he too saw the election of Lincoln as not an end but a means to an end. But for Douai that end was "still greater victories for the cause of humanity."[102] For the communist Weydemeyer, however—and Willich as well—the end was the overthrow of class society, that is, socialist transformation. That process required workers to take power, an impossibility as long as slavery was in place. The "cause of humanity" was the language of the pre-communist Marx who spoke of "human emancipation." After the publication of *Capital* in 1867, Douai proclaimed his adherence to the Marxist program and became one of its leading propagandists in the United States. As with Willich, Marx's scientific work bore fruit again. This political harvest required the kind of practice in which Weydemeyer and the Marx-Engels team, separated by a vast ocean, were willing to invest the time and energy.

The convergence of the Marx party with Willich and Douai was possible because of their common political work—their efforts to mobilize opposition to slavery in the German American working class—because despite differences they were all fighters. Willich and Douai were militants of a movement that engaged most veterans of 1848. In that sense they were not unique. This should not come as a surprise. Marx and Engels never saw their program as a scheme or catechism but rather the generalized lessons of the real movement of the working class. "Communism is not a doctrine," Engels argued many years earlier, "but a *movement*; it proceeds not from principles but from *facts*."[103] Willich, Douai, Weydemeyer and many others were all participants in the working-class component of the antislavery movement—exactly as they should have been. Only on that basis could the communist wing distinguish itself—by distilling the lessons of the movement in its entirety. Thus, they saw themselves as the most conscious component of that movement, those who had the clearest understanding of its historical significance and its future. As the *Manifesto* put it, "in the [working class] movement of the present, they [communists] also represent and take care of the future of that movement."

The next stage in the movement began with the slavocracy's attack on and conquest of Fort Sumter, South Carolina, in April 1861—the explosive commencement of the "general conflagration" that Engels anticipated. Again, the Marx party would take its position alongside other working-class fighters. "When the Civil War began with the attack . . . most of the German radical organizations disbanded because the majority of their members had enlisted in the Union forces. The New York Communist

Club did not meet for the duration of the war since most of its members had joined the Union Army."[104] Weydemeyer was among the first communists to don the Union blue.

Tocqueville died two years to the month before the outbreak of the war. His correspondence indicates that he followed developments in America closely, identifying himself as one point as "partly an American citizen." He anticipated impending events with unmistakable dread. The very real likelihood of war depressed him. Tocqueville's aristocratic worldview prevented him from seeing what the enslaved and the abolitionists could—war as an opportunity for the overthrow of slavery. Nothing in his political core or perspective allowed him to see that such a decisive contest might actually advance the democratic process. Neither could he envision that immigrants from Germany would make a significant contribution in the outcome of that contest. Their "rapid introduction into the United States," he wrote in 1854, "men foreign to the English race was the greatest peril that America would have to run, and what makes the final success of democratic institutions still an unresolved problem."[105] The prospect that Tocqueville's "absolute democracy" was going to war, a civil war at that, challenged, in his eyes, the claims he was famous for about the exemplary character of the U.S. polity.[106]

For Marx, on the other hand, war meant that the "defiled republic" could finally cleanse itself of the stench of chattel slavery. Above all, this historic confrontation by rival social systems provided an opportunity for working people, including German communists, to participate in that momentous showdown—to ensure that the democratic revolution, located this time on the soil of the adolescent United States, would not fail as it had in 1848–1849 in the old world of Europe.

Notes

1. Consistent with my chronological approach of presentation, I am employing here the original 1848 *Manifesto* rather than Engels's more common 1888 English translation which says "whenever."

2. This is the reason that Engels employed "whenever" rather than "as soon as" in his 1888 translation of the *Manifesto*—an acknowledg-

ment that the hope implied in "as soon as" that he and Marx held about the bourgeoisie was unfulfilled; see preceding note. For more details, see Hal Draper, *The Adventures of the Communist Manifesto* (Berkeley: Center for Socialist History, 1994), p. 321.

3. Alexis de Tocqueville, *Democracy in America*, Vol. 1 (New York: Vintage Books, 1945), p. 6.

4. **6**, pp. 471–72.

5. **18**, pp. 67–69.

6. André Jardin, *Tocqueville: A Biography* (New York: Farrar, Staus, Giroux, 1998), pp. 333–34. For a recent assessment of Tocqueville's posture toward Algeria, also critical, but from a different perspective, see Cheryl B. Welch, "Colonial Violence and the Rhetoric of Evasion," *Political Theory* 31, no. 2 (April 2003):

7. Alexis de Tocqueville, *Oeuvres Complètes*, III, 1 (Paris: Editions Gallimard, 1962), p. 311.

8. Ibid., p. 324.

9. Ibid., p. 342.

10. **46**, pp. 234, 242.

11. **12**, p. 132.

12. Ibid., p. 221.

13. **40**, pp. 142, 249. In the *Marx-Engels Collected Works*, English words in the original are given in small caps.

14. Alexis de Tocqueville, *Selected Letters on Politics and Society*, ed. Roger Boesche (Berkeley: University of California Press, 1985), pp. 359–60.

15. August H. Nimtz, Jr., *Marx and Engels: Their Contribution to the Democratic Breakthrough* (Albany: State University Press of New York, 2000).

16. **6**, p. 323.

17. Though Marx never made the argument (at least as far as the written record is concerned) the logic of his method, politics, and reading of the United States could lead one to conclude that it is this reality, the vigor of social or class inequality, that explains why racial inequality took off with such a vengeance—exactly at the moment when the former was entrenching itself. Racial inequality, in other words, became a convenient and conscious way to camouflage class inequality. Barbara Fields makes a related argument in "Slavery, Race and Ideology in the United States of America," *New Left Review*, no. 181 (May–June 1990).

18. Ibid., pp. 334–35.

19. This is the central argument of Donald L. Robinson's *Slavery in the Structure of American Politics, 1765–1820* (New York: Harcourt Brace Jovanovich, Inc., 1971). This reality figured significantly in recent U.S.

politics, specifically, the role of the electoral college—one of the compromises reached at Philadelphia—in the "fiasco" of the 2000 presidential election.

20. **6**, p. 167. He said as much the same six months earlier in a letter; **38**, p. 101.

21. Michael Goldfield, *The Color of Politics: Race and the Mainspring of American Politics* (New York: The New Press, 1997), pp. 86–87.

22. **38**, p. 101. In this letter to Pavel Annenkov, Marx anticipated, almost verbatim, his aforementioned comments on slavery in the polemic with Proudhon.

23. **6**, p. 100.

24. Karl Marx, *Grundrisse* (Middlesex, England: Penguin Books, 1973), p. 513.

25. Charles Sellers, *The Market Revolution: Jacksonian America, 1815–1846* (New York: Oxford University Press, 1991) p. 396.

26. **9**, p. 211.

27. For details, see "Critique against Kriege," **6**, pp. 34–51.

28. David Herreshoff, *The Origins of American Marxism: From the Transcendentalists to De Leon* (New York: Pathfinder Press, 1967), particularly, chapter 2.

29. Bruce Levine, *The Spirit of 1848: German Immigrants, Labor Conflict and the Coming of the Civil War* (Urbana: University of Illinois Press, 1992), p. 105.

30. Philip S. Foner, *American Socialism and Black Americans: From the Age of Jackson to World War II* (Westport, Conn.: Greenwood Press, 1977), p. 14.

31. Levine, *Spirit of 1848*, pp. 151–52.

32. **6**, 41–42.

33. **6**, 43.

34. Kriege's second, above-cited comment about abolition was published in November 1846 (Levine, *Spirit of 1848*, p. 322 fn. 8), at least eight months after the circular. The Brussels committee sent a second circular in October 1846 that Marx largely wrote, but it has yet to be found.

35. Anthony Gronowicz, *Race and Class Politics in New York City before the Civil War* (Boston: Northeastern University Press, 1998), p. 126. It's interesting to note that not every refugee from the 1848 revolution believed in the immutability of two-party politics as it existed then. "Fritz Anneke," with whom Marx and Engels had collaborated in the revolution, "remained 'convinced that the old parties are on the verge of dissolution'"(Levine, *Spirit of 1848*, p. 152). This suggests that the position of Kriege and others that German workers had no alternative to

the Democratic Party was not shared by those who still retained a revolutionary perspective.

36. Stanley Nadel, *Little Germany: Ethnicity, Religion, and Class in New York City, 1845–1880* (Chicago: University of Illinois Press, 1990), pp. 118–19.

37. While it's true that New York City white workers were intimately linked to the cotton trade and thus to the slavocracy, the response of the British working class during the Civil War, as will be seen in chapter 3, makes clear that there was no ineluctable proclivity of workers in such situations to support the slavocracy.

38. Philip Foner, *American Socialism*, p. 13.

39. Even Chartists who migrated to the United States, advanced workers from Europe who, owing to the longevity of their movement, might be expected to have behaved otherwise, found the call of the Free-Soilers hard to resist. See Ray Boston, *British Chartists in America, 1839–1900* (Totowa, N. J.: Rowman & Littlefield, 1971), p. 54, 63.

40. See chapter 1, p. 9

41. **38**, p. 406.

42. Ibid., p. 454.

43. **39**, p. 62.

44. Marx, *Grundrisse*, p. 884.

45. **38**, p. 454.

46. Jardin, pp. 306–7.

47. Seymour Drescher, *Tocqueville and Beaumont on Social Reform* (New York: Harper Torchbooks, 1968), p. 149.

48. See Lawrence C. Jennings, *French Anti-Slavery: The Movement for the Abolition of Slavery in France, 1802–1848* (New York: Cambridge University Press, 2000), chapter 7, for the details and reason for this retreat.

49. Ibid., p. 187.

50. His correspondence indicates that he was a confidant of Charles Summer, the famous abolitionist senator from Massachusetts. See Tocqueville, *Selected Letters*, p. 358.

51. Herbert Morais, "Marx and Engels on America," *Science and Society* 12, no. 1 (winter 1948): 9.

52. I am taking some liberty here with Marx's polemic. The quotation is actually from a letter he wrote some months earlier that outlined his argument against Proudhon. See respectively, **38**, p. 101, and **6**, p. 167–68.

53. For details, see my *Marx and Engels*, chapters 3 and 4.

54. Again, for details, see ibid., chapter 5.

55. Alan S. Kahan, *Aristocratic Liberalism: The Social and Political Thought of Jacob Burkhardt, John Stuart Mill, and Alexis de Tocqueville* (New York: Oxford University Press, 1992), p. 72.

56. **38**, pp. 402–3.

57. Coy F. Cross, *"Go West Young Man!: Horace Greeley's Vision for America* (Albuquerque: University of New Mexico Press, 1995), pp. 21–22. Another account says "Greeley could reasonably claim a collective readership of some one and a half million Americans"(Richard Kluger, *The Paper: The Life and Death of the* New York Herald Tribune [New York: Alfred A. Knopf, 1986], p. 92).

58. For the complete list see Hal Draper, *The Marx-Engels Register: A Complete Bibliography of Marx and Engels' Individual Writings* (New York: Schocken Books, 1985), pp. 160–72. "Approximately" refers to the number of articles whose authorship, as Draper indicates, is uncertain.

59. **40**, p. 409.

60. "During the 1850's, Carey served as a consultant to Greeley on economic matters, and the *Tribune*—the North's 'economic oracle'—reflected his views"(Eric Foner, *Free Soil, Free Labor, Free Men: The Ideology of the Republican Party before the Civil War* [New York: Oxford University Press, 1995], pp. 19–20). For details of Marx's critique of Carey's views, see Marx, *Grundrisse*, pp. 883–89.

61. Again, I am employing the original 1848 *Manifesto* and not the later translation of Engels of 1888, which says "whenever" instead of "as soon as."

62. **40**, p. 410.

63. Nadel, p. ix.

64. F. I. Herriott, "The Conference in the Deutsches Haus Chicago, May 14–15, 1860," Illinois State Historical Library, *Transactions of the Illinois State Historical Society for the Year 1928*, no. 35, 1928, p. 181.

65. Philip Foner, *American Socialism*, p. 14.

66. Levine, *Spirit of 1848*, pp. 169–80.

67. Nadel, p. 139.

68. Philip Foner, *The Workingmen's Party of the United States: A History of the First Marxist Party in the Americas* (Minneapolis: MEP Publications, 1984), p. 10. Weydemeyer's American Labor Union had also been open to women and one of the veterans of 1848, Mathilde Giesler Anneke, actively worked with him during its brief existence; see Levine, *Spirit of 1848*, pp. 124–25, for details.

69. **40**, p. 616 n. 297, **41**, p. 81, **40**, p. 374.

70. Karl Obermann, *Joseph Weydemeyer: Pioneer of American Socialism* (New York: International Publishers, 1947), p. 94.

71. Loyd D. Easton, *Hegel's First American Followers: The Ohio Hegelians: John B. Stallo, Peter Kaufman, Moncure Conway, and August Willich, with Key Writings* (Athens: Ohio University Press, 1966), p. 190.

72. Levine, *Spirit of 1848*, p. 223. "Democracy," it should be understood, referred to the Democratic Party—the party of the slavocracy.

73. Herriott, p. 156.

74. For details, see ibid., pp. 217–22.

75. **41**, p. 117.

76. Philip Foner, *American Socialism*, p. 26.

77. For details, see ibid., pp. 15–23.

78. Ibid., p. 25.

79. Herriott, p. 189.

80. Ibid., p. 181, and Philip Foner, *American Socialism*, p. 26.

81. James M. Bergquist, "The Political Attitudes of the German Immigrant in Illinois, 1848–1860," Ph.D. Diss., Northwestern University, 1966, p. 296.

82. Levine, *Spirit of 1848*, p. 248.

83. Herriott suggests that this was the case on the basis of the position the Baltimore delegates took on the eve of Chicago (pp. 155–56).

84. Levine, *Spirit of 1848*, 249.

85. John W. Blassingame, ed., *The Frederick Douglass Papers, Series One: Speeches, Debates, and Interviews*, Vol. 3: 1855–1863 (New Haven: Yale University Press, 1985), p. 381–82.

86. http://ourworld.compuserve.com/homepages/JanHochbruck/Cincinn.html.

87. **41**, p. 210.

88. For details, see Obermann, pp. 108–13, and *Joseph Weydemeyer: Ein Lebensbild* (Berlin: Dietz Verlag, 1968), pp. 367–69.

89. Levine, p. *Spirit of 1848*, 250.

90. Both Nadel, p. 136, and Levine, *Spirit of 1848*, pp. 249–53, provide details, especially the latter for the national picture.

91. **41**, p. 242.

92. Philip Foner, *American Socialism*, p. 29.

93. Ibid.

94. Philip Foner and Herbert Shapiro, eds., *Northern Labor and Antislavery: A Documentary History* (Westport, Conn.: Greenwood Press, 1994), pp. 287–88.

95. Stewart Sifakis, *Who Was Who in the Civil War* (New York: Fact on File Publications, 1988), p. 720.

96. **40**, p. 377.

97. **39**, p. 290.

98. __40__, p. 482.

99. Easton, p. 190.

100. On the details of Marx's critique and the split in the Communist League, see my *Marx and Engels*, pp. 143–48.

101. Easton, p. 180. His translation is more elegant than that of the *MECW*, __24__, p. 52.

102. Philip Foner, *American Socialism*, p. 29.

103. __6__, p. 303.

104. Philip Foner, *The Workingmen's Party*, p. 10.

105. Alexis de Tocqueville, *Selected Letters on Politics and Society*, ed. Roger Boesche (Berkeley: University of California Press, 1985), p. 309.

106. Sheldon Wolin, *Tocqueville between Two Worlds: The Making of a Political and Theoretical Life* (Princeton, N.J.: Princeton University Press, 2001), p. 556.

3

"A Last Card Up Its Sleeve"
The Overthrow of Slavery

Marx declared at the beginning of 1860—with Engels's concurrence—that the "the most momentous thing happening in the world today is the slave movement . . . in America, started by the death of [John] Brown . . . and in Russia [with the ending of serfdom]. . . . a 'social' movement [that] promises great things." From then on the pair gave their attention to developments beyond Europe with unprecedented focus. They related to events not simply as interested observers but as active partisans on behalf of the abolitionist cause. More than any other development, it was the U. S. Civil War that brought Marx back into active politics. As was true for other veterans of 1848, the war against the slave owners was an opportunity to resume the worldwide democratic revolution that had been derailed in Europe and to do all in their power to ensure its triumph. As communists they saw such a victory, especially in a setting as critical as the United States, as the next necessary step to the emancipation of the working class, a required precursor for "human emancipation."

Explaining the Civil War

It is instructive that it was the "slave movement" in the United States—along with the comparable developments in Russia—that Marx looked to as opening a new stage in the worldwide revolutionary process. "I have just seen in the *Tribune* that there's been another slave revolt in Missouri, which has been put down, needless to say. But the signal has now been given."[1] He was referring, in his letter to Engels, to the apparently spontaneous uprisings and other instances of slave resistance spurred by John Brown's rebellion, October 16–18, 1859, and his execution on December 2, 1859. For Marx, the focus was not on Brown himself or his action but rather what it ignited. If he was generalizing from this account in the *Tribune*, December 30, 1859, Marx was prescient. On the basis of detailed research, Herbert Aptheker concluded that in spite of the many exaggerated accounts "there yet remains good evidence of real and widespread disaffection among the slaves" in the aftermath of the rebellion.[2]

Marx's expectations were at least partially fulfilled. This speaks volumes about the analytical method he and Engels employed—an underappreciated historical fact. Even before becoming a communist—and no doubt a necessary prerequisite for his subsequent trajectory—the rebel youth Marx was an optimist about the prospects for "suffering humanity": "No people wholly despairs, and even if for a long time it goes on hoping merely out of stupidity, yet one day, after many years, it will suddenly become wise and fulfill all its pious wishes."[3] According to the opening paragraphs of the *Manifesto*, written four years later in 1848, all of history—that is, "the history of class struggles"—revealed that the oppressed had always fought back and taken initiatives: "Freeman and slave. . . . carried on an uninterrupted, now hidden, now open fight, a fight that each time ended, either in a revolutionary re-constitution of society at large, or in the common ruin of the contending classes." The communist Marx and Engels were predisposed to look for any signs of fighting back on the part of modern slaves. They considered it an elementary obligation of their current to fight to make sure that such struggles ended not in "common ruin" but in a "revolutionary" outcome. Often ignored therein is the assumption that there was nothing inevitable about the revolutionary process. This impelled the need for conscious political intervention.

The *Manifesto* as well as providing broad analysis, is also a call to action. Its final section, concretely applied to U.S. reality, required communists to ally with the bourgeoisie to overthrow slavery since "Communists everywhere support every revolutionary movement against the existing social and political order of things." The standard charge, then, that their historical, materialist method left little room for the agency of the oppressed or political action ignores the real record of Marx and Engels and their U.S. adherents.[4]

What about the larger claim that the slave movement was the opening shot in the revival of the international democratic revolution? Engels essentially said as much a year later in January 1861 in his comment about "things . . . hotting up" in the United States. Marx and Engels were virtually unique in European radical circles in their appraisal of the long-term consequences of the Brown rebellion.[5] While it is praiseworthy that they credited those who are sometimes today called the subalterns in initiating this historic process, wasn't this an overstatement? After all, it was not until the attack on Fort Sumter some sixteen months after Brown's rebellion that the Civil War—which would in fact lead to the overthrow of slavery—actually began. Nevertheless, a case can be made that the attack on Harpers Ferry—a multiracial endeavor—figured significantly in what eventually occurred. As Marx remarked, "the signal has now been given." It had real consequences—the fears it sent through the ranks of the slave owners. The horror of the Spectator at the gathering in Cincinnati that not only commemorated Brown but urged that his example be emulated was symptomatic of the cause of their anxiety. This underscored why the 1860 presidential election so dramatized this both for advocates and opponents of abolition. Would the new president encourage or discourage the hopes that the rebellion engendered? Even with a temporizing president-elect such as Lincoln—but who was elevated to the White House on a platform in opposition to the peculiar institution— the slave owners in the deep South, with the John Brown rebellion still very much on their minds, concluded that their interests were no longer sustainable within the framework of the union.

In the context of Lincoln's victory, the rebellion and the terror it inspired in the heart of the slavocracy, combined to compel the slave owners to make their fateful decision, based on their utopian illusions they could win the war, against a historical tide they were incapable of comprehending. In another time and context they might have been willing to live with an Abraham Lincoln. In the aftermath of the Brown uprising and what it ominously foretold they were clearly not so disposed. Recent scholarship sustains this interpretation. "The final crisis of the Union is commonly thought of as starting with the election of Lincoln in November 1860, but the entire presidential campaign had taken place in an atmosphere of crisis that extended back into the preceding year. . . . [W]ith the apprehension aroused by John Brown still keenly felt, a new wave of fear swept through the South. . . . Chief Justice Roger B. Taney was not alone in believing that the news of Lincoln's election might be the signal for a general slave uprising."[6] At the beginning of 1860, Marx and Engels did not, therefore, exaggerate when they characterized the "slave movement," as "the most momentous thing happening in the world today." They could not know in advance the rich and complex developments that would unfold, but they accurately recognized Brown's actions as initiating the most important political advance in the nineteenth century—the overthrow of slavery in the United States.

The New "Struggle in the Press"

With the outbreak of the Civil War, Marx and Engels, as Union partisans, gave their undivided attention to its every detail. For both of them the heart of the matter was the slavery question. Marx proved to be even more insightful as he accurately predicted the overall course of events within a week of the beginning of hostilities.

> There can be no doubt that, in the early part of the struggle, the scales will be weighted in favour of the South, where the class of propertyless white adventurers provides an inexhaustible source of martial militia. In the LONG RUN, of course, the North will be victorious since, if the need arises, it has a last card up its sleeve, in the shape of a slave revolution.[7]

Marx's view that the slaves would be the decisive factor in the war proved to be true. His optimism, anchored in his historical materialist method, would serve him well since the South was indeed successful in the early military campaigns. This led to many supporters of the Union to be pessimistic about its prospects. Though also hopeful at the outset because of the North's sheer population advantage, Engels began to harbor doubts, as well.

Their primary political task was to mobilize European working-class opinion in support of the Northern cause. A new "struggle in the press" was the primary vehicle for the campaign. Marx had to read everything he could on U.S. political and economic developments prior to the war in order to make the case to his readers. This meant putting the completion of *Capital* on the back burner. He and Engels adopted a "Civil War" division of labor; Marx focused on the political economy of the irrepressible conflict and Engels on its military conduct. The two newspapers they had at their disposal—only for about a year and a half as it turned out—were the *Tribune*, which had a sizeable readership in English-speaking Europe, and *Die Presse*, a liberal daily published in Vienna with about twenty-six thousand subscribers.[8] For U.S. abolitionists like Wendell Phillips, Marx's *Tribune* articles proved invaluable in their efforts to "strengthen ties between British and American abolitionists and influence British opinion to favor the Northern cause."[9]

The challenge before Marx was the need to refute, particularly for the *Tribune* readers in England, the arguments of the country's bourgeois press—among them *The Economist*, *The Saturday Review*, *The Examiner*, and especially *The Times*—that the war had nothing to do with slavery or abolition but rather concerned only secession. *The Times* and the others represented the interests of textile mill owners and related capitalists who had intimate material relations with the suppliers of their cotton. The way in which they explained the war was hardly accidental. The deep well of abolitionist sentiment in England required such papers to present it in any way but as a war to overturn the slavocracy. British bourgeois editorialists had to camouflage their pro-Confederacy sympathies with calumnies against the North for its supposedly anti-abolitionist posture.

In September 1861, Marx took on the particulars of this argument for *Tribune* readers in his first sustained publication on the war. Marx conceded that the North explained its actions only in defense of the union and not the abolition of slavery. But it was the South that initiated the war and did so, according to the Confederacy's vice-president, A. H. Stephens, and constitution, to defend the peculiar institution.

"It confessed to fight for the liberty of enslaving other people, a liberty which, despite the Northern protests, it asserted to be put in danger by the victory of the Republican party and the election of Lincoln." It was hypocritical of the British bourgeois press to feign disappointment with the North for not defending its actions as a war against slavery. "If Anti-Slavery and idealistic England felt not attracted by the profession of the North, how came it to pass that it was not violently repulsed by the cynical confessions of the South?" As for the charge that the North had never really challenged slavery, Marx then sketched out U.S. political history to show how the slavocracy, in alliance with the northern wing of the Democratic Party, sought to impose its will on the rest of the country—"the general formula of the United States history since the beginning of this century"—with a number of successes including the Kansas-Nebraska Act. But the victories were costly because they incurred the increasing hostility of antislavery forces in the North. "If the positive and final results of each single contest told in favor of the South, the attentive observer of history could not but see that every new advance of the slave power was a step forward to its ultimate defeat." The material basis for the North's advantage was the growth in population and influence of the "North-West . . . from 1850 to 1860." The formation and eventual victory of the Republican Party was the concrete political expression of this fact.[10]

Marx then defended the Republican Party against the charge of *The Economist* that its platform, calling for limiting slavery to the states in which it was already established, was disingenuous. He reminded his readers that it was the same newspaper that had argued only two years earlier that by "dint of an *economical law*" slavery would be ended if denied the power to expand. Two years later, however it changed its tune to say that a non-expansionist policy could not guarantee "extinction"—another pretext to slander the Republicans and give backhanded support to the slavocracy. But, as Marx pointed out, it was exactly the anti-expansionist Republican platform that provoked the first threats of secession from the slavocracy in December 1860 in the immediate aftermath of Lincoln's electoral victory. The slave owners also knew that their survival depended on slavery's expansion—the workings of an "*economical law.*" But unlike the editors of *The Economist* they had also understood for some time that "keeping up their *political* sway over the United States" was essential for the realization of such a "law." The Republican victory had now threatened that "sway."

But if *The Economist* and those who held similar views were really sincere they would now support the North since it "had arrived at the fixed resolution of circumscribing Slavery within its present limits, and of thus extinguishing it in a constitutional way," Marx argued. Implementing the Republican program, in other words, would lead eventually to slavery's extinction. Since *The Economist* was neither sincere in its demand that the North wage a "'war for the emancipation of the Negro race'"—what they counterposed to the Republican stance—they shuddered from even considering the "repulsive" possibility of "summoning the slaves to a general insurrection." Like Tocqueville, they could only conceive of the abolishment of slavery within constitutional means. Yet when offered such an opportunity they managed to find a excuse for not supporting the North. "Thus the English eagerness for the Abolitionist war is all cant," Marx pointedly remarked.

Marx concluded by speculating on the real reasons for British ruling class duplicity. He ended with a long quote from a liberal weekly *The Spectator*, that suggested that a victory of the North would ensure a much stronger United States, while dissolution of the union would leave the two regions at each others throats for some time and thus "draw out of our side the thorn of American rivalry."[11] Whether this reflected Marx's own opinion is not clear but it certainly meant that he considered the objections of the British bourgeois press to the Lincoln administration and the Northern cause to be disingenuous, at best.

In two subsequent articles a month later for *Die Presse* Marx elaborated on some of these themes, among others. He dispensed forthwith the argument that the war was really about free trade versus protectionism, with the South advocating the former and the North the latter.

The actual history of tariff enactments, as he convincingly demonstrated, undermined such a claim. As well, it was a patently self-serving claim for Britain's manufacturing class— advocates of free trade—an excuse to justify their support for the Confederacy. Marx then provided details on how the slavocracy established its hegemony over the course of the preceding half century, a process he referred to in his *Tribune* article as the "general formula" of U.S. history; for *Die Presse* readers such details were necessary to clinch his argument.

Marx reviewed the history of constitutional, legislative, and court actions, which first limited and then expanded slavery, from the North-West Ordinance, the Missouri Compromise, and the Fugitive Slave Act, to the Kansas-Nebraska Act and the Dred Scott case. With considerable insight Marx argued that in the "foreign, as in the domestic, policy of the United States, the interests of the slaveholders served as the guiding star." Efforts to acquire Cuba, "unceasing piratical expeditions of the filibusters against the states of Central America, and the conquest of Northern Mexico" were all done for the "manifest purpose . . . [of] conquest of new territory for the spread of slavery and of the slaveholders' rule." Finally, Marx charged, on the basis of a claim by Stephen Douglas, Lincoln's presidential opponent and Southern sympathizer, that the trade of Africans, which had been formally banned in 1807, was effectively reopened in 1859. This dramatic increase in illegal trafficking of slaves was for Marx further evidence that the "300,000 slaveholders" had no intention of giving up the source of their wealth and were prepared to do whatever was required to maintain their dominion over the rest of the nation. An important tool in that domination, Marx noted, was Southern control over the U.S. Senate which required, as John Calhoun—"the slaveholders . . . statesman *par excellence*"—had taught, "a continual formation of new slave states." The equal representation of states in the Senate, regardless of the size of their populations, insured the South's "hegemony" in national politics.[12]

Marx then addressed another significant dimension of slave-owner rule, its relationship to the "so-called poor whites" in the South. There were "millions" of them—their "numbers have been constantly growing through concentration of landed property and whose condition is only to be compared with that of the Roman plebeians in the period of Rome's extreme decline." How were they controlled, given the relatively small number of slave owners, a "narrow oligarchy"? Marx answered: "Only by acquisition and the prospect of acquisition of new Territories, as well as by filibustering expeditions, is it possible to square the interests of these 'poor whites' with those of the slaveholders, to give their restless thirst for action a harmless direction and to tame them with the prospect of one day becoming slaveholders themselves."

The forcible incorporation of Northern Mexico into the United States was clearly on Marx's mind. He sought to explain the material basis for what would later be called the false consciousness of poor antebellum Southern whites, thus offering insights into the establishment and maintenance of ideological hegemony. These concerns will be revisited in this chapter.

In the second *Die Presse* article, his last substantial published writing on the politics of the Civil War, Marx disputed the "advice" of the British bourgeois press that the North should allow the South to go its own way and allow for the emergence of "two independent countries"—confirmation of his suspicion that Britain's ruling class was first and foremost interested in removing the "thorn of American rivalry." His thesis was that the South's initiative at Fort Sumter was not for "a war of defense, but a war of conquest . . . for the spread and perpetuation of slavery." He then surveyed all the border and Deep South states in order to show how the oligarchy imposed its will on the non-slave holding portions. "Were it to relinquish its plans of conquest, the Southern Confederacy would relinquish its capacity to live and the purpose of secession." The same logic that drove it to extend itself regionally, therefore, would lead it to do the same nationally. Thus, Marx concluded, "The present struggle between the South and North is . . . nothing but a struggle between two social systems, the system of slavery and the system of free labour. The struggle has broken out because the two systems can no longer live peacefully side by side on the North American continent. It can only be ended by the victory of one system or the other."[13]

More than any other, it was this claim that undergirded all of Marx's judgements about the war, its course, and outcome. This formula recognized that the North, regardless of how the Lincoln administration interpreted or defined its actions and goals, was objectively pursuing a war to overthrow slavery, "the root of the evil. . . . Events themselves drive to the promulgation of the decisive slogan—*emancipation of the slaves*." On display was one of the key features of Marx and Engels's method, specifically, the assertion that a genuine sociohistorical process can have an objective reality independent of how its protagonists understand and explain their role in it. In this particular example, the qualifier "can have an objective reality" is appropriate. At a certain stage, to be seen shortly, consciousness—on the part of Lincoln—became decisive. The slavocracy, Marx argued, was far more conscious of *its* tasks at the outset than Lincoln. For Lincoln and the North, of which he was truly commander in chief, to emerge triumphant, his consciousness, Marx knew, would have to catch up with reality. In addition to the explanations of the Civil War put forward by the British bourgeois press, Marx's historical materialist method also took to task a related claim, popular in middle-class circles and one with which Tocqueville would have been comfortable—that the conflict had its origins in the so-called cultural divide between the North and South. Tocqueville, owing to his *Democracy in America*, may have been responsible, at least to some degree, for the popularity of this facile notion in such a milieu. After all, he attributed the differences between both regions to "manners" and "habits." Marx would have agreed that there were indeed significant cultural differences between both areas. Engels in fact, early in the war, drew on some of these to explain their different military capabilities.[14] But Marx and Engels, as materialists, rejected the idea that "culture" transcended economic and social relations. The basis of the cultural divide was the very different material terrain upon which both regions stood—two profoundly different "social systems."

There are two very significant issues that Marx raised in his arguments that are worth pursuing at this time. One concerns race, color, and class. For the first time, at least in the U.S. context, Marx addressed this most contentious of issues, in the form of a few trenchant comments. In regard to the subjugation of the non-slave owning whites of the South to the slavocracy—in the second *Die Presse* article—he wrote: "Between 1856 and 1860 the political spokesmen, jurists, moralists and theologians of the slaveholders' party had already sought to prove, not so much that Negro slavery is justified, but rather that colour is a matter of indifference and the working class is everywhere born to slavery." Then, three paragraphs later, in regard to the claim that the logic of the slave owners was to extend their system to the North, he wrote: "In the Northern states, where Negro slavery is in practice impossible, the white working class would gradually be forced down to the level of helotry. This would fully accord with the loudly proclaimed principle that only certain races are capable of freedom, and as the actual labour is the lot of the Negro in the South, so in the North it is the lot of the German and the Irishman, or their direct descendants."[15]

The two comments, which to my knowledge have never been treated in the scholarly literature, are most instructive. They offer a window into Marx's thinking and approach to the race-class nexus, thoughts that anticipate better-known subsequent pronouncements. Both reveal Marx's view that the exploitation of labor, or class subordination, had its own logic and, in the United States setting at least, had a structural-historical givenness independent of race/color distinctions. The exploiters, regardless of their pronouncements, were fundamentally indifferent about the race and color of those they exploited.

Marx's second comment recognized that in certain settings, again the U.S. case, claims about racial superiority and inferiority could facilitate the exploitation process. Some layers of society were more potentially exploitable than others. In the particular historical reality of mid-nineteenth century America, German and Irish working-class immigrants were only a step above Blacks in the racial hierarchy. Given the logic of labor exploitation, workers with "white" skin would suffice if those with "black" were unavailable. Note that Marx employed "race" to refer to color as well as national origins. This reflected the two different usages in German-speaking Europe and the United States. But while race, however defined, facilitated the process of class subordination, it was the logic of the latter itself that framed race and its utility as a category. As long as slavery was in place in the South, all workers, regardless of color and location, would be vulnerable to enslavement. Whether Marx really believed that the slavocracy could actually impose its system on the North is uncertain. His historical materialist perspective would suggest otherwise. But exactly because the method did not assume historical inevitability—for reasons already discussed—a struggle had to be waged in order to avoid such an outcome. What he wrote may have been just for that reason—the "struggle in the press."

Neither is it clear what sources Marx drew upon to make his claims. There is, nevertheless, evidence which suggests that his assertions were plausible given prevailing opinions at the time. For example, George Fitzhugh's *Cannibals All! or, Slaves without Masters*, probably the most famous apologia for the peculiar institution, and published in 1857, would have likely been known by Marx. As part of the attempt to prove his central thesis that wage labor was more exploitative than slave labor, Fitzhugh repeatedly stated that white workers were as much slaves as black chattel. And, as "modern civilization advances, slavery becomes daily more necessary."[16] Marx may have had Fitzhugh in mind in his first comment. Two decades earlier, Calhoun had argued in a famous speech for the necessity of slavery. "There never has yet existed a wealthy and civilized society in which one portion of the community did not, in point of fact, live on the labor of the other."[17] He too was indifferent to the race or color of "the other."

It must be noted that most Southern defenders of the peculiar institution shifted by the 1840s their argument to an explicit racial justification—the alleged innate inferiority of Blacks. They did so under the pressure of the demands of the Southern white male plebian class for full political equality. The sentiments expressed in the above-cited comments of Fitzhugh and Calhoun were incompatible with such aspirations. The change in rhetoric in no way, however, represented a change of heart from the earlier positions that defended racial slavery on the basis of class exploitation.[18]

As for Marx's second comment regarding the social status of German immigrants vis-á-vis Blacks, the advice of a popular German-language guide to the United States seems corroboratory. "'[B]y treating black men with a certain familiarity and good nature,' the plebeian immigrant 'lowers himself even more in the estimation of the [social] circle to which he belongs.' Sometimes, thus, 'in answer to the question, "Was he a white man?" one will hear, "No, sir, he was a Dutchman."[19] The immigrants, in other words, had to learn how to be "white," otherwise they might be mistaken for being within the same social rank of Blacks. Although Marx, in his second comment, referred specifically to German and Irish immigrants as potential "others" or slaves, he would not have been surprised by a story about how former slave owners sought to solve their labor problems after the end of the Civil War. "One Alabama planter brought in thirty Swedes in 1866, housed them in slave cabins and fed them the usual rations. Within a week the laborers had departed, informing him 'they were not slaves.'"[20] The planter, as Marx would have understood, couldn't afford to be choosy about the color of those whose labor he needed. He instantiated exactly the logic of labor exploitation that Marx warned about.

Both the tone and spirit in which Marx wrote about the conquest of Northern Mexico is clearly at variance with what Engels said more than a decade earlier. In the same vein in which he applauded in 1848 French imperialism in Algeria (see chapter 2), Engels, then, and in the following year, wrote approvingly of Washington's expropriation of Mexico. It advanced, he argued, the interests of the bourgeoisie by making possible the "creation of fresh capital, that is, for calling new bourgeois into being, and enriching those already in existence."[22] The conquest of Northern Mexico was, therefore, "waged wholly and solely in the interest of civilisation," particularly because the "energetic Yankees"—unlike the "lazy Mexicans"—would bring about the "rapid exploitation of the California gold mines" and, hence, for the "third time in history give world trade a new direction."[23] Though these were Engels's opinions, there is nothing to suggest that they differed from those Marx held at that time. As late as 1853 the latter expressed similar views about British imperialism in India.[24] Such views were informed more by the trial and error application of their newly arrived at historical materialist perspective and less by the concrete empirical terrain. As developing, pioneer communists, their advanced outlook was affected by prevailing political and cultural attitudes, as well as the isolation of the European working class from their colonial brothers and sisters locked in semi-feudal bondage.

Better acquaintance with the American reality led to a different assessment. Rather than the bourgeoisie it was the slavocracy that was served by the conquest. This prevented the full institution of capitalist relations of production in the acquired possessions and thus the growth of the working class. The benefits, in other words, that came with the acquisition of California were compromised by the "barbarity" of slavery's extension.

Marx, therefore, just as Engels had done in relation to Algeria, changed his position on Mexico (he did the same for India).[25] This argument is given added credence by subsequent comments and pronouncements he made about Mexico. For example, he reported favorably in December 1861 that Mexico had refused in 1845 to meet with Washington's emissary to even discuss the sale of its Northern territories.[26] In 1848 or 1849 he, like Engels, would have viewed Mexico's refusal disfavorably—an obstacle to the U.S. bourgeoisie's "civilizing" mission.

Interestingly, in the same month, Engels, in a passing comment, described the Mexican-American War as one in which "Mexico defended herself."[27] It's hard to imagine that he would have employed such language in 1849. Then, in 1862, when Louis Bonaparte, with the backing of England and Spain, sought to take advantage of Washington's preoccupation with the Confederacy by undertaking an imperialist venture into Mexico, Marx came to the defense of the country and its new liberal government headed by Benito Juárez. French aggression, he told *Tribune* readers, was "one of the most monstrous enterprises ever chronicled in the annals of international history."[28] When Bonaparte's forces began to suffer setbacks at the hands of the Mexicans, he exclaimed to Engels: "If only the Mexicans (*les derniers des hommes!* [the dregs of humanity!]) were once more to best the *crapauds* [i.e., Bonaparte's generals]."[29] The success of the so-called dregs exhilarated Marx. His celebratory tone measured the distance he and Engels had traveled from the initial application of their theoretical perspective.

From a "Constitutional" to a "Revolutionary" War

To return to Marx's subsequent assessment of the Civil War, the South was, as he had anticipated, more successful in the opening phase of the war. In fact, the Confederacy could claim more victories than the North well into the second year of the war, making many Union supporters, Engels in particular, increasingly pessimistic about its prospects. Engels wrote for the partnership on the military aspects of the conflict—the consequences about which Marx would later comment. The question not only for Lincoln but for Marx and Engels as well was how could the North turn things around and eventually win. Within weeks of the war's commencement, Marx, as already noted, supplied an answer—a thesis to which he continually returned: "In the long run, of course, the North will be victorious since, if the need arises, it has a last card up its sleeve in the shape of a slave revolution."[30] The fundamental issue hinged, he argued, on whether Lincoln would transform the war from a merely "constitutional" matter to one that was "revolutionary," from one that focused simply on the secession issue to one in which the North applied "its great radical remedy"—"Abolition of Slavery!" In spite of his hesitancy, Lincoln, Marx foresaw, would have to increasingly take revolutionary steps, including use of his "last card," to ensure victory. But as late as December 1861, the president "had admonished Congress that the Civil War must not degenerate into 'a violent and remorseless revolutionary struggle.'"[31]

While history would prove Marx correct, the route to his prescription for triumph was complicated and frustrating. Marx criticized Lincoln for dismissing John Frémont, the commander of Union troops in Missouri in November 1861. Months earlier, as Marx commented in another article, "Lincoln pusillanimously revoked Frémont's" order that freed slaves of rebel slaveholders in Missouri. The revocation and later dismissal of Frémont were, for

Marx, examples of Lincoln's efforts to appease the interests of slave owners in the states that hadn't joined the Confederacy, which reinforced avoidance of the question of abolition. "Lincoln, in accordance with his legal tradition, has an aversion for all genius, anxiously clings to the letter of the Constitution and fights shy of every step that could mislead the 'loyal' slaveholders of the border states," he wrote.[32] With remarkable foresight Marx predicted that the dismissal would make Frémont "a rival of candidates for the presidency in the future," for those who wanted a candidate that would be uncompromising with any slave owner. Frémont was well known since he had been the Republican standard bearer in the 1856 presidential election, a contest in which the party's abolitionist stance was more resolute than in 1860 when Lincoln was its candidate.

If Frémont's dismissal frustrated Marx, Lincoln's removal of George McClellan from the post of commander in chief of Northern military forces in February 1862 lifted his spirits—a sign perhaps that "Old Abe" finally meant business. For McClellan, the war was for the "restoration of the Union on its *old* basis, and therefore must above all be kept free from revolutionary tendencies." Rather than free slaves, his "army was trained to catch slaves!"[33] His demotion signaled for Marx a "turning point" in the conflict.

Though more optimistic, Marx continued to criticize Lincoln for wanting to appease the border state slave owners. Particularly repugnant, owing to this strategy, was the policy that "no [Union] general could venture to put a company of Negroes in the field," with the result "that slavery was finally transformed from the Achilles' heel of the South into its invulnerable horny hide. Thanks to the slaves, who do all the productive work, all able-bodied men in the South can be put into the field!" Again, for Marx the key to victory was a "slave revolution," the need for the North to pursue a "revolutionary kind of warfare and to inscribe the battle-slogan of 'Aboliton of Slavery!' on the star-spangled banner." The arming of Blacks, free, runaway, and captured slaves, would deprive the South of its ability to carry on the war. Lincoln "errs only if he imagines that the 'loyal' slaveholders are to be moved by benevolent speeches and rational arguments.

They will yield only to force."[34] In a letter to Engels, written, apparently, on the eve of the *Die Presse* article, he argued that the North would be compelled to "wage the war in earnest, have recourse to revolutionary methods and overthrow the supremacy of the BORDER SLAVE STATESMEN. One single NIGGER REGIMENT would have a remarkable effect on Southern nerves."[35] Like Marx, Frederick Douglass had repeatedly called for the arming of the slaves, insisting from the outset, "'The Negro is the key of the situation—the pivotal point upon which the whole rebellion turns.'"[36]

By August 1862, Marx saw signs that Lincoln and the North were beginning to recognize what it would take to be victorious. Measures enacted by the recently adjourned Congress were most encouraging. One of them, the Homestead Act, "which the northern masses had long striven for in vain"—through the Free-Soil movement—garnered greater political support from the northern laboring classes. Another measure, the recognition by Washington for the first time of the government of Haiti, the Republic forged by freed slaves in rebellion, fulfilled a long-sought goal of the abolitionists. But even more significant, "[a]nother law, which is now being put into effect *for the first time*, provides that these emancipated Negroes may be militarily organised and put into the field against the South." The North had finally begun to use the "last card up its sleeve." On the basis of these and the other laws, Marx concluded that "no matter how the dice may fall in the fortunes of war, even now it can safely be said that Negro slavery will not long outlive the Civil War."[37]

When Lincoln issued his Emancipation Proclamation less than two months later—"from January 1, 1863, slavery in the Confederacy shall be abolished"—Marx no doubt felt vindicated about his prognostication. Though there is no way that Marx would have known, the rationale for it, as Lincoln explained to his Cabinet in July, was uncannily similar to what he argued in his August article for *Die Presse*. "Emancipation," the president said, "had become 'a military necessity, absolutely essential to the preservation of the Union . . . We must free the slaves or be ourselves subdued. The slaves [are] undeniably an element of strength to those who [have] their service, and we must decide whether that element should be with us or against us . . . Decisive and extensive measures must be adopted . . . We [want] the army to strike more vigorous blows. The Administration must set an example, and strike at the heart of the rebellion.'"[38] It was as if Lincoln anticipated and gave heed to Marx's advice about the need for "a revolutionary kind of warfare" and how to deal with the slavocracy: "They will yield only to force."

The Proclamation, Marx declared, was "even more important than the "recent Union success at Antietam, Maryland"—"the most important document in American history since the establishment of the Union, tantamount to the tearing up of the old American Constitution." Whether an overstatement—to be discussed later—his prediction that "Lincoln's place in the history of the United States and of mankind will, nevertheless, be next to that of Washington" proved certainly to be accurate. From the perspective of a historical materialist, Lincoln was "a *sui generis* figure in the annals of history: He is not the product of a popular revolution. This plebeian . . . an average person of good will, was placed at the top by the interplay of the forces of universal suffrage unaware of the great issues at stake."

Then Marx bestowed his highest compliment ever on the United States: "The new world has never achieved a greater triumph than by this demonstration that, given its political and social organisation, ordinary people of good will can accomplish feats which only heroes could accomplish in the old world!"[39] Superior social relations combined with particular institutional arrangements, among them the electoral system, brought out the best in Lincoln. Marx's method also allowed him to understand the revolutionary tasks before Lincoln certainly sooner, if not better, than the president himself.

A Comradely Disagreement

The Emancipation Proclamation notwithstanding, Marx's partner remained doubtful about the North's prospects. Engels's pessimism contrasted sharply to Marx's optimism. Their different assessments constitutes the only documented and sustained political disagreement between the pair, lasting for well over two years. Engels began raising doubts as early as May 1862.

"What makes me lose confidence," he frankly confessed, "isn't so much the military situation as such, which is what it is only as a result of the indolence and indifference apparent throughout the North. Where amongst the people, is there any sign of revolutionary vigour?"[40] Two months later, he worried aloud, "it is this complete absence of any resilience among the people at large which proves to me that it is all up." Unfortunately, "what clinches the matter" argued Engels, was the resoluteness of the South, whose military victories "threaten to carry their offensive into the North. On top of that, they are really fighting quite splendidly."[41]

"I don't quite share your views," replied Marx at the beginning of August in 1862. Thus began a series of letters in which Marx laid out the basis for his optimism—the essence of which has already been cited. In addition, Marx took up another issue first broached in the opening chapter of this book, the nature of the U.S. political system.

What was especially frustrating for Engels was the failure of the North to organize itself with the single-minded determination that the Confederacy had so far achieved. "They shrink from conscription, from resolute fiscal measures, from attacking slavery, from everything that is urgently necessary; everything's left to amble along at will, and, if some factitious measure finally gets through Congress, the honourable Lincoln hedges it about with so many clauses that it's reduced to nothing at all." In his reply, Marx answered the specifics of Engels's complaints including his already discussed solution to the slavery question. He also chided him on more than one occasion: "It strikes me that you allow yourself to be influenced by the military ASPECT of things A LITTLE TOO MUCH."[42]

The slave question and the other issues, Marx pointed out, were part of a larger problem. "The way in which the North is waging the war is none other than might be expected of a *bourgeois republic*, where humbug has reigned supreme for so long. The South, an oligarchy, is better suited to the purpose."[43] Then, a month and a half later: "Like others, I am of course aware of the distasteful form assumed by the movement *chez* the Yankees; but, having regard to the nature of a 'bourgeois' democracy, I find this explicable."[44] Marx, unfortunately, didn't elaborate but it's possible to surmise, on the basis of the details of his replies to Engels, what he meant. In the most immediate sense, the constitutional arrangements prevented the institution of a powerful executive or certainly a presidential or military dictatorship as eventually emerged in the Confederacy. In a more fundamental sense, and again unlike the slavocracy, the bourgeois democratic state of the North was obligated to represent the interests of a more diverse ruling class which, therefore, placed limits on the ability of that state to act in as concerted a way as the Confederacy.

For example, the inadequate "fiscal measures" about which Engels complained, Marx noted, "are clumsy as, indeed, they are bound to be in a country where IN FACT taxation has hitherto been non-existent (so far as the country as a whole is concerned)."[45] Exactly because of the diversity of ruling class interests that had to be represented in the northern state, there was less consensus about how to finance that state and, hence, the absence of a national tax policy. One of the outcomes of the war, not surprisingly, was the institution of a nationwide fiscal and monetary policy for the first time. These steps toward centralization reflected the interests of a more homogenous ruling class, the triumphant bourgeoisie of the North.

If the United States continued to be for Marx the purest example of a bourgeois democracy, the crisis of the Civil War revealed the many limitations associated with such a polity, at least at that stage in its life. "For all that, I'm prepared to bet my life on it that these fellows [the Confederacy] will come off worst, 'STONEWALL JACKSON' notwithstanding."[46] And a few weeks later, "events over there [in America] are such as to transform the world."[47]

Not the least problematic character of U.S. bourgeois democracy was the electoral process. While it could produce a Lincoln it could also produce irresoluteness or ambiguity, especially in time of war. In his first analysis of a U.S. election, Marx attempted to make some sense of the 1862 elections, which could only be described, at first glance, as a "defeat" for Lincoln's administration. The Democrats made significant gains at both the state—New York in particular—and national levels, gaining a majority in the House of Representatives. Anti-Black sentiment benefitted Democrats in both elections. In prescient anticipation of the notorious draft riots that would wrack New York City the following year, Marx wrote that the "Irishman sees the Negro as a dangerous competitor." Elsewhere, the "efficient farmers in Indiana and Ohio hate the Negro almost as much as the slaveholder. He is a symbol, for them, of slavery and the humiliation of the working class, and the Democratic press threatens them daily with a flooding of their territories by 'niggers.'" Contrary, therefore, to the usual charge that Marx ignored or wasn't aware of racism among white workers, he not only addressed it but provided a plausible explanation for its existence.

The 1862 elections, Marx argued, revealed something more important. Unlike the presidential election of 1860, the Republicans this time, in the aftermath of the Emancipation Proclamation, "made common cause with the Abolitionists." Thus, the gains they made, which were not insignificant, registered the increase in pro-abolitionist sympathy. "Before the war such a result would have been impossible."[48] Again, Marx was the optimist. For Engels, on the other hand, the elections—especially those in New York—were further evidence of the North's lack of resolve. "[T]he only apparent effect of Lincoln's emancipation so far is that the North-West has voted Democrat for fear of being overrun by Negroes." In response to his partner's take on the complexities of bourgeois democracy and its electoral process, he made a most instructive comment:

> Desirable though it may be, on the one hand, that the bourgeois republic should be utterly discredited in America too, so that in the future it may never again be preached ON ITS OWN MERITS, but only as a means towards, and a form of transition to, social revolution, it is, nevertheless, annoying that a rotten oligarchy, with a population only half as large, should evince such strength as the great fat, helpless democracy.[49]

What Engels confirms—as discussed in the first chapter—is that bourgeois democracy for him and Marx was to be supported not as an end in itself but as a means to an end. There is nothing to suggest here that Marx differed with him on this point. In the context of the exchange, it might be argued that Engels was more frustrated with bourgeois democracy whereas Marx was more sober about its limitations. All of this, of course, has to be seen within the larger historical materialist framework that the two operated within. Bourgeois democracy was superior to prior modes of political organization because it facilitated the fight for a more superior set of social relations. And as a democrat like Marx, he defended it, limitations and all, against the polity of the retrograde slavocracy.

As the war continued without any decisive turns after Lincoln's Proclamation, it would be almost two years before Marx and Engels made any significant comments on developments in the United States.[50] The time was fall 1864, the presidential campaign. "I consider," Marx told Engels, "the present moment, *entre nous*, to be extremely critical. If Grant suffers a major defeat, or Sherman wins a major victory, SO ALL RIGHT. Just now, at election time, chronic series of small CHECKS would be dangerous. I fully agree with you that, to date, Lincoln's re-election is pretty well assured, *still 100 to 1*. But election time in a country which is the archetype of democratic humbug is full of hazards that may quite unexpectedly defy the logic of events. . . . This is undoubtedly the most critical moment since the beginning of the war. Once this has been SHIFTED, OLD LINCOLN CAN BLUNDER ON to his heart's content."[51] Events would once again prove Marx, and this time Engels, to have been remarkably insightful. Just as he predicted, Lincoln did indeed win the election, overwhelmingly in the electoral college though closer in the popular vote. General William Tecumseh Sherman's military victory in Georgia on the eve of the election, as both had suspected—though Engels was "doubtful" about the incumbent's chances—proved to be decisive. Finally, as Marx confidently noted, Lincoln's victory ensured the defeat of the Confederacy. With the results in, Frederick Douglass called the election "the most momentous and solemn that ever occurred in our country or in any other. . . . to determine the question of life or death to the nation."[52] Modern research also—as will be seen later—concurs with Marx's opinion about the crucialness of the election. Lincoln's defeat would have in all likelihood resulted in a negotiated settlement of the war to the advantage of the slaveocracy.

By the summer of 1864 Engels began to be a bit hopeful about the North's situation. When he and Marx received a letter in October that year from Weydemeyer, with whom they had been out of touch since the beginning of war—for reasons to be discussed—they got for the first time an insider's view of developments, particularly regarding the conduct of the war. Weydemeyer's insights, Marx's continuing optimism, and, most importantly, the progress registered by Sherman's victory eventually conquered Engels's doubts, as his reply to Marx's letter in the aftermath of Lincoln's reelection, made clear.

> Despite the numerous blunders made by the Northern armies
> . . . the tide of conquest is rolling slowly but surely onward,
> and, in the course of 1865, at all events the moment will un-
> doubtedly come when the *organised* resistance of the South will
> fold up like a pocket-knife.

Engels then put the war in historical perspective.

> A people's war of this kind, on both sides, has not taken place
> since great states have been in existence, and it will, at all
> events, point the direction for the future of the whole of Amer-
> ica for hundreds of years to come. Once slavery, the greatest
> shackle on the political and social development of the United
> States, has been broken, the country is bound to receive an im-
> petus from which it will acquire quite a differed position in
> world history within the shortest possible time, and a use will
> then soon be found for the army and navy with which the war
> is providing it.[53]

Six months later Engels's prognosis was realized at Appomattox, just as Marx had been predicting from the outset. While he could not have foreseen the particulars, Engels's general forecast about America's future was also remarkably accurate, including the anticipation of U.S. imperialism—"a use will then soon be found for the army and navy"—at home (the subjugation of the Plains

Indians, as it turned out, was a significant chapter in this process) and abroad, testimony to the power of the theoretical perspective that he and Marx employed. Following Lincoln's re-election, Marx, in a letter to his uncle Lion Philips, put the war in historical and global perspective. "When you reflect. . . . how at the time of Lincoln's election 3½ years ago it was only a mat-ter of making *no further concessions* to the slave-owners, whereas now the avowed aim, which has in part already been realised, is the *abolition of slavery*, one has to admit that *never* has such a gigantic revolution occurred with such rapidity. It will have a highly beneficial influence on the whole world."[54]

The Judgement of Modern Scholarship

Just as was posed in the first chapter about Marx's earlier pro-nouncements on American democracy, to what extent has mod-ern scholarship substantiated or challenged his views on the Civil War? Given both the breadth and depth of the Civil War lit-erature and the secondary importance of such an assessment for this inquiry, this exercise pretends in no way to be exhaustive. It hopes only to make judgements based on the general consensus of the literature.

Rather than take up all of Marx's positions, the focus here is only on his major claims: (1) that the war was first and foremost about slavery owing to the fundamental incompatibility of two social systems—one based on slave labor and the other on free labor—and that the peculiar institution would be ended who-ever the winner; (2) that the Union had an inherent advantage from the outset because of the "last card up its sleeve," abolition and a "slave revolt"; (3) that the North was hampered in its con-duct of the war by the "democratic humbug," bourgeois democ-racy; (4) that the period leading up to Lincoln's reelection was the most "critical" in the war; and, lastly (5), that a victory for the North would advance the democratic struggle elsewhere—"a highly beneficial influence on the whole world."[55]

As for the first claim, this is in one sense, to employ current parlance, a "no-brainer." If the war wasn't about slavery when it began, Lincoln made it so with the issuance of the Emancipation Proclamation. But this begs the question about Marx's argument that slavery was the issue to begin with. This is not a trivial issue since a body of literature and practice, that of modern day Confederacy sympathizers (the "Lost Cause" contingent) continues to argue in one form or another—like the bourgeois press in England in 1861—against slavery being the real cause of the war. Present day research reveals that "Slaves," for sure, "had a different understanding of the sectional struggle."

> Unmoved by the public pronouncements and official policies of the federal government, they recognized their centrality to the dispute, and knew that their future depended upon its outcome. With divisions among white Americans erupting into open warfare, slaves watched and waited, alert for ways to turn the military conflict to their own advantage, stubbornly refusing to leave its outcome to the two belligerents. Lacking political standing or public voice, forbidden access to the weapons of war, slaves nonetheless acted resolutely to place their freedom—and that of their posterity—on the wartime agenda. Steadily, as opportunities arose, they demonstrated their readiness to take risks for freedom and to put their loyalty, their labor, and their lives in the service of the Union. In so doing, they gradually rendered untenable every Union policy short of universal emancipation and forced the Confederate government to adopt measures that severely compromised the sovereignty of the master. On both sides of the line of battle, Americans came to know that a war for the Union must be a war for freedom.[56]

This assessment, made on the basis of primary materials in the most definitive collection to date of the testimonies of the slaves themselves, indicates that Marx and Engels, though thousands of miles away, were more in tune with the enslaved than were their enslavers or the modern day apologists for the latter.

The consensus of current research is that slavery was indeed at the heart of the dispute. James McPherson, arguably the leading Civil War scholar, is most clear about this. He argues effectively that slavery, indisputably, was crucial for understanding the very

different ways of life—materially, ideologically, and politically—
that became increasingly apparent in the decades leading up to the
war; Bruce Levine's aptly titled *Half Slave and Half Free: The Roots of
Civil War*, discussed earlier, makes a similar case. McPherson,
drawing on a suggestion by C. Van Woodward, argues further that
the changes underway in the North by the third and fourth
decades of the century put into motion the tensions that would tear
the nation apart—the emergence of what Marx and Engels would
have labeled as two very different modes of production with all of
the sociopolitical consequences that Marx wrote about in his three
Tribune and *Die Presse* articles. "The North. . . . hurtled forward ea-
gerly toward a future of industrial capitalism that many Southerners found distasteful if not frightening; the South remained
proudly and even defiantly rooted in the past."[57] This last point is
instructive with regard to Tocqueville. It was exactly at the time of
his visit to the United States that the fateful changes McPherson
describes were getting underway Both *Democracy in America* and
his diary reveal that Tocqueville too, for all the reasons discussed
earlier, was more attuned to and comfortable in the aristocratic
world of the slaveholders than the new one coming into being
north of the Mason-Dixon line.

What about Marx's claim in August 1862 that "no matter
how the dice may fall in the fortunes of war . . . it can safely be
said that Negro slavery will not long outlive the Civil War." This
is more difficult to evaluate as the literature is not explicit one
way or another. Since the North did win after issuing the Emancipation Proclamation, the question really turns on what would
have happened with a Confederacy victory? That elements of
the slaveocracy seriously considered abolishing slavery in the final months of the war, in a futile hope to save itself from defeat,
suggests that Marx was probably right. The hollow gesture was
too little, too late. It failed to muster the necessary votes in the
Confederacy legislature; its passage would have put into question the very basis of the secession in 1861. That the vote, however, was as close as it was registered the depths of abolitionist
sentiment building in the South. Proof of this was the authoriza-
tion of the Confederate Congress in March 1865, a month before
Appomattox, to enlist Black soldiers. In anticipation of this move

two months earlier, Engels wrote that "[I]f the South arms its Negroes, that will be so much the better for the North. However, they will take good care not to. At the last moment, if at all. The Negroes are not so stupid as to allow themselves to be massacred for the whip that flays their backs."[58] When the question of slavery came up at a meeting with General William T. Sherman in April 1865 after Appomattox, Confederate Generals Joseph Johnston and John Breckinridge agreed "that the institution was dead. Indeed Johnston actually joked that the Confederacy itself had driven a few nails into slavery's coffin by its recent legislation to enlist slaves as soldiers in return for emancipation."[59] Had the war continued on inconclusively for a while, a favorable vote for abolition may have been a real possibility, thus, fulfilling Marx's assertion. There is also good evidence that if, for some unlikely reason, the South had won without freeing its slaves, the latter would have resorted to armed struggle and/or flight, given heightened hopes and experiences learned as a result of the war. This reinforces Engels's comment about the revolutionary potential of slaves in arms. The probability is high that slavery, as Marx had expected, was one way or another destined for the grave as a result of the conflagration.

Whether abolition would have ensured victory for the Confederacy takes us to the second claim of Marx—"the last card" thesis. Marx explained that the North, from the outset, had a unique advantage over the South: the option of transforming the war from one about secession to one to end slavery and in the process recruit and arm the former slaves on its behalf. This was the sword of Damocles hanging over the destiny of the slavocracy. Lincoln, facing a military stalemate and possible defeat, concluded in the summer of 1862 that he had to utilize this weapon, just as Marx was now arguing. Joseph Glatthaar, in an article written about a decade ago, addresses this issue more directly than any other recent writing. He documents the "critical contributions of blacks to the defeat of the Confederacy" and concludes:

> In 1861 few foresaw the pivotal position of blacks in the American balance of power. Through their actions as slaves and free men and women, blacks helped to force supporters of the

Union to re-examine their approach to war. Unionists had to fight a war against the Rebels and adopt more vigorous methods of prosecution, such as the destruction of property and the use of blacks in the armed forces. For the Confederacy, they were a crucial workforce, providing food and essential labor for a wide range of civilian and military projects. Their steady loss to the Federals caused supply shortages, various hardships, and escalating inflation, all of which took a terrible toll on Confederate fighting men and civilians. Then, by converting blacks into soldiers, the Union not only deprived the Confederacy of a great resource, but employed it against the foe. As Lincoln explained to Grant in 1863, "I believe it is a resource which, if vigorously applied now, will soon close the contest. It works doubly, weakening the enemy and strengthening us." In time he proved right.[60]

Glatthaar states in the opening pages of the article that at "the outbreak of the war, leadership on neither side envisioned the varied and dramatic contributions that blacks would make to Confederate defeat." This is only partially true. As well as figures like Frederick Douglass, the leadership of the communist movement, specifically, Marx, not only envisioned the strategic weight of Black soldiers in combat, but did what he could to get Union supporters to see it too. Glatthaar unearthed almost everything that Marx anticipated.[61]

This is the appropriate place to take up Marx's optimism, which tended at times—certainly for the first two years of the war—to verge on assuming the inevitability of a Northern victory owing to the "abolition option." Although such a reading is understandable, two points should be noted.

In his published writings Marx was more cautious than in his letters to Engels with whom he was involved in a uniquely, I think, unguarded and friendly debate. Precisely because Marx was not a voluntarist or "inevitablist," he employed journalism, as well as political activism, to fight for the outcomes he desired. Secondly, for almost two years from the end of 1862, Marx made no significant pronouncements about the war's direction, even—since he no longer had access to a public venue—in his correspondence. When he finally offered an opinion, about two months before the 1864 presidential election, he advised caution about the war's outcome. Thus, a case can be made that Marx began to harbor doubts—though not to the extent of his partner—about a victory for the North, despite once having stated that the latter would triumph "IN THE LONG RUN."

Marx's note of caution anticipated the opinion of McPherson: "*There was nothing inevitable about Northern victory in the Civil War.* . . . There were several major turning points," one of which was "Sherman's capture of Atlanta in September 1864."[62] Marx agreed with Engels that the outcome of Sherman's campaign could prove decisive in what was a very uncertain period in the conflict—"the most critical moment since the beginning of the war." Sherman's success, McPherson contends, "turned Northern opinion from deepest despair in the summer to confident determination by November," thus guaranteeing Lincoln's election. Elsewhere, he asserts that the late summer–early fall 1864 period framed the "gravest" crisis of Lincoln's presidency.[63] In all likelihood, therefore, McPherson's view parallels Marx's claim that this moment was "the most critical" in the war.

What about the third claim that the North's difficulties had much to do with its failure to resort to the dictatorial measures that the slavocracy employed? Not surprisingly, this is not addressed in any sustained way in the literature because of the academy's implicit—and traditional—assumption that dictatorial methods can never have positive value. The term "dictatorship" was not saddled for mid-nineteenth century users with all the negatives that came in the following century. For Marx and Engels, the "dictatorship" of a class, specifically, the working class, or "dictatorial" measures that served the interests of the proletariat were justifiable.[64] Unbeknownst to most of his admirers, even Tocqueville defended dictatorship, specifically, what he called a "military dictatorship" to crush the worker's uprising in Paris in June 1848, the imposition of which he enthusiastically aided and abetted.[65] The question of whether dictatorial measures might have brought the Civil War to a more rapid end—as Marx and Engels thought—and thereby reducing combat fatalities and shortening the reign of terror that slaves daily experienced, is rarely posed. (The employment of such methods will be a very pertinent question in evaluating Reconstruction in the next chapter.)

In the most detailed and authoritative account of the measures Lincoln did take, particularly the suspension of writ of habeas corpus, Mark Neely concludes that the "Democratic [party] depiction of Lincoln as a tyrant was to have more influence on history than it merited, but like many political caricatures, it contained a certain element of truth. To be sure, there was nothing of the dictator in Lincoln. . . . But he did not by habit think first of the constitutional aspect of most problems he faced. His impulse was to turn to the practical."[66] In a follow-up study on the Confederacy, Neely concludes that the "Confederate government restricted civil liberties as modern democratic nations did in war. We did not know this until now. . . . [The image] of a people united in a long history of constitutionalism and uncompromising dedication to southern rights . . . was as false as any forgery and misled later historians, but the true canvas presenting a rougher image is now emerging into view."

Compared to the North, the regulation of dissent was simultaneously more sweeping and less controversial in the Confederacy. Thus, Neely's meticulous research appears to confirm Marx and Engels's assessments of Lincoln and the North—the absence of a dictatorship—and, secondly, in the South, the probable existence of an "oligarchy." Had Neely factored in the reality of slaves and other Blacks in the South, then their characterization of the South would be clearly warranted.

Neely's point about Lincoln's approach to the Constitution has relevance for Marx's claim that Lincoln's issuance of the Emancipation Proclamation was "tantamount to the tearing up of the old American Constitution." This is clearly an issue broader than the scope of this work. Suffice it to say that there is a respected body of scholarly opinion that agrees with if not the letter of Marx's comment, at least its spirit. George Fletcher argues in his recent book, *Our Secret Constitution: How Lincoln Redefined American Democracy*, that in both the Emancipation Proclamation and the Gettysburg Address Lincoln consciously drew on the authority of the Declaration of Independence and not the U.S. Constitution. "Lincoln's posture toward the 1787 Constitution was less than reverent. He treated the founding charter of the government more as a guideline to action than as a set of absolute restrictions on his actions. His decisions, particularly in the early stages of the war, suggest a willingness to assert extraconstitutional executive power and, thus, to permit the exigencies of war to restructure the government." The Gettysburg Address itself, Fletcher continues, served as the preamble for a "new constitutional order" that originated in the abolition of slavery. This was a radical move on Lincoln's part. It provoked the emergence of "reactionary forces that sought to mystify and entrench the values of 1787," to which the peculiar institution, its political weight and prerogatives were hardly an anathema.[67]

The Marx-Engels claim that a Northern victory would advance the democratic struggle on a worldwide basis has wide support in modern scholarship. McPherson certainly subscribes to this position, even citing Marx as evidence, specifically, his well-known passage from *Capital*, published two years after the end of the war: "As in the eighteenth century, the American war of independence sounded the tocsin for the European middle classes, so in the nineteenth century, the American Civil War sounded it for the European working-class." McPherson, with added emphasis on the significance of the overthrow of slavery, documents both Marx's claim about Europe and Engels's allusions to developments elsewhere. "[P]erhaps it was more than coincidence that within five years of that Union victory, the forces of liberalism had expanded the suffrage in Britain and toppled emperors in Mexico and France. And it is also more than coincidence that after the abolition of slavery in the United States the abolitionist forces in the two remaining slave societies in the Western Hemisphere, Brazil and Cuba, stepped up their campaign for emancipation, which culminated in success two decades later."[68]

Though nothing suggests that Marx and Engels anticipated the outcomes in either Brazil or Cuba, everything indicates that they would not have been surprised at what occurred in both countries. Other breakthroughs in the democratic movement had their roots in the outcome of the Civil War, not the least of which was the first wave of the struggle for equality for women in the United States— further testimony to Marx and Engels's prescience.

One of the most striking aspects about the many expectations Marx had about the outcome of the Civil War, as well as developments leading to it, is that they were arrived at from afar, on the basis of limited sources and data—especially compared to what was available to those who lived in the United States. Additionally, Marx had about six months to cram his studies in order to write sustained pieces for a readership that included Abraham Lincoln, who closely followed the *Tribune* (unfortunately, there is no way to know if Lincoln read articles from *Die Presse*). Most significantly, Marx grasped the revolutionary tasks before Lincoln—the need to transform the defensive war for preservation of the Union into a revolutionary one to overthrow slavery—at least sixteen months earlier than the president himself. Herein lies the advantage that Marx derived from the historical materialist perspective, the revolutionary experiences of 1848–1849, and the revolutionary optimism which issued from the combination of revolutionary theory and practice.

Revolutionary Practice

The effort, through the "struggle in the press," to win the English- and German-speaking proletariat in Europe to the side of the North was Marx and Engels's primary practice during the course of the war. At a certain stage of the crisis it was necessary for supporters of the Union cause, particularly the proletariat, to organize a movement in Europe to prevent "their" governments from intervening in behalf of the Confederacy. This effort was most successful in Britain. The breakthrough occurred only after Lincoln issued the Emancipation Proclamation. According to trade union leader George Howell, " 'once it became clear that slavery was the issue the workers rallied to the North with almost singular unanimity.'"[69] Royden Harrison argues persuasively that it was rank-and-file proletarian support for the Northern cause that threw decisive forces against British intervention on the side of the "the rebels," since a significant element of the trade-union leadership and its newspapers were either sympathetic to the Confederacy or nonsupportive of the North.[70]

In addition to reporting on this campaign, Marx assisted in the organization in March 1863 of the largest of many English trade union-sponsored meetings in solidarity with the North. Marx undertook this through the initiative of a party member, Johann Eccarius, who had close contact with the English labor movement and its leaders.[71] The anti-interventionist sentiment and movement, Marx felt, was the decisive factor in preventing the British government from coming to the Confederacy's defense—in essence, the English working class's finest hour. Royden Harrison reports that "British workers organised five pro-Federal meetings in 1862, fifty-six such meetings in 1863 and eleven more in 1864. . . . these figures understate the amount of working-class activity."

The fact that English workers, many of whom lost their jobs because of the Union blockade against the export of southern cotton to England and elsewhere, were in the forefront of this campaign particularly gratified Marx.[72] Given the almost unanimous pro-Confederacy propaganda directed at the proletariat by the British bourgeois press, along with many trade union papers, Marx told *Tribune* readers in America that "simple justice requires to pay a tribute to the sound attitude of the British working classes, the more so when contrasted with the hypocritical, bullying, cowardly, and stupid conduct of the official and well-to-do John Bull."[73] For his mainly German readership of *Die Presse*, he wrote: "This is a new, brilliant proof of the staunchness of the English popular masses, of that staunchness which is the secret of England's greatness."[74] A year later Lincoln came close to echoing Marx. "Self-interest, Lincoln wrote the workers in Manchester, could easily have directed them into supporting the Confederacy; instead, they had made their decision on high principles and cast their lot with the Union. British workers had gone through a 'severe trial' in resisting Confederate efforts to attract their support for an unjust cause. Their stand provided 'an instance of sublime Christian heroism which has not been surpassed in any age or in any country.'"[75] The stance of the British working class and the promulgation of the Emancipation Proclamation in January 1863 were some of the reasons why Marx confidently told Engels a month later, "the ERA OF REVOLUTION has now FAIRLY OPENED IN EUROPE once again." His involvement in the mass rally of March was a harbinger of his return to organized political activity a year later.

Textile workers weren't the only British economic victims of the Civil War. Marx and his family endured new hardships, mainly for two reasons. First, Engels, upon whom they had always relied financially, couldn't be as generous in his support since the funds he had access to, through his family's textile business in Manchester, diminished significantly as a result of the war. Second, the money that Marx earned through his regular writing for the *Tribune* came to a halt by March 1862; for *Die Presse* by the end of the year. Marx was informed by the *Tribune*'s editor, Charles Dana, that for economic reasons related to the war the paper couldn't afford to publish his articles. Dana, who had hired Marx, was a Fourierist socialist and abolitionist. He had fallen out of favor with Greeley, the publisher and, unbeknownst to Marx, had been fired, for apparently political reasons. At about this time Greeley had become increasingly pessimistic about prospects for the North and began a campaign to get Lincoln to compromise with the Confederacy. The kind of writing that Marx submitted clearly did not mesh with Greeley's conciliatory schemes.[76]

Britain's working-class anti-interventionist movement not only returned Marx to action, but also helped to bring into existence the International Working Men's Association (IWMA), or First International. Invited to participate in its founding meeting in September 1864, Marx immediately threw himself into getting the new organization off the ground and soon emerged as its de facto leader. The "General Rules," which he drafted, stipulated not only how its members should behave toward one another but "all men, without regard to colour, creed, or nationality."[77] One of his first assignments—highlighted at the very beginning of this book—was to compose a message to Lincoln on behalf of the Association, congratulating him on his reelection. Writing the message, Marx admitted to Engels, proved to be "far more difficult than writing a proper book."[78]

In addition to reiterating some of the points he had made about the Civil War in his journalism, the letter highlighted

Marx's most penetrating and revealing observation about class, race, and American democracy—position that go to the heart of this book.

> While the working men, the true political power of the North, allowed slavery to defile their own republic; while before the Negro, mastered and sold without his concurrence, they boasted it the highest prerogative of the white-skinned labourer to sell himself and choose his own master; they were unable to attain the true freedom of labour or to support their European brethren in their struggle for emancipation, but this barrier to progress has been swept off by the red sea of civil war.[79]

Marx's lines are pregnant with insight. First, white workers in the United States had made a Faustian pact with the slaveocracy that in turn placed severe limits not only on "free labor" (as Lincoln often referred to it) but on bourgeois democracy itself—an enormously important fact that the great cheerleader for the American experiment, Tocqueville, failed to see. In exchange for the "wages of whiteness," the peculiar institution was given a new lease on life. Noel Ignatiev writes that his book, *How the Irish Became White*, "may be understood as a meditation on how the Irish, an important contingent of the 'true political power of the North,' came to boast the white skin as their highest prerogative."[80]

Second, Marx anticipated the point he would concisely state three years later in *Capital*: "Labour cannot emancipate itself in the white skin where in the black it is branded." Encapsulated here is not only his broader political strategy—the full attainment of bourgeois democracy as the precondition for the socialist revolution—but as well his particular view about race and class (ideas foreshadowed in his 1861 *Die Presse* article discussed earlier). That is, the working-class expresses itself in many faces as well as different skin colors. But in the final analysis it is still labor. Implicit here is the assumption that race is no more than, as it would later be termed, a social construction or invention, while class is far more than a construct. Class for Marx was first and foremost about social relations of production. It had an ontological quality that went beyond the particular constructions given to it. Marx didn't ignore the self-understandings of workers. To the contrary, only by duly acknowledging them—as his assertion about workers in "white skin" makes clear—would it be possible to successfully challenge such conceptions in order to advance working-class emancipation.

The third insight was the interconnectedness between the overthrow of slavery and racism as a precondition for the liberation of workers in America and the advancement of the workers' movement elsewhere, specifically, in Europe. The birth of the IWMA, in part the product of the working-class anti-interventionist movement in Britain and other countries, was for him the concrete expression of that linkage.

Lastly, this was not simply a congratulatory message but as well an effort to impart to Lincoln, whom he called in his letter "the single-minded son of the working class," a specific, concrete assessment, in nonsectarian language, of what was unfolding—an analysis to which Lincoln, as McPherson has suggested, was capable of appreciating and applying in his own words.[81] With boldness and confidence Marx, in other words, politically engaged the president of the United States. That Lincoln "acknowledged the services of the [IWMA] for the good cause" was a measure of the organization's standing, evidence that Marx had good reason to believe such an intervention might have some payoff.[82] The IWMA wasn't the only body to congratulate the president. It pleased Marx to no end that "Lincoln answered us so courteously and the 'BOURGEOIS EMANCIPATION SOCIETY' [one of whose leading members was John Stuart Mill] so brusquely and purely formally. . . . The difference between Lincoln's answer to us and to the bourgeoisie has created such a sensation here that the West End 'clubs' are shaking their heads at it. You can understand how gratifying that has been for our people."[83]

Marx's congratulatory message reflected his support for Lincoln in the 1864 election just as he and the Marx party had done in 1860. This is noteworthy since it raises the larger issue of Marx's electoral strategy, one that, unfortunately, can only be briefly addressed here. In 1864, Marx and Engels backed Lincoln despite their many reservations. Abolitionists and Radical Republicans in the United States, including many German Americans, were less certain. Many of them, in fact, hoped that John

Frémont, the Republican Party's presidential candidate in 1856—winning thirty-three percent of the popular vote—would be their standard bearer and, therefore, nominated him at a rump convention in June 1864.[84] In a public letter, Frederick Douglass expressed his support for Frémont's nomination.[85]

Frémont, it may be remembered, had been reprimanded by Lincoln for taking the unauthorized step, in the early months of the war, of freeing the slaves of rebel slave owners in Missouri. In the eyes of abolitionists, this made him a hero and the president a villain. Just as Marx had expected there were electoral repercussions. Veterans of 1848 and Marx party members could have, with justification, expected that Marx and Engels would approve of the Frémont nomination. After all, their well-known—at least within their circles—*Address to the Central Authority in March 1850* had argued that workers should not support bourgeoisie candidates but rather should pursue independent working-class political action in the electoral arena. But their strategy was tailored to the reality of Germany in 1848–1849, where the bourgeoisie had unequivocally demonstrated that it had no stomach for waging an unconditional fight to overthrow the retrograde, precapitalist social formation of feudalism. The bourgeoisie in the United States, on the other hand, with Lincoln in the lead, demonstrated that it was still committed to a fight to overthrow slavery. And as long as they were willing to do so, communists were obligated to fight alongside them. Thus, Marx and Engels's continued support to Lincoln and the Republican Party.

At this moment, the "most critical since the beginning of the war" in Marx's opinion, Weydemeyer played a crucial role. Because he knew Frémont well, having served with him in the Union army in Missouri, and was well respected by radical German Americans as the leading Marx party member, he helped to convince both parties to end the candidacy with the argument that it would only play into the hands of the slavocracy and the compromisers in the North.[86] Weydemeyer did this largely through a paper, *Die Neue Zeit*, that he was editing in St. Louis, the largest city in the all-important border state of Missouri. Frémont withdrew his name from consideration at the end of September 1864, less than two months before the election.[87] Had he

remained in the race, his candidacy would have split the abolitionist vote and no doubt prevented a Lincoln victory—which he
acknowledged in his withdrawal statement. The *Tribune* editori-
alized that "his withdrawal . . . is wise, timely, auspicious, and
we believe it assures even the vote in Missouri to Lincoln and
[vice-presidential candidate Andrew] Johnson." As a special correspondent from St. Louis for the *Tribune* reported, the "leading
Germans of this city who were friendly to Fremont advised his
withdrawal."[88] Weydemeyer was clearly one of the "leading
Germans." In the aftermath of the war, the issue of support to the
Republican Party, critical or uncritical, would continue to challenge communists in the United States.

As well as the "struggle in the press" and participating in
and organizing the anti-interventionist movement in Europe,
the practice of the Marx party also involved armed struggle.
Party members in the United States, like most radical German
Americans, immediately enrolled in the Union army after the
attack on Fort Sumter. Marx and Engels even provided financial assistance for at least one close contact living in Britain to
get to the war front.[89] They were motivated not just by the
need to maintain the Union, which was typically the case for
most Northern volunteers, but by abolitionist sentiments.[90]
Weydemeyer thought that the western war front, particularly
the border state of Missouri, would play a decisive role in the
Union's fortunes and signed on in July 1861 when Frémont
sought out veterans of the 1848–1849 revolutions residing in
New York. Weydemeyer served with distinction in the Missouri campaign and rose to the rank of colonel. When his first
term of duty ended in September 1863, he took on the editor-
ship of the *Neue Zeit.* He returned to active duty a year later
and assumed command over the forces defending St. Louis
and environs—of enormous importance for the Union—until
June 1865 when he was mustered out of the army as a deco-
rated combat veteran.

"Of the Germans who have joined the war," wrote Engels to
Weydemeyer in November 1864, "Willich appears to have given
the best account of himself."[91] Having trained at the Royal Prussian Military Academy, he led a unit in 1849. Engels served as his

adjutant. Willich was the most experienced military cadre of the Marx party milieu. His service was of such outstanding quality that he was promoted to the rank of major general, the only communist to have ever been so honored in the history of the U.S. military.[92] What distinguished him from other Union officers was his revolutionary approach to soldiering and commanding. He "had the respect and affection of the common soldiers under him because he shared their privations, was always in the lead when the fighting was thickest, and treated them 'like men, not dogs.'... On returning to camp he would put his troops at ease, address them as 'citizens,' and proceed to a lecture on socialism"—again, a first and last in U.S. military history. In good communist fashion, he published a pamphlet upon retiring from the army in 1866, in which he excoriated the Union conduct of the war, especially the treatment of the rank and file soldiers by the officer class, and called for the creation of a real citizens army in order to defend against the next expected threat to "human liberty."[93]

Countless other German Americans joined the Union cause and served with distinction, many no doubt who had been influenced by the ideas of the Marx party, be it Marx, Engels, or Weydemeyer.[94] For veterans of 1848–1849, the Civil War was an opportunity to continue the fight they had waged more than a decade earlier. Prussian feudal autocracy was not unlike the Southern slavocracy. Little wonder, then, that they called the war their "Zweiter Freiheitskampf," the "second fight for liberty."[95]

Marx and Engels's Contribution

What I've presented thus far about Marx and Engels's praxis in the American theatre is unproblematic in the sense that the historical record is transparent. At this point I want to make a case about the consequences of their practice for which the evidence is not conclusive but only suggestive. It concerns their intervention through Weydemeyer and other comrades in the German American community in the years leading up to and during the Civil War. The significance of this argument can best be appreciated by considering what Ignatiev, as noted above, has to say about the Irish American experience. That is, the Irish as a whole and their working class in particular were more likely to oppose rather than back the Union cause, as suggested by their support to the party of the slaveocracy, the Democrats, to their involvement in the New York City draft/race riots in 1863, an "insurrection against the government that was waging the war" against the slaveocracy.[96]

It is true that the Irish workers were not unique. For much of the first half of the nineteenth century the alliance between the slaveocracy and northern labor was "characteristic of the white labor radicalism of the day."[97] In the decade preceding the Civil War, however, white workers in their majority adopted an antislavery stance and supported the Republican Party in the 1860 elections. The evidence suggests—and I stress suggests—that of all white workers, German Americans were the ones most likely to have been opponents of the slaveocracy on the eve of the war. In contrast to the Irish, they were in their majority active partisans for the Union cause.

What I want to argue is that one, if not the most important, of the reasons for this difference between the Irish and German immigrants was the impact that the political émigrés from the 1848 revolution—the "Red '48ers," and the Marx party in particular—had on the political consciousness of the latter. Prior to the 1850s, German-born workers had also been susceptible to illusions about the slaveocracy. Kriege's anti-abolitionist approach to the Free-Soil question, discussed in the previous chapter, reflected this tendency. With the coming of the Red '48ers, however, veterans from another revolution who were committed to the overthrow of feudal-like institutions such as slavery and actively supported the extension of the democratic revolution, German Americans and, especially workers, came under the influence of a group of fighters whose vanguard role in that community was out of proportion to their numbers. The '48ers, made their impact mainly through journalistic endeavors. The Germans, hence, had something that the Irish lacked—committed and seasoned fighters from a real revolutionary movement who saw the struggle against slavery as an opportunity to carry out the democratic revolution in a new setting. No such leadership existed, unfortunately, in the Irish community.

Even before the war, Blacks viewed Germans favorably. In Frederick Douglass's opinion, "a German has only to be a German to be utterly opposed to slavery. In feeling, as well as in conviction and principle, they are anti-slavery."[98] Douglass and other Blacks embraced the revolutionary struggles in Germany in 1848–1849. In 1851, "a society of free blacks in Cleveland expressed sympathy for and offered 'material aid' to the cause of German freedom."[99] One is hard pressed to find similar Black sentiments about the Irish. Clearly, the fact that Irish workers were comparatively more unskilled meant that they had more legitimate fears about competition with Black workers and were thus more vulnerable to the racist appeal. It was no accident, as McPherson notes, that "[u]nskilled workers and Irish-Americans were proportionately under-represented in the Union army."[100] However unskilled the Irish may have been as a group, the central point I argue is that the absence of a pro-abolition leadership is more decisive in explaining their relative lack of support for the Union cause.

The Marx party's unique contribution to the German American community was its effective opposition to the myth that labor had more to gain from the slaveocracy than capital. It supplied the ammunition for the political struggle. While the abolitionists did their best to counter the appeals of the slaveocracy to northern white workers, relying mainly on moral suasion, only the Marx party, on the basis of its historical materialist perspective, could really explain why "labour cannot emancipate itself in the white skin where in the black it is branded." Gilbert Osofsky says of the abolitionists:

"The Garrisonian condemnation of the labor system of slavery was more often moral than economic. . . . . Here was an individualist, middle-class work ethic that automatically banned any class approach to relief of Irish-American economic conditions. . . . . Despite the effort of the Garrisonians to understand the situation of Irish-Americans and to defend them against religious and nativist prejudices, they were unable to view the immigrants' attitude on slavery as other than a moral failure. Moreover a middle-class, individualistic conception of personal freedom hindered any adequate response to the economic conditions of the Irish, though this limitation was scarcely peculiar to abolitionists. Given the individualistic attitude of the period, it is difficult to see what course toward the Irish a pragmatic, nonmoralistic social analysis could have suggested."[101]

It was precisely a "nonmoralistic social analysis" that the Marx party both supplied and for which it received a positive response among German American workers, despite the "individualistic attitude of the period." Yet, even the best of perspectives had to be fought for. Through the struggle in the German American press and party organizing, that is, *politics*, led largely by Weydemeyer in collaboration with Marx and Engels, the Marx party made its presence felt. Because of their common theoretical and political program, they could act collectively. For example, Weydemeyer's successful efforts to end the Frémont candidacy were undertaken despite a long absence of direct contact with Marx and Engels. Such initiatives embodied the theoretical unity that is the real measure of a political party.

If this argument is valid, then the Marx party's contribution to "democracy in America" was of major consequence. Without the support of German American workers in key places like Illinois it is unlikely that Lincoln would have been nominated and elected president. As McPherson persuasively argues, without Lincoln the conditions would not have existed for the fight to overthrow slavery. His decision to use force to end the Confederacy's secession—his awareness of the support he had for such a move among the German American workers in Cincinnati and elsewhere may have helped to stiffen his resolve—was a necessary condition for initiatives the slaves took and the conversion of the war into one against slavery. The British anti-interventionist movement to which Marx made a singular contribution was a major factor in staying European intervention on behalf of the Confederacy—a fact that Lincoln recognized.

In the war itself, Weydemeyer in particular played a key role in the defense of St. Louis, a strategically important front for the Union. Whether the city's defense was a factor in the Union victory, it was, in turn, the necessary condition for the end of slavery. Of greater significance was Weydemeyer's role in the successful effort to convince Frémont to withdraw from the 1864 presidential election—the most important in U.S. history—and, thereby, preventing a likely defeat for Lincoln. Without Lincoln in office, a temporary compromise with the slavocracy was the probable outcome. Lastly, without the overthrow of slavery the worldwide democratic movement would have been considerably delayed.[102] My argument is speculative. Yet, if true it would mean that Marx and Engels's practice, in conjunction with their co-thinkers in America, had an enormous impact not only after their deaths but, as is generally unacknowledged, even in their own lifetime.

To conclude, the outstanding feature of Marx and Engels's activities and those of their comrades in America before and during the Civil War is that they were integrally involved in the most important struggle against racism in history, the overthrow of slavery in the United States—the foundation upon which all modern struggles for progressive social change stand. The war was also the longest revolutionary upheaval that Marx and Engels ever lived through and necessarily enriched their understanding of that process. It's no accident that six years later Marx titled the most popular work in his lifetime—the events of the 1871 workers uprising of the Paris Commune—*The Civil War in France*. The actions of the Marx party during the U.S. Civil War were hardly inconsequential. Its programmatic insights, based on the historical materialist framework, allowed its members to correctly view the uprooting of slavery as the precondition for the overthrow of capital. Capital itself, as will be seen in the next chapter, understood this all too well.

Tocqueville did not live long enough to see the Civil War. One can only speculate about what his reaction might have been. But there was nothing in his record to suggest that he would have enthusiastically embraced the cause of the Union or assisted it in the manner of Marx and Engels to score a victory over the slavocracy—a triumph that did more to advance the global democratic struggle in the nineteenth century than any single other event.

Notes

1. **41**, p. 5.
2. Herbert Aptheker, *American Negro Slave Revolts* (New York: International Publishers, 1987), p. 353.
3. **3**, p. 134.
4. This is exactly the problem with Reinhardt's reading of the *Manifesto*—pp. 109–22—again, the limitations of a textual analysis.
5. For an overview of European reaction, see Seymour Drescher, "Servile Insurection and John Brown's Body in Europe," in *His Soul Goes Marching On: Responses to John Brown and the Harpers Ferry Raid*, ed. Paul Finkelman (Charlottesville: University Press of Virginia, 1995). Interestingly, the only individual who had a position close to Marx and Engels was the Russian revolutionary Nicholas Chernyshevskii (p. 291 n. 42); his views about Russian developments would later exercise a powerful influence on both of them.
6. Don E. Fehrenbacher, "Kansas, Republicanism, and the Crisis of the Union," in *Major Problems in the Civil War and Reconstruction*, ed. Michael Perman (Boston: Houghton Mifflin Co., 1998), p. 61. On the fiftieth anniversary of Brown's uprising, W. E. B. DuBois wrote that his final written message, in defense of his actions, "did more to shake the foundations of slavery than any single thing that ever happened in America"(*John Brown* [New York: International Publishers, 1969], p. 365).
7. **41**, p. 277. English words in the original are given in small caps.
8. On the particulars about Marx's affiliation with *Die Presse* see **40**, pp. 429-37.
9. Irving Barlett, *Wendell Phillips: Brahmin Radical* (Boston: Beacon Press, 1961), p. 241.
10. **19**, pp. 8–10.
11. Ibid., pp. 13-16.
12. **19**, pp. 37–38. The 2000 presidential election "fiasco"—the undemocratic character of the electoral college and what happened in Florida, a former confederate state—has its roots in these antebellum arrangements.
13. **19**, p. 50.
14. **41**, p. 296.
15. **19**, pp. 49–50.
16. George Fitzhugh, *Cannibals All! or Slaves without Masters*, ed. C. Vann Woodward (Cambridge: Harvard University Press, 1988), p. 30.
17. Bruce Levine, *Half Slave and Half Free: The Roots of Civil War* (New York: Hill and Wang, 1992), p. 139.

18. Ibid., p. 143. See also, George Frederickson, *White Supremacy: A Comparative Study in American and South African History* (New York: Oxford University Press, 1981), pp. 154–55.

19. Bruce Levine, *The Spirit of 1848: German Immigrants, Labor Conflict and the Coming of the Civil War* (Urbana: University of Illinois Press, 1992), p. 150.

20. Eric Foner, *Reconstruction: America's Unfinished Revolution, 1863–1877* (New York: Harper & Row, 1988), p. 213.

21. **19**, pp. 40, 36, 42.

22. **6**, p. 527.

23. **8**, p. 365.

24. See chapter 2, p. 46.

25. **40**, p. 249. In an otherwise faithful and sympathetic reading of their views Jeffrey Vogel fails to note this reassessment. See his "The Tragedy of History," *New Left Review*, no. 220 (November–December 1996): 40–41. See also my "The Eurocentric Marx and Engels and Other Related Myths" in Crystal Bartolovich and Neil Lazarus, eds., *Marxism, Modernity, and Postcolonial Studies* (Cambridge: Cambridge University Press, 2002).

26. **19**, p. 103.

27. **18**, p. 527.

28. **19**, p. 71.

29. **41**, p. 431.

30. **41**, p. 277.

31. Eric Foner, *Reconstruction*, p. 7.

32. **19**, p. 87.

33. **19**, pp. 179–80.

34. **19**, pp. 227–28.

35. **41**. p. 400. As for "NIGGER," which Marx employed in more than one context and of obvious concern not only for those of us with visible roots in Africa, the *MECW* editors note that in the nineteenth century it did not have the "more profane and unacceptable status" of later history (**42**, p. xl). The epithet "Nigger regiment," in fact, was often hurled at the North by Confederate sympathizers who detested the idea that Blacks might be armed by the former. Whether the editors' point is an apologia is irrelevant. It's true that even Harriet Tubman employed the term for self-description (William K. Klingaman, *Abraham Lincoln and the Road to Emancipation, 1861–1865* [New York: Viking Penguin, 2001], p. 88).

Marx began to use "nigger" during the Civil War as he was familiarizing himself with the U.S. reality. In published writings he always employed quotation marks; in letters often without. Only once, it seems, did he use it in a derogatory sense, in a diatribe against Ferdinand Lassalle (**41**, p. 389–90) in 1862, that is, in the year when he first used the word (for the context see, Hal Draper, "Lassalle and Marx: History of a Myth," in *Karl Marx's Theory of Revolution: Vol. IV* [New York: Monthly Review Press, 1990], pp. 241–69). Marx and Engels, like all mortals, were products, clearly, of the world in which they lived. Their comments in personal correspondence that were unambiguously racist, sexist or anti-Semitic must be seen in context and in relation to their entire corpus of writings and actions. For what it's worth, Marx was fondly known by close friends and family as "Moor" owing to his dark features and had a son-in-law, Paul Lafargue, a mulatto, who was also fondly called in family circles, "African," "Negro," and "Negrillo." This suggests that one should be cautious and not rush to judgement based on the vapid criteria of "political correctness."

36. Eric Foner, *Reconstruction*, p. 5.

37. **19**, pp. 228–29.

38. James M. McPherson, *Drawn with the Sword: Reflections on the American Civil War* (New York: Oxford University Press, 1996), p. 77.

39. **41**, p. 250.

40. **41**, p. 364.

41. **41**, pp. 387–88.

42. **41**, p. 416.

43. **41**, p. 416.

44. **41**, p. 421.

45. **41**, p. 400.

46. **41**, p. 416.

47. **41**, p. 421.

48. **19**, p. 264.

49. **41**, p. 428.

50. After 1862 neither had access to a public venue to air their views—for reasons to be discussed shortly—and thus the need here to rely on their correspondence.

51. **41**, p. 562.

52. John W. Blassingame, ed., *The Frederick Douglass Papers, Series One: Speeches, Debates, and Interviews*, Vol. 4: 1864–1880 (New Haven: Yale University Press, 1991), p. 33.

53. **42**, p. 39.

54. **42**, p. 48.

55. The "Marxist" historian Eugene Genovese, in a 1968 article, "Marxian Interpretations of the Slave South" (in *Towards a New Past:*

Dissenting Essays in American History, ed. Barton J. Bernstein [New York: Pantheon Books, 1968]), sought to critique Marx and Engels's Civil War writings. Some of what he says is interesting and worthy of a reply, but not here. None of the five claims discussed here is the target of his criticisms; one of the latter will be addressed in the next section.

56. Ira Berlin, Barbara J. Fields, Thavolia Glymph, Joseph P. Reidy, and Leslie S. Rowland, eds. *Freedom: A Documentary History of Emancipation, 1861–1867: Selected from the Holdings of the National Archives of the United States. Series I, Volume I, The Destruction of Slavery* (Cambridge: Cambridge University Press, 1985), p. 2.

57. McPherson, *Drawn with the Sword*, p. 22.

58. **42**, p. 61.

59. William C. Davis, *An Honorable Defeat: The Last Days of the Confederate Government* (New York: Harcourt Brace, 2001), p. 160.

60. Joseph T. Glatthaar, "Black Glory: The African-American Role in Union Victory," in *Why the Confederacy Lost*, ed. Gabor S. Boritt (New York: Oxford University Press, 1992), p. 161.

61. Among Civil War scholars there is a debate related to the role of the slaves in the defeat of the Confederacy—whether Lincoln or the slaves were responsible for slavery's abolition. McPherson in "Who Freed the Slaves?" (*Drawn with the Sword*), takes issue with what he calls the "black self-emancipation thesis" and argues for the primacy of Lincoln. In response, Ira Berlin, "Who Freed the Slaves? Emancipation and Its Meaning" (see, Michael Perman), argues that "Both Lincoln and the slaves played their parts . . . complementary roles"(p. 296). While persuasive, Berlin, unfortunately, doesn't address the post-Emancipation Proclamation issue that McPherson does, specifically, the 1864 presidential election. While Marx would probably be more sympathetic to Berlin's response, his historical materialist approach put the actions of Lincoln as well as the slaves in broader perspective, beyond what he and McPherson offer.

62. McPherson, *Drawn with the Sword*, p. 134.

63. James M. McPherson, *Abraham Lincoln and the Second American Revolution* (New York: Oxford University Press, 1991), p. 122.

64. For the most thorough treatment of the matter, see Hal Draper, *Karl Marx's Theory of Revolution: Volume III. The "Dictatorship of the Proletariat"* (New York: Monthly Review Books, 1986).

65. For details, see my *Marx and Engels: Their Contribution to the Democratic Breakthrough* (Albany, N.Y.: State University Press of New York, 2000), pp. 126–27.

66. Mark Neely, *The Fate of Liberty: Abraham Lincoln and Civil Liberties* (New York: Oxford University Press, 1991), p. 210.

67. George P. Fletcher, *Our Secret Constitution: How Lincoln Redefined American Democracy* (New York: Oxford University Press, 2001), pp. 37, 56. For an alternative reading, see Harry V. Jaffa, *A New Birth of Freedom: Abraham Lincoln and the Coming of the Civil War* (Lanham, Md.: Rowman & Littlefield, 2000), particularly, chapter 2.

68. McPherson, *Drawn with the Sword*, pp. 224, 227. For details on how the course of the Civil War impacted developments in Brazil, see Ana Maria Rios, " 'My Mother was a Slave, Not Me!' Black Peasantry and Regional Politics in Southeast Brazil: 1870–1940," Ph.D. diss., University of Minnesota, 2001, chapter 3.

69. Henry Collins and Chimen Abramsky, *Karl Marx and the British Labour Movement: Years of the First International* (London: Macmillan and Co., 1965), p. 21.

70. Royden Harrison, "British Labour and American Slavery," in *Before the Socialists: Studies in Labour and Politics, 1861–1881* (London: Routledge and Kegan Paul, 1965).

71. Hal Draper, *The Marx-Engels Chronicle: A Day-by-Day Chronology of Marx and Engels' Life and Activity* (New York: Schocken, 1985) p. 116. Harrison, op. cit., p. 72, on the other hand, disputes the claim that Marx "organised the meeting" saying rather that it was really the work of the positivist academic Edward Beesly; this isn't, however, inconsistent with Draper's claim.

72. Harrison, op. cit., p. 65. The sharp increase in meetings in 1863 substantiates the point that it was only after Lincoln issued the Emancipation Proclamation, which took effect at the beginning of 1863, that the British proletariat "rallied to the North with almost singular unanimity."

73. **19**, p. 138. Modern scholarship has by and large confirmed Marx's insights about the role of England's working class in restraining the efforts of official England in intervening on behalf of the Confederacy. The most recent assessment can be found in Howard Jones, *Abraham Lincoln and a New Birth of Freedom: The Union and Slavery in the Diplomacy of the Civil War* (Lincoln: University of Nebraska Press, 1999), pp. 154–57. See also his *Union in Peril: The Crisis over British Intervention in the Civil War* (Chapel Hill: The University of North Carolina Press, 1992), pp. 155–56, 260. In addition to Harrison's article, op. cit., Philip Foner's, *British Labor and the American Civil War* (New York: Holmes and Meier, 1981) is still the most authoritative historiographical treatment of the issue. Kevin Logan's

article, "The *Bee-Hive* Newspaper and British Working Class Attitudes toward the American Civil War," *Civil War History* 22 (December 1976), offers two reasons why workers opposed slavery. "First, the working class had supported abolition of slavery in the British Empire, and could see the Emancipation Proclamation as a positive step. Second, the English worker, at least on an abstract level, could identify with the slave as a fellow worker. Many English workers thought of themselves as 'wage slaves,' and could readily sympathize with a movement to abolish slavery of every kind" (pp. 347–48).

74. **19**, p. 154.

75. Howard Jones, *Abraham Lincoln*, p. 156. According to Jones, the "president had played no small role in molding British workers' opinion toward the war. American funds, kept hidden from public knowledge, helped to finance the huge meetings in England that praised the Union and exalted emancipation" (p. 155).

76. On Greeley's evolution, see McPherson, *Abraham Lincoln*, pp. 121–25.

77. **20**, p. 15.

78. **42**, p. 49.

79. **20**, p. 20. One of Genovese's criticisms of Marx (see above fn. 55) is that his characterization of Northern workers as "the true political power of the North" was an "excursion into fantasy." Unfortunately, Genovese doesn't elaborate. Marx may very well have been looking to the future rather than presenting a description of then current U.S. reality.

80. Noel Ignatiev, *How the Irish Became White* (New York: Routledge, 1995), p. 69

81. McPherson, *Drawn with the Sword*; see especially, inter alia, part IV, "The Enduring Lincoln." The historian Herbert Mitgang quotes the following from Lincoln: "Labor is prior to, and independent of, capital. Capital is only the fruit of labor, and could never have existed if labor had not first existed. Labor is the superior of capital, and deserves much the higher consideration. Capital has its rights, which are as worthy of protection as any other rights" (*The Nation*, September 30, 1996, p. 6).

82. **21**, p. 362.

83. It seems likely that Lincoln would have recognized Marx's name as one of the fifty-four signatories of the message. As noted above, Lincoln was the *Tribune*'s best-known reader. He had followed the paper closely for many years, including the period when Marx was one of its

regular correspondents. This might explain—along with the conscious efforts of his administration to cultivate working-class support for the Union in Britain—why Lincoln apparently thought more highly of the congratulatory message from the IWMA.

84. For an overview of radical German American support for Frémont, see Levine, *Spirit of 1848*, pp. 260–63.

85. James M. McPherson, *The Negro's Civil War: How American Negroes Felt and Acted during the War for the Union* (New York: Vintage Books, 1965), pp. 303–4.

86. See Kark Obermann, *Joseph Weydemeyer: Pioneer of American Socialism* (New York: International Publishers 1947), pp. 127–28, *Joseph Weydemeyer: Ein Lebensbild* (Berlin: Dietz Verlag, 1968), pp. 380–81, on the particulars.

87. Andrew Rolle, *John Charles Frémont: Character as Destiny* (Norman: University of Oklahoma Press, 1991), suggests that he withdrew after getting Lincoln's agreement to dismiss from his cabinet a longtime enemy; he then presents evidence that no such deal was ever made (pp. 232–33). In a footnote, he reveals that German American support in Missouri was indeed crucial in unifying the party behind Lincoln (p. 317 n.12)—further evidence, then, for the claim here about Weydemeyer's role.

88. *New York Daily Tribune*, 1864 September 29, p. 1. Frémont's two letters of withdrawal were printed in the September 23 edition of the paper along with its editorial. That the German vote in the election was important is testified to by the German-language edition of the Republican Party platform that the pro-Lincoln paper made available for its readers.

89. **41**, p. 321.

90. A perusal of the most popular songs sung by German American soldiers testifies to this sentiment. See "The German-American Songbook," http://ourworld.compuserve.com/homepages/Jan-Hochbruck/songbook.

91. **42**, p. 40.

92. The most authoritative account of his exploits can be found in Loyd D. Easton, *Hegels' First American Followers: The Ohio Hegelians: John B. Stallo, Peter Kaufman, Moncure Conway, and August Willich, with Key Writings* (Athens: Ohio University Press, 1966), pp. 191–97.

93. August Willich, *The Army, Standing Army or National Army?: An Essay* (Cincinnati: A. Frey, 1866), p. 23.

94. For details on their participation as well as others in the war, see A. E. Zucker, ed. *The Forty-Eighters: Political Refugees of the German Rev-*

olution of 1848 (New York: Columbia University Press, 1950), particularly chapter 7. See Levine, *Spirit of 1848*, chapter 10, for an overview.

95. http://ourworld.compuserve.com/homepages/Jan-Hochbruck/intro., p. 1.

96. Ignatiev, p. 88.

97. Ignatiev, p. 79.

98. Levine, *Spirit of 1848*, p. 150.

99. Ibid., p. 149.

100. McPherson, *Drawn with the Sword*, p. 92.

101. Gilbert Osofsky, "Abolitionists, Irish Immigrants, and the Dilemmas of Romantic Nationalism," *American Historical Review* 80, no. 4 (October 1975): 899, 903, 911.

102. On this and the other claim here about Lincoln's unique role in the overthrow of slavery, see McPherson, *Drawn with the Sword*, chapters 13 and 14.

4

A Dream Deferred
The Failed "Attempt to Reconstruct Democracy in America"

> In the United States of North America, every indepen-
> dent movement of the workers was paralysed so long
> as slavery disfigured a part of the Republic. Labour
> cannot emancipate itself in the white skin where in the
> black it is branded.
>
> —Marx, *Capital*

Marx and Engels expected that the overthrow of slavery would
put the class question on the political agenda in a qualitatively different way for the first time in the United States. As long as the peculiar institution was in place the full development of capitalist
property relations would remain fettered and deformed, thus re-
tarding the process of proletarianization. This would inevitably delay the fulfillment of the historic mission of the proletariat, the
forging of real democracy as the necessary prelude to human
emancipation. Slavery not only "defiled" the republic but was also
an obstacle to the political emancipation of the working class. The
"perogatives of the white-skinned labourer" vis-á-vis "the Negro"
had hindered his ability to recognize his real class interests.

As capitalist development proceeded in an unprecedented
way in the aftermath of the slavocracy's defeat, U.S. labor took
initiatives just as Marx and Engels anticipated. It also appeared
that race might take a back seat to class consciousness and independent working-class political action. The program of Radical
Reconstruction heralded a new era in American race and, thus,
class relations. Such hopes were dashed with the presidential

election Compromise of 1877, the long-term consequences of which were catastrophic for the U.S. working class, in all its hues. Not until the Second Reconstruction exploded in the 1960s would this historic setback be overcome.

Reconstruction

When Lincoln was assassinated in April 1865, Marx, on behalf of the General Council (hereafter, GC) of the International Working Men's Association (First International) wrote a letter to the new president, Andrew Johnson, with this advice: "Yours . . . has become the task to uproot by the law what has been felled by the sword, to preside over the arduous task of political reconstruction and social regeneration. A profound sense of your great mission will save you from any compromise with stern duties . . . to initiate the new era of the emancipation of labour."[1]

Marx told Engels what he meant by "stern duties": "*Johnson* is STERN, INFLEXIBLE, REVENGEFUL, and as former POOR WHITE has a deadly hatred of the oligarchy. He will make less fuss about these fellows, and because of the treachery, he will find the TEMPER of the North commensurate with his INTENTIONS." In his reply, Engels thought that "Johnson will insist on confiscation of the great estates, which will make the pacification and reorganisation of the South rather more acute. Lincoln would scarcely have insisted on it."[2] "Political reconstruction and social regeneration" for Marx and Engels entailed a thoroughgoing dismantling of the slavocracy, including the expropriation of its property, through the use of "stern duties"—something that Lincoln, based on his earlier pronouncements, appeared indisposed to carry out.

Marx and Engels's optimism about Johnson wasn't unique. Abolitionist Wendell Phillips initially "nursed the hope that . . . Johnson might be the man who would lead the nation to protect and rehabilitate the Negro."[3] Not surprisingly, then, Marx and Engels reacted with alarm when Johnson did not heed Marx's advice and began to compromise with the old slave owners. Within a couple of months of his inauguration, Marx told Engels: "Johnson's policy likes me not. . . . excessively VACILLATING and weak. . . . The reaction has already set in in America and will soon be much fortified if the present lackadaisical attitude is not ended immediately."[4]

For Engels too, "Mr Johnson's policy is less and less to my liking . . . NIGGER-hatred is coming out more and more violently, and he is relinquishing all his power vis-à-vis the old lords in the South." Engels then pointed to the solution. "Without COLOURED SUFFRAGE nothing can be done, and Johnson is leaving it up to the defeated, the ex-slaveowners, to decide on that. It is absurd."[5] Nevertheless, Engels was optimistic about the long run. The defeated slave owners would gladly sell their remaining properties to "immigrants and speculators from the North. The latter will arrive soon enough and make a good number of changes. I think the MEAN WHITES will gradually die out. Nothing more will become of this RACE; those who are left after 2 generations will merge with the immigrants to make a completely different RACE." As for the former slaves, they "will probably turn into small SQUATTERS as in Jamaica. Thus ultimately the oligarchy will go to pot after all, but the process could be accomplished immediately at one fell swoop, whereas it is now being drawn out."

As it turned out these fragments constitute Marx and Engels's most explicit and extant thinking about the fate of the former slaves and merit discussion. To what extent Marx concurred with Engels's views is not clear. It can be confidently assumed that he agreed that granting the former slaves political rights including the right to vote would be the way to counter Black oppression. As for economic rights, particularly access to land ownership, it seems that Engels did not envision a land reform in favor of the former slaves. This may have had to do with his expectation that capitalist speculators for the North would prevent such a transformation from taking place. Marx would have agreed—for reasons to be seen shortly—that the commodification of former plantation land was very much on the agenda in the aftermath of the Confederacy's defeat. This in no way suggests that this expectation constituted a political position. Had the two formulated a political program for the situation at hand, they would have undoubtedly called for a redistribution of land to the former slaves. Engels proved to be partially correct insofar as the freedmen never acquired any meaningful amount of the plantation lands. But rather than becoming squatters as in Jamaica they ended up in their majority as sharecroppers, a form of peonage.[6]

In hindsight, Engels was overly optimistic about the disappearance of the "mean whites." They proved to be more enduring than Engels, and perhaps Marx, thought. Tellingly, Engels didn't consider "nigger-hatred" to be immutable. That it proved to be more intractable had much to do with what he and Marx saw as Washington's irresolute behavior after Appomattox—its failure to execute the necessary "stern duties" toward the defeated slave owners. If Lincoln had been reluctant to use dictatorial methods against the rebels, Marx and Engels initially hoped that Johnson would be less squeamish.

Notwithstanding Engels's optimism about the long term, in September 1865 the GC of the IWMA composed an "Address to the People of the United States," copies of which were sent to every branch of the International. Unlike the earlier message to Johnson, it isn't clear if Marx penned it but the document clearly reflected what he and Engels had said in their letters.[7] Given the role Marx was playing in the organization by this time, such an address would not have been issued without his agreement. After congratulating the American people for their victory over the slaveocracy, the letter then asks to "add a word of counsel for the future."

> Injustice against a fraction of your people having been followed by such dire consequences, put an end to it. Declare your fellow citizens from this day forth free and equal, without any reserve. If you refuse them citizens' rights while you exact from them citizens' duties, you will sooner or later face a new struggle which will once more drench your country in blood. The eyes of Europe and of the whole world are on your attempts at reconstruction, and foes are ever ready to sound the death-knell of republican institutions as soon as they see their opportunity. We therefore admonish you, as brothers in a common cause, to sunder all the chains of freedom, and your victory will be complete.[8]

In no uncertain terms the organization that Marx led "admonished" the "American people" for having failed so far to grant full political equality to the former slaves and warned that if

they delayed in so doing they could expect to have a new rebellion on their hands. There is nothing to suggest that Marx and
Engels ever veered from this perspective.

In the last months of the Civil War Weydemeyer was active
in Missouri in calling for the immediate abolishment of slavery
"without compensation."[9] Even without documentation, it is
reasonable to infer that he, like Marx and Engels, opposed Johnson's conciliatory stance toward the former slave owners. The
record is clear that the German American socialist milieu in
which he worked, in New York and Chicago, actively sought to
counter Johnson's policies. At almost the same time that Marx
and Engels began to denounce Johnson, like-minded activists in
both cities organized meetings and issued manifestos that con-
demned his policies and called for the "stern duties" from which
Johnson recoiled. In Chicago, the *Arbeiter Verein* sponsored a
mass meeting that criticized Johnson's policies. They voted, just
as the German Unionbund in New York had stated in its manifesto, that Congress should "decree universal suffrage for black
and white alike and provide an economic foundation, through
land distribution for the ex-slaves, without which even political
and civil rights would become meaningless."[10]

After one year of the Johnson administration, in May 1866,
Marx told Engels: "The phase of the Civil War over, only now
have the UNITED STATES really entered the revolutionary
phase."[11] He may have been referring to the bloody riot in
Memphis at the beginning of the month in which scores of
Blacks were murdered by racist gangs, evidence that Johnson's
conciliatory approach only emboldened the counterrevolution.
Among some, this sparked hope that such horrors would gal-
vanize opposition to Johnson's policies and institute real reconstruction. Thus, when the president's congressional allies
were defeated at the polls in November, Marx was "delighted.
. . . The workers in the North have at last fully understood that
white labour will never be emancipated so long as black labour
is still stigmatised."[12] Virtually the same language would be
immortalized a year later in *Capital*. Modern scholarship confirms the significance of these congressional elections. They
are "the most important off-presidential election in our history,"

according to renowned historian Samuel Eliot Morison,[13] "For the first time in America history," states Eric Foner, "civil rights for blacks played a central part in a major party's national campaign. . . . More than anything else, the election became a referendum on the Fourteenth Amendment."[14] The outcome, as Rogers Smith notes, "led to the most significant legislative session in U.S. history from the standpoint of citizenship and civil rights, the 39th Congress of 1866–1867."[15]

Marx continued in an optimistic vein about such developments as his comment in the preface to *Capital* suggests: "Mr. Wade, vice-president of the United States, declared in public meetings that, after the abolition of slavery, a radical change of the relations of capital and of property in land is next upon the order of the day. These are signs of the times. . . . They do not signify that tomorrow a miracle will happen. They show that, within the ruling classes themselves, a foreboding is dawning, that the present society is no solid crystal, but an organism capable of change, and is constantly changing."[16] "Mr. Wade" was Senator Benjamin Wade from Ohio, the president of the senate who was next in line for succession, i.e., "vice-president." What Marx was referring to was "a widely publicized speech" that Wade delivered in Kansas earlier in 1867 in which he also declared that "Property . . . is not equally divided, and a more equal distribution of capital must be wrought out."[17]

Liberal supporters of Reconstruction reacted with horror at Wade's sentiments. "The [*New York*] Times lambasted the Radicals for desiring 'a war on property . . . to succeed the war on Slavery,' and *The Nation* linked Wade's speech with the confiscation [of land] issue, organized labor's demand for an eight-hour day, and the rise of Fenianism among Irish-Americans as illustrations of how 'demagogues' had abandoned 'true radicalism'—equality before the law and equal economic opportunity—in favor of 'special favors for special classes of people.'"[18]

In hindsight, such fears—the "foreboding . . . within the ruling classes"—signaled the beginning of liberal capitalist abandonment of Reconstruction. Two decades earlier, during the 1848 revolutions in Europe, liberals responded in like manner. Tocqueville, like later liberal Republicans, also worshiped at the altar of private property. He too would have found the eight-hour-day movement and "Fenianism" as offensive as land confiscation. Though Marx may have been unaware, Wade's pro-labor sympathies were well known amongst his colleagues, one reason it seems why the Johnson impeachment campaign fell short by one vote of removing the president. Wade would have assumed the presidency upon such an ouster. This specter was enough to sober property-conscious jurors at Johnson's Senate trial. Though probably unacquainted with its details, nothing in this drama would have surprised Marx. He had long understood the political dynamics of private property relations, both theoretically and, as a result of the 1848–1849 experiences, politically.

While the 1866 elections encouraged Marx, it's worthwhile to point out that he reiterated in *Capital* a year later his point about the deep linkage between labor and racial discrimination. "In the United States of North America, every independent movement of the workers was paralyzed so long as slavery disfigured a part of the Republic. Labour cannot emancipate itself in the white skin where in the black it is branded." Note the similarity between this and what he wrote to Lincoln three years earlier: "While the working men, the true political power of the North, allowed slavery to defile their own republic; while before the Negro, mastered and sold without his concurrence, they boasted it the highest prerogative of the white-skinned labourer to sell himself and choose his own master; they were unable to attain the true freedom of labour or to support their European brethren in their struggle for emancipation."

His point to Lincoln about "white-skinned labour" being "unable to attain the true freedom of labour," becomes in *Capital* "every independent movement of the workers was paralyzed." He initially maintains use of the past tense. But in the next sentence—"Labour cannot emancipate itself . . . "—he shifts to the present, referring to 1867. This suggests Marx recognized that the battle to end the "prerogatives of white-skinned labour," two years after Appomattox, had yet to be won. He certainly knew about the rapid backsliding of Johnson, who had by mid-1867— not long after Marx had sent the last proofs of *Capital* to the printer—become "*a dirty tool of the SLAVEHOLDERS.* "[19] Not only was victory over the slavocracy still to be consolidated but white workers could use some advice—their own liberation from the exploitation of capital couldn't be accomplished at the expense or denial of the fullest equality for fellow workers of a different skin color.

Marx argued that the overthrow of slavery brought the class question to the fore because it exposed the fundamental contradiction between capital and labor—as the *Manifesto* put it, bourgeois society "has simplified the class antagonisms." But this did not mean that he thought socialist revolution was imminent. His qualification of Wade's above-cited comment is instructive: "These are signs of the times . . . They do not signify that tomorrow a miracle will happen." In the very last page of *Capital* Marx was more explicit. While the end of the war had allowed for the "creation of a finance aristocracy of the vilest type"—land speculation for the railroads—"the very centralization of capital" meant that the "great republic has therefore ceased to be the promised land for emigrating workers." This was due to the massive exodus from Europe which "throws men onto the labour-market there more rapidly than the wave of immigration to the West can wash them away" to the "promised land." In spite of the "gigantic strides" in capitalist production the process of proletarianization "has by no means yet proceeded so far as to reach the normal European level," Marx concludes.[20] The material conditions for socialist revolution in the United States, in other words, were not yet in place.

The process was more retarded in the United States exactly because of the westward migration, that is, access to land. Marx had earlier highlighted this point in one of a series of presentations to the GC of the IWMA in 1865, which became the basis for his famous pamphlet *Value, Price and Profit*. Access to western lands insured the "continuous conversion of wages labourers into independent, self-sustaining peasants. The position of a wages labourer is for a very large part of the American people but a probational state, which they are sure to leave within a longer or shorter term."[21] Engels reiterated this point, with all its political implications, in another GC discussion in 1871. "In the densely populated states [of the United States] the labor movement was organised but the extent of unoccupied land prevented [it from] getting stronger than it was."[22]

For Marx and Engels the abolition of chattel slavery helped to accelerate the deepening and expansion of capitalist relations of production throughout the United States, thereby bringing into existence for the first time a hereditary proletariat and thus the necessary prerequisite for socialist revolution. Nothing they ever said about the consequences of the war in this regard went further than this affirmation of orthodoxy. They were therefore sober about what lay ahead—and what did not. As Marx pointed out in 1868, "Socialist literature does not exist in the UNITED STATES. There are only workers' papers."[23] About three years before the Civil War, Marx wrote in *Grundrisse*, his notebooks, that "even the antitheses of bourgeois society itself appear only as vanishing moments."[24] There had yet to emerge, at least in 1867, after the overthrow of slavery—as Marx's remarks in *Capital* reveal—a real "antithesis" to capitalism in America.

In an interview with a reporter from the New York *World* in 1871, Marx responded to a question about the relationship of the IWMA to the United States: "The chief centres of our activity are for the present among the old societies of Europe. Many circumstances have hitherto tended to prevent the labor problem from assuming an all-absorbing importance in the United States. But they are rapidly disappearing, and it is rapidly coming to the front there with the growth as in Europe of a laboring class distinct from the rest of the community and divorced from capital."[25] This is clearly consistent with everything that he and Engels had been saying about the United States. In the final years of his life, Marx devoted much of his research to two developments. One was the proletarianization process in America, specifically how "rapidly" it was proceeding, especially in the West. He had intended to include the results of such investigations in the second and third volumes of *Capital*. The other process was the "rapidity" with which capitalist property relations were undermining feudal relations of production in czarist Russia. Not for the first time were Marx's inquiries prescient.

Birth of a New Labor Movement

It was within this overall *longue durée* framework that Marx and Engels approached the newly revived labor movement in the United States and, less explicitly, the initial and hesitant steps toward an alliance of labor in both "white and black skin." Once slavery had been confined to the dustbin of history, their theory had predicted the qualitative deepening of capitalist property relations and, hence, the emergence of working-class opposition and organization. Thus Marx was cheered by news that, within weeks of the victory over the slavocracy, American workers had launched a nationwide campaign to win the eight-hour workday. Weydemeyer, in August 1866, put the significance of the undertaking for the class struggle in the United States in historical context: "With the eight-hour movement . . . the labor question, i.e. the modern labor question—the question of hired labor, which is better known under the euphemistic name of 'free labor'—steps before the social forum, strips off the secondary character which heretofore adhered to it on this continent, raises itself to a social question."[26] The initiative had not just theoretical but also political import for the class struggle in Europe as well as the United States. In his "Instructions" to the first congress of the IWMA in 1866 in Geneva, Marx pointed to the vanguard actions of the workers as an example to be emulated. "We propose *8 hours work* as the *legal limit* of the working day. This limitation being generally claimed by the workmen of the United States of America, the vote of the Congress will raise it to the common platform of the working classes all over the world."[27]

Thus began the first international campaign to institute the eight-hour workday. In the preface to *Capital* Marx wrote: "Just as in the eighteenth century the American War of Independence sounded the tocsin for the European middle class, so in the nineteenth century the American Civil War did the same for the European working class." In addition to the stimulus that the war against slavery provided for independent, European, working-class political action in the form of the anti-interventionist movement—which in turn helped inspire the formation of the IWMA—Marx was also referring to the newly organized eight-hour campaign and its anticipated impact on the other side of the Atlantic, one which he was doing everything in his power to encourage.

The Geneva meeting coincided with the inaugural conference of the National Labor Union (NLU) in Baltimore. It adopted the eight-hour day as one of its main goals. The formation of the NLU, truly the first national labor organization in the United States, signaled for Marx and Engels the revival of the American labor movement on a new and more advanced basis. This development commanded their attention, for the first time, toward the question of union organizing in the United States. Marx remarked, "I was exceedingly pleased at the American workers' congress which took place at the same time in Baltimore. The watchword there was organisation for the struggle against capital, and remarkably enough, most of the demands I had put up for Geneva were put up there, too, by the correct instinct of the workers."[28] *Capital* made its timely debut a year later.

Engels explained to a close contact in America: "I hope you will be able to bring Marx's book to the attention of the German-American press and of the workers. With the 8-hour agitation that is in progress in America now, this book with its chapter on the *working day* will come at just the right time for you over there, and, in other respects too, it is likely to clarify people's minds on a variety of issues. The future of the party in America will be greatly beholden to you for any step you can take in that direction."[29] Engels's efforts reveal, once again, that he and his partner did not view the course of the class struggle as inevitable. They were prepared to do all in their capacity to advance it—endeavoring to assure, for example, that "socialist literature" would "exist" for the first time in America. Unbeknownst to Marx and Engels, on the same day the Baltimore conference began, Weydemeyer succumbed to cholera. Only in hindsight would it become clear what his loss would mean for the nascent communist movement—what Engels called the "party"—in the United States.

If the eight-hour-day campaign represented the best effort of the new labor movement in America, it's obsession with currency reform as a solution to the economic crisis that workers and farmers increasingly faced revealed for Marx and Engels its limitations. That the NLU made the latter one of its priorities at the Baltimore meeting testified for them the still yet infantile character of the movement. Time and experience, the *longue durée*, would be needed to overcome such immaturity.

Another issue that registered the limitations on the new labor movement was the NLU's attitude toward workers in "black skin." Some of its final declarations and statements of its leaders were more advanced on this issue. These recognized, at least, at the level of rhetoric, the necessity of Black and white workers uniting. But the reality of the organization was its failure in its short life to vote with its feet. In a speech in 1868, President William Sylvis, said, for example, "No man in America rejoiced more than I at the downfall of Negro slavery. But when the shackles fell from the limbs of those four millions of blacks, it did not make them *free* men; it simply transferred them from one condition of slavery to another; it placed them upon the platform of the white workingmen, and made all slaves together. . . . We are now all one family of slaves together, and the labor reform movement is a second emancipation proclamation."[30] A few months later in a circular he declared: "Our people are being divided into two classes—the rich and the poor, the producers and the non-producers. . . . The working-people of our nation, white and black, male and female, are sinking to a condition of serfdom. Even now a slavery exists in our land worse than ever existed under the old slave system."[31]

Andrew Cameron, another central NLU leader, also recognized the importance of Black-white labor unity. Cameron wrote the organization's first address to American workers in which he wondered whether white workers would be willing to embrace their Black coworkers if the latter extended a friendly hand. To not do so, "we would inflict greater injury upon the cause of labor reform than the combined efforts of capital could accomplish. . . . So capitalists North and South would foment discord between the whites and blacks and hurl one against the other . . . to maintain their ascendancy and continue the reign of oppression . . . What is wanted is for every union to help inculcate the grand ennobling idea that the interests of labor are one; that there should be no distinction of race or nationality; no classification of Jew or Gentile,

Christian or infidel; that there is one dividing line, that which separates mankind into two great classes, the class that labors and the class that lives by others' labor."[32] Not surprisingly, pronouncements such as these earned an invitation from Marx on behalf of the GC to the NLU to send a delegate to the second and third IWMA congresses. This was exactly the kind of language that encouraged Marx to believe that indeed the class question was on the agenda in the United States in an unprecedented way.

Their rhetoric notwithstanding, Sylvis and Cameron failed to bring the NLU ranks to their perspective. Sylvis's premature death in September 1869 was a major blow as Marx underscored in a letter to Engels: "Much to be regretted is the sudden death of Sylvis (aged 41). . . . just *before* the meeting of the LABOR UNION CONGRESS, for which purpose he travelled across the United States agitating for nearly a whole year. Part of his work will thus be lost."[33] As was true with Weydemeyer's death three years earlier, only in retrospect would the real impact of Sylvis's death to the fledgling labor movement be fully registered.

To what extent Sylvis focused on the challenge of actually forging Black-white unity in his efforts to promote the 1869 congress of the NLU is not known. Black workers, having observed and experienced the vacillation of the NLU for three years, decided to form their own organization in December 1869, the Colored National Labor Union.[34] What is certain is that there were very real obstacles to multiracial solidarity, among them the NLU's incessant focus on currency reform. Its panacea, the issuance of "greenbacks," was understood by Blacks as repudiation of the national debt, the product of the means by which slavery had been overthrown. Thus their staunch opposition to the NLU's greenback panacea and apparent support for paying the debt.

More than any other factor, the reality of the racial order, not only in the ranks of labor but in the larger society, effectively obstructed unity. The disagreement between both groups of workers on how to respond to racist bigotry proved insurmountable. While the most class-conscious white workers had concluded as early as 1864 that labor needed its own political party—an example of "independent working class political action" that Marx inscribed on the banner of the IWMA—Black workers continued to look to the Republicans, the party of Lincoln, as their best hope for political salvation. Indeed, though the GOP, a bourgeois party, continued to backslide after reaching the highpoint of advancing civil rights for Blacks, 1867–1870, they were at least a known quantity. The Black masses were understandably reluctant to take a chance with a labor party, whose potential base continued to be permeated by deeply racist practices. The extant record doesn't reveal the extent to which Marx and Engels were familiar with this reality or if they tried to intervene to advance Black-white unity.

Engels's efforts to get *Capital* into the hands of U.S. workers was part of his and Marx's deliberate effort to assist in the maturation of the new labor movement. The formation of the IWMA in 1864 gave Marx the organizational vehicle to carry out that project. But he faced an immediate obstacle in that the ranks of the Marx party had considerably dwindled as a result of the Civil War. "I lost contact years ago with all my acquaintances in America. I am still in touch only with Meyer in St. Louis, the friend of our J. Weydemeyer (deceased last year [1866])."[35] This did not deter him from making an effort to establish links with the newly emerging labor movement.

Invitations were extended to the NLU to send delegates to IWMA congresses beginning with the second gathering in Lausanne in 1867. By 1869 the NLU finally sent a delegate, Andrew Cameron, to the Basel congress. Though not officially a branch of the IWMA, the NLU communicated with the GC. In 1869 the latter received an address written by Marx that focused on a brewing diplomatic conflict between Washington and London that threatened to lead to war. While the statement's purpose was to promote antiwar sentiment and to encourage solidarity between American and British workers, it noted how the Civil War had given birth to a more rapacious U.S. bourgeoisie at the expense of workers—an issue that Marx had raised in *Capital* and one to which he would often return. "Yet for all this the civil war did compensate by freeing the slave and the consequent moral impetus it gave to your own class movement."[36] A war with England, he argued, would only set back the new U.S. working-class movement.

In the meantime, the New York Communist Club was revived by returning war veterans and new recruits from Germany. Frederick Sorge, who, as noted earlier, joined the Club when it was first organized in 1857, soon emerged as its head. Adolph Douai, who Weydemeyer worked with to insure Lincoln's election, became an active member and did much to popularize *Capital* in the German American labor press. The Club merged with partisans of Marx's rival Ferdinand Lassalle and then reconstituted itself, first as a branch of the NLU and then the IWMA, in December 1869. Composed almost exclusively of German American workers, Section I of the International, as it became known, showed some interest in Black workers when it "appointed a committee to promote the organization of Negro workers. However, it sent no delegate to the convention of the Colored National Labor Union held that same month in Washington, even though it was widely publicized that whites would be welcomed as fraternal delegates."[37]

There are only two explicit mentions of Black workers in IWMA records. One is in a report that Sorge wrote in June 1871 to the GC about the state of the U.S. labor movement. "A great strike occurred lately in Washington amongst the colored laborers for an increase of their extremely low wages. They were momentarily defeated by the stepping in of white laborers. The result will probably be the emancipation of the colored workingmen from the grip of the political suckers who kept them till now almost exclusively in the ranks of the so-called Republican Party."[38] Why Sorge thought such an outcome would occur is not clear but it reveals once again the political blinders on white labor that side-tracked effective collaboration between it and Black toilers.

The other mention is in Sorge's intervention in a discussion at the Hague Congress of the IWMA in 1872 in which he says: "the working class in America consists in the first place of Irishmen, then of Germans, then of Negroes, and in the fourth place of American-borns, since the Americans prefer to speculate, lounge about in offices, etc."[39] Sorge's comment is intriguing because he recognized Blacks as workers but not, apparently, as "Americans" even though, unlike "Irishmen" and "Germans," they were clearly born in the United States. Also, "Americans" were the least important workers because they evidently didn't labor as hard as the other three groups. The latter fact explains why "Negroes" weren't "Americans." To read more into Sorge's comment would be speculative.[40]

There is no evidence that Marx, either on behalf of the GC or as its corresponding secretary for German Americans, ever explicitly promoted Black-white unity in any of the U.S. sections of the International—a matter to be revisited. Marx, however, did make an intervention in Section I in 1870 on an issue that has some relevance—Irish self-determination. With the rise of a new wave in Irish nationalist activism at the end of the 1860s known as Fenianism, Marx felt that the IWMA, with its headquarters in Britain, had to take a position. The situation he faced, as he explained to Engels, is that "One has to struggle here not only against prejudices, but also against the stupidity and wretchedness of the *Irish* spokesmen in Dublin."[41] The reality of anti-Irish sentiment amongst the English working class and misleadership within the Irish community—specifically, the dead hand of the clergy—required programmatic clarity and direction for the International.

Marx initiated a discussion in the GC at the end of 1869. The research that he had been doing, he told Engels, convinced him to rethink his earlier position: "For a long time I believed it would be possible to overthrow the Irish regime by ENGLISH WORKING CLASS ASCENDANCY. . . . Deeper study has now convinced me of the opposite. The English WORKING CLASS will *never accomplish anything* BEFORE IT HAS GOT RID OF IRELAND. The lever must be applied in Ireland. This is why the Irish QUESTION is so important for the social movement in general."[42] If Marx had once prioritized the initiatives of the English working class, by the end of 1869 his eyes were now on the oppressed Irish nation. This shift was not unlike the adjustments that he and Engels had made earlier in relation to the struggles for national liberation in Algeria and Mexico.[43] While indeed their historical materialist method explains Marx's initial position on the Irish situation, that same method, with its dialectical calibrations, disposed them to be partisans of any initiatives of the oppressed—what they often called "the real movement." In other words, the liberation of the nationally oppressed did not have to wait on the revolutionary actions of the workers in advanced capitalist oppressor nations. The actions of the former could be a spur to the latter.

Having won the GC over to his new position, Marx wrote to Section I in New York in April 1870 to convince them of the importance of the issue not only in Britain but also in the United States. (See the appendix for details.) In New York, where the Irish comprised a significant layer of the working class, clarity on this issue was crucial in winning their allegiance to the International. He explained how the English ruling class used anti-Irish sentiment to divide the working class in England and then drew a parallel to the United States. "The ordinary English worker hates the Irish worker as a competitor who forces down the STANDARD OF LIFE. In relation to the Irish worker, he feels himself to be a member of the *ruling nation* and therefore, makes himself a tool of his aristocrats and capitalists *against Ireland*, thus strengthening their domination *over himself*. He harbours religious, social and national prejudices against him. His attitude towards him is roughly that of the POOR WHITES to the NIGGERS in the former slave states of the American Union. . . . This antagonism is kept artificially alive and intensified by the press, the pulpit, the comic papers, in short by all the means at the disposal of the ruling class." He then urged the section to take part in the IWMA's campaign to counter this by helping to forge an alliance between Irish, German, "naturally, also, with the English and American workers who wish to join in . . . is the greatest thing you could undertake now. This must be done in the name of the 'International.' The social significance of the Irish question must be made clear."[44]

Marx's comments challenge the oft-made claim that he ignored racism in the working class. Be it Britain or the United States he had no problem in acknowledging its pernicious presence in the proletariat. More important than such recognition, though, was Marx's understanding how it was perpetuated and the necessity of waging a struggle against it. For modern sensibilities, Marx's catalogue of the role of religion, the media, and popular culture as mechanisms for infusing and perpetuating such false consciousness is pertinent. Yet, for the United States it appears that he may have thought this was a regional problem—in the former Confederate states where the vast majority of Blacks resided. Second, if the Irish case was instructive for Marx—as it indeed seemed to be—then this might explain why he urged Section I to embrace the Irish cause but said nothing about Blacks. After all it was "the real movement"—the active mobilization of Irish nationalists—that put the Irish question on his radar screen and convinced him to reconsider earlier positions. In the United States, on the other hand, there had yet to appear in the aftermath of the Civil War any independent mobilization of Blacks to challenge the continuing racism—at least comparable to what the Irish were doing. The Colored National Labor Union survived for only two years, effectively coming to an end in 1871. Its failure was due in large part to the undying faith of the Black community's leadership in the Republican Party and, thus, unwillingness to embark—as Sorge had erroneously expected—upon an independent project.[45] The absence of any major mobilization of Blacks to actively counter such practices may therefore explain Marx's silence. Only from the vantage of hindsight—arguably years if not decades later—would it be obvious that by then the counterrevolution to overthrow Reconstruction was already underway. It is unlikely that Marx and Engels—especially from afar—were aware of the extent to which the reversal had commenced.

In the meantime, the U.S. sections of the IWMA continued to grow. No event proved to be as decisive in the International's destiny as the Paris Commune. For the first time in history, from March to May 1871, the proletariat held power in its hands. Marx's famous homage to the Communards, *The Civil War in France*—a title inspired by the U.S. conflagration—put both the IWMA and himself on the world's political map, also for the first time. The number of U.S. sections increased threefold by the end of the year. "The most important news" from America, Marx told the August 15th meeting of the GC, "was that Wendell Phillips, the great anti-slavery leader, had joined the ranks of the International."[46] Some years later Engels explained to August Bebel, his closest comrade in Germany, who Phillips was: "the great anti-slavery man who, with the exception of John Brown, did more than anyone else for the abolition of slavery and the prosecution of the war, and is the foremost speaker in America—maybe the world."[47] Phillips's membership was further confirmation for Marx and Engels that the overthrow of slavery had indeed placed the class question at the top of the U.S. political agenda. Even with the effective end of the IWMA in 1874—the result of ruling-class attacks and an internal struggle between the Marxists and the anarchists—they held to this view.[48] Only in retrospect would they realize that there was still unfinished business from the Civil War, the continuing "branding" of Black labor.

Marx was nevertheless sober about the prospects for socialist revolution in America. In one of his most didactic letters on strategy and tactics—to one of the leaders of Section I—Marx put the work of the International and the workers movement in broad historical perspective. He explained how "the political movement of the working class"—an example being the fight for the eight-hour workday in the United States— differed from "economic struggles." Unlike the latter, the former has as its "final object the "conquest of POLITICAL POWER for this class." And to do so assumed "a certain degree of PREVIOUS organisation." But it was through the "economic struggles," such as strikes against individual capitalist firms, that "previous" structures came into being. "Where the working class is not yet far enough advanced in its organisation to undertake a decisive campaign against the collective power, i.e. the political power, of the ruling classes, it must at any rate be trained for this by continual agitation against, and a hostile attitude towards, the policies of the ruling classes."[49] Marx's admonition to a U.S. IWMA leader is not coincidental. It was just the kind of advice that was needed in a setting where the emergence of a hereditary working class was just underway and hardly, therefore, propitious for a socialist project. Hence, the importance of what he called on another occasion the day-to-day "guerilla" struggles in which the working class "trained" to organize the political movement that would eventually take power and institute "real democracy." In other words, the strategy for the *longue durée.*

Marx on Race

This is the appropriate place to address Marx's views on race in general and Blacks in particular, given the apparent silence in his thinking about Black-white working-class unity in the aftermath of the Civil War.

As noted in chapter 2, the record prior to the war is, except for a fragment here and there, virtually blank. On the eve of and during the war, as chapter 3 explains, Blacks are seen first and foremost as the necessary troops to overthrow slavery. In the aftermath of the war the portrait became more complex. Almost all of his extant private thoughts in this period were addressed directly or indirectly to his son-in-law Paul Lafargue. In 1868, Marx's daughter Laura married Lafargue, who traced his origins to Africa; his maternal grandmother was a Haitian mulatto. He also had roots in the indigenous peoples of the Americas. There is no evidence that this was of concern to the Marxs when Paul proposed and was granted permission to marry Laura. For Marx, the most important concern was that Lafargue be financially able to support his daughter in order not to subject her to the kinds of privations she experienced with her often financially beleaguered father. Because Lafargue was a communist activist, an ally in the IWMA, his future father-in-law was all too aware of the hardships associated with such a life.[50] Lafargue's most authoritative biographer writes that "Although, of course aware of [his] racial origins, the Marxs showed no signs of real prejudice. . . . their references to Lafargue's one-eighth black background were couched in affectionate and joking terms and seen as a source of amusement, not concern."[51] According to the same biographer, Lafargue, throughout his life, "remained sensitive to the issues of color. When, at an international congress [1911], the American Marxist Daniel DeLeon asked Lafargue about his origins, he promptly replied, 'I am proudest of my negro extraction.'"[52]

During parental discussions about the impending engagement and marriage, Marx, first made his comment to Lafargue's father that appeared a year later in *Capital*. "You will have been just as delighted by the defeat of President Johnson in the latest elections as I was. The workers in the North have at last fully understood that white labour will never be emancipated so long as black labour is still stigmatised."[53] Implied here is a shared sense of opposition to the racist practices of the Johnson administration and optimism—undue as history would reveal—that with the 1866 congressional elections white workers in America had come to recognize the class advantages of fighting racism. This suggests that Marx had already engaged Lafargue's father on the topic of race. It can also be assumed that it was precisely because the father's son had known roots in Africa Marx felt he had the license to express himself.

The next extant reference that Marx made about Lafargue's origins came during the young couple's honeymoon. In a letter addressed to both Laura and Paul, father-in-law Marx remarked that "his sending books to me, at such a critical juncture, speaks volumes for the innate kindness of the 'young man.' This simple fact would go far to prove that he must belong to a better than the European race."[54] About a year later in 1869 in a comment meant for Lafargue, Marx wrote: "And compliments to the African. It will give him great pleasure to hear . . . that the first 'black' ambassador of the United States has been appointed by [President] Grant."[55] "African" was one of a number of terms of affection used within the family and amongst friends to refer to Lafargue, others being "creole," "negrillo," "gorilla," and even "nigger."[56] (Marx, as already noted, was known in the same circles as "Moor" owing to his dark features.) The comment itself suggests that Marx thought the situation for Blacks was genuinely improving under Grant—possible evidence that Marx and Engels were, like most people on the scene, not aware that Reconstruction was on its deathbed.

One last example from this period is Marx's letter to Paul and Laura about a year later in 1870. Grandfather Marx began by expressing concern for their sick one-year-old son and offered an opinion. "The poor dear little fellow must have suffered severely from the cold so adverse to 'la nature mélanienne' [dark-skinned constitution]." "Apropos," he mentioned Gobineau's four-volume work, *Essai sur l'inégalité des races humaines* [Essay on the Inequality of the Human Races], which he had apparently been reading.

He dismissed what he characterized as Gobineau's claim that "*'la race blanche* [the white race]' is a sort of God amongst the other human races." Though they remained friends to the end, Tocqueville, too, disagreed with Gobineau's white supremacist stance. As for the latter's "spite against the *'race noire* [black race],' " Marx offered an explanation: "to such people it is always a source of satisfaction to have somebody they think themselves entitled to *mépriser* [despise]." Nevertheless, "he declares *'le négre' ou 'le sang noir'* ['the black' or 'the black blood'] to be *la source matérielle de l'art* [the material source of art], and all artistic production of the white nations to depend on their mixture *avec 'le sang noir,'* [with the 'black blood']."

All of this is instructive given the context. While clearly critical of white chauvinism, he noted approvingly Gobineau's essentialist views about Blacks and the arts. Given his opinion about *la nature mélanienne*, it's not surprising that he would be susceptible to such thinking. Four years earlier—about the time that Lafargue began dating Laura, but perhaps coincidentally—Marx and Engels debated the merits of a work which claimed that geological differences largely explained national and racial differences. Marx thought the thesis to be credible, while Engels considered it "to be totally mistaken or incredibly one-sided and exaggerated."[57] Though Marx seemed to accept his partner's critique, he still recommended the book to others because it was "an advance over Darwin."[58] His *nature mélanienne* thesis may very well have originated with the disputed work and suggests that Engels hadn't fully disabused him of this particular brand of essentialist thinking about race.

Again, it's no coincidence that these fragments, Marx's most explicit views on Blacks and race, are directed in one way or another to his son-in-law Lafargue, with whom he had license to explore these issues. They reveal Marx the real human being who, as his historical materialist perspective would explain, was very much the product of the world in which he lived. On the one hand, they disclose his desire to convince both daughter and son-in-law that he had enlightened ideas on race and was an opponent of white chauvinism. He even proffered a still valuable insight on the racist mind—the need to feel superior to others.

On the other hand, he continued to carry with him the essentialist baggage that informed even the then most advanced ideas on the subject. These fragments offer a window into Marx's thinking, but they should be seen just as that. Far more important were his actions, how he voted with his feet—the criterion he and Engels always employed to evaluate themselves and others.

Overthrow of Reconstruction

The Paris Commune went down to bloody defeat in May 1871. The consequences for the workers' movement was underscored by Marx at a conference of the IWMA in London in September. "Reaction exists throughout the Continent, it is general and permanent—and even in the United States and in England in another form."[59] Though the conference minutes are not explicit, Marx no doubt was referring to the ruling-class backlash to the Commune in the United States. When New York riot police carried out a savage attack against mainly Catholic Irish demonstrators in July protesting against a Protestant Irish American parade, which resulted in over sixty civilian deaths and another one hundred wounded, Sorge told the GC that the city's "ruling classes had the 'Commune' on the brain."[60] The Commune was for the bourgeoisie in the nineteenth century what the Bolshevik revolution would be for its heirs in the twentieth century. America was no exception. Like John Brown's raid at Harpers Ferry for the slave owners, Paris, in an increasingly global reaity, became a nightmare for the country's newly triumphant bourgeoisie. It's reaction, in hindsight, foreshadowed and enhanced the already growing backlash to Reconstruction.[61]

Four years earlier Marx, in the introduction to *Capital*, pointed to the aforementioned speech of Senator Benjamin Wade, president of the Senate and next in line for the presidency, and the fears it generated among the U.S. ruling class about the redistribution of property in the aftermath of slavery's abolition. Such trepidations, combined with a sense that there could be an American version of the Commune, began to erode support for Reconstruction in Republican circles.[62] An important contingent of these figures, who dubbed themselves "Liberal Republicans," began with the 1872 elections to lead the retreat. Though it appeared for a brief moment in 1875 that Congress and the Grant administration might actually enact and enforce civil rights for the former slaves, Washington's commitment to Reconstruction had in fact evaporated. The presidential election of 1876 registered this reality. The 1877 compromise that was reached to resolve the inconclusive vote brought in new president Rutherford Hayes on the condition that Washington's betrayal would become official policy. Though it would take almost two decades for the process to be completed, the brutal fact is that it was underway and irreversible.[63] The result, as U.S. Marxist and 1930's Teamster struggle leader Farrell Dobbs aptly declared, was that "not only Afro-Americans but the entire working class had suffered the worst setback in its history."[64] The "branding" of Black labor went forth with a vengeance and with all the consequences implied in Dobbs's observation.

It's not clear to what extent Marx and Engels understood what happened in 1877. The extant record yields little. One problem has to do with Engels's move, after two decades in Manchester, to London in 1870, to within a ten-minute walk from the Marx household. Their correspondence, hence, and unfortunately, would never be as rich as it had till then. The only evidence of some awareness was a comment Marx made to Engels in a letter in July 1877 about the massive railway strike underway in the eastern United States—what labor historian Philip Foner called the "first nationwide rebellion of labor."[65] "What do you think of the workers of the [United States] . . . This, the first outbreak against the ASSOCIATED CAPITAL oligarchy that has arisen since the CIVIL WAR, will, of course, be suppressed, but may well provide a point of departure for the constitution of a serious workers' party in the [United States]. There are two favourable circumstances on top of that. The policy of the new President will turn the negroes, just as the big expropriations of land . . . for the benefit of the Railway, Mining, etc. companies will turn the peasants of the West—whose grumbling is already plainly audible—into militant allies of the workers."[66] In reply, Engels wrote: "I was delighted by the business of the strike in America.

The way they throw themselves into the movement has no equivalent on this side of the ocean. Only twelve years since slavery was abolished and already the movement has got to such a pitch."[67]

Their comments suggest two points. One, Marx was aware of the 1877 compromise/betrayal since Hayes's succession would now mobilize "negroes," against, apparently, the "policy of the new president," that is, the deal that had been cut in Washington. Evidently, he had no expectation before the compromise that Blacks were ready to go into action. The situation had not deteriorated enough to force them to do so. Sorge, as noted earlier, had informed Marx that the Black leadership was solidly wedded to the Republican Party and only now, he thought—erroneously as it turned out—would they be willing to break. The terms under which Hayes took office made the betrayal that had been under way for some years unmistakably real.

Second, Marx felt it would take a viable workers' party to bring about an alliance between Black and white labor, on the one hand, and workers and farmers on the other. This was clearly consistent with the struggle for independent working-class political action that he had waged in the now defunct IWMA. Engels's response is also instructive, particularly his usage of "already." It means that he and Marx were surprised by the upheaval. It may be recalled that they took a *longue durée* approach to the U.S. class struggle. While certainly encouraged and supportive of the strike Marx correctly foresaw that it would, "of course, be suppressed." Not until a hereditary proletariat was in place would the working class be able to really put its stamp on American politics.

Marx was right that the strike was "a point of departure for the constitution of a serious workers' party," specifically, the Socialist Labor Party (SLP) which was launched at the end of the year. On the other hand, he was unduly optimistic about that development being the basis for the Black–working class–farmer alliance. The limitations of the SLP, as history showed, were in part responsible for its failure to come about. But the overthrow of Reconstruction and the beginning of the institution of the Jim Crow system constituted the main obstacle to the realization of that alliance. Though slavery had been abolished, the continued branding of Black labor made that an impossibility. Nevertheless, Marx's hopes pointed the way forward for what had to be done—a key issue discussed in the conclusion of this book.

There are two related aspects of the overthrow of Reconstruction worth exploring since they indirectly relate to Marx's activities. One was ruling-class fear of another Paris Commune. No one did more to promote the Communards as heroes as Marx and, hence, no one's name, as well as the IWMA, which he headed, was more associated with the uprising. Reporters from around the world flocked to his study for interviews, giving him and the International, as noted earlier, unprecedented publicity. This in large part explains why Wendell Phillips, a partisan of the Communards, joined the organization. The fear of another Commune by liberals played a role in their about-face from Reconstruction, its potentially radical character as an attack on property.[68] No one outraged the Liberal Republicans more than Massachusetts Congressman Benjamin Butler, a member of their party. He not only embraced the demand for an eight-hour workday, women's suffrage, Irish self-determination but, horror of horrors, the Commune. "The juxtaposition of Butler and Karl Marx as advocates of the 'spoilation' of property occurred more frequently in the reform press than the modern reader might imagine."[69] The association of Marx's name with all that the liberals dreaded meant that he figured, at some level, and probably unbeknownst to him, as a bête noire in Reconstruction's demise.[70]

The second and related fact is that the individual who led the charge against Reconstruction in the Republican Party was an old opponent of Marx and Engels. Carl Schurz, senator from Missouri, had crossed swords with both of them in the 1848–1849 revolutions in Germany. He was the object of Marx's ridicule in his bitter satire about exile politics in the aftermath of the revolutions, *The Great Men of the Exile*. Two years earlier in 1850 Marx and Engels described the wing of the revolution that Schurz belonged to as "the most timorous petty-bourgeois democrats," that is, those democrats who feared pushing—as the Marx party did—the revolution too far to the left.[71] In the intrigues of the exile setting Schurz was portrayed by Marx as "a little intriguer with great ambitions" who sees himself as "destined to be the future president of the German Republic."[72] Schurz paid Marx back in kind in his autobiography *Reminiscences*. Many years later he remembered his first encounter with Marx: "I have never seen a man whose bearing was so provoking and intolerable. . . . I remember most distinctly the cutting disdain with which he pronounced the word 'bourgeois'; and as a 'bourgeois,' that is as a detestable example of the deepest mental and moral degeneracy he denounced everyone that dared to oppose his opinion."[73] In contextualizing the encounter, at a meeting of democrats in the heat of the unfolding revolution, Schurz emphasized the views of the group that he represented. "Most of us indeed recoiled from the wild excesses which had stained with streams of innocent blood the national uprising in France during the Reign of Terror. But we hoped to stir up the national energies without such terrorism."[74] Such views hint at why he so detested "Marx the ogre." His fears in 1848–1849 also foreshadow his trajectory in the aftermath of the victory over the slave owners.

If it's true that Schurz once aspired to become president of republican Germany, he could take solace in the fact that he eventually rubbed shoulders with a real republican president, Lincoln. His 1848 credentials, activism in founding the Republican Party and getting Lincoln elected, achievements on the field of battle for the Union, a leading Radical Republican until about 1868, election to the Senate from the all-important state of Missouri, and the leading figure in German American politics made him a real force in the GOP. Just as important, he, perhaps more than anyone in the Republican Party, led the charge for getting Reconstruction off the ground. All of this served him well in the campaign he formally launched in 1872, a break with the Grant administration in the name of "Liberal Republicanism." Two years earlier he began talking of the need to reconcile the differences between the North and South, to put behind what once divided the two regions. A month and a half after the bloody New York riot, which followed the Commune by two months, he told a Nashville audience, "Never were circumstances more urgent than after a great civil war and social revolution . . . as to call for the unbiased consideration and the most unselfish and devoted efforts of every citizen."[75] By "every citizen" he meant the "wise and generous men of the South" and, hence, the need to restore the vote to the former supporters of the confederacy.

Another Liberal Republican, Charles Francis Adams, Jr., made clear why this was important. He expressed "a common concern among reformers when he wrote that Americans were lifting voting restrictions despite the development of a 'Celtic proletariat on the Atlantic coast, an African proletariat on the shores of the Gulf, and a Chinese proletariat on the Pacific.' Disfranchisement of the white southern 'intelligent class' would only make things worse."[76] For Schurz, restoration of the vote to the former confederates was justifiable because "equality of rights" for the former slaves was now "an irreversible fact."[77]

Schurz sold his Liberal Republican program on the twin altar of reform and local control. For the northern middle class, the siren call for clean government, the end of patronage and political machines, i.e., civil service reform, was appealing. And for his southern audiences the promise to return government to local control was just the music the old slavocracy in its new incarnation longed to hear. "But," as Eric Foner frankly put it, "whether he quite appreciated it or not, his program had no other meaning than a return to white supremacy."[78] His actions bore a striking resemblance to the stance that he and his milieu adopted in the 1848 events— the desire to avoid a radical outcome for fear of another "Reign of Terror." Like Schurz, Tocqueville too, as an actor in the 1848 revolutions, thought that he could finesse an outcome in France that was neither radical nor reactionary.[79] Just as history gave lie to Tocqueville's expectations about the dictator Louis Bonaparte, it did the same to Schurz's claim about the "irreversible fact" of Black rights. One can easily imagine the two as allies in the revolutionary aftermath of the Civil War. Although Schurz was unable to prevent Grant's reelection in 1872, his campaign laid the ideological and political underpinnings for the Compromise of 1877.[80] That he was rewarded with an appointment as Secretary of the Interior in the new Hayes administration is no accident.

The interesting question here is whether the specter of Marx entered into Schurz's calculations. His autobiography, written in the aftermath of these events, reveals that he still harbored an intense dislike for Marx. It's also certain that Schurz was well-informed about developments in the politics of the German American community including its most radical circles, that is, the arena is which Marx exercised some influence. He would have known about Marx's efforts to win the fledgling labor movement to the IWMA and his collaboration with the German-speaking Section 1 in New York. Obviously he knew about Marx's links to the Commune and the campaign of the IWMA to publicize it in the United States through his pamphlet.[81] While there is no smoking gun in the published public and private utterances of Schurz, there is, in combination with the circumstantial evidence, enough to suggest that in leading the retreat his old foe weighed heavily on his brain.[82] Of those who led it, Schurz alone knew Marx personally and opposed virtually everything he stood for by the time of the Commune, if not before. The main issue that divided them in the 1848 revolutions, how far left to push the revolution, also pitted them against one another two decades later in the U.S. theater of action. As the red scare figured in the defeat of the 1848–1849 revolutions in Germany, it also had a role in the overthrow of Reconstruction. Marx, the embodiment of the "scare" for Schurz, may very well have been, if not the elephant in the room, at least a shadow on the minds of those looking for reasons to end what had been until then America's most democratic moment.

Finally, Heather Cox Richardson's recently published research shows convincingly why northern Republicans like Schurz had every reason to fear Marx. The puzzle that she seeks an answer to is why this layer of the party, which had once been enthusiastic about Reconstruction, was willing to abandon the former slaves to the terror of the counterrevolution. Drawing largely on the northern press, which represented different factions of U.S. ruling elites, she concludes that in "the years after the Civil War, mainstream Northerners increasingly perceived the mass of African-Americans as adherents of a theory of political economy in which labor and capital were at odds and in which a growing government would be used to

advance laborers at the expense of capitalists. For these Northerners, the majority of ex-slaves became the face of 'communism' or 'socialism,' as opponents dubbed this view of political
economy . . . Ultimately, Northerners turned against African-
Americans not because of racism, although they were certainly
racists. Northerners turned against freedpeople after the Civil
War because African-Americans came to represent a concept of
society and government that would destroy the free labor
world," that is, a view that assumed that labor and capital had
mutually compatible interests. "Black citizens, it seemed,
threatened the core of American society."[83]

No one did more than Marx to promote the idea that capital
and labor were fundamentally "at odds"—what Schurz knew
better than any of the northern Republicans who led the retreat.
Of all the key actors in the party, Schurz alone would have
known what his erstwhile opponent wrote in *Capital*—published
in 1867—since it would be almost two decades before it became
available in English. When the Commune in Paris exploded in
1871, almost at the same time that the newly proletarianized
freedmen in South Carolina took their most militant actions, he
may have remembered with trepidation the attention Marx gave
in the introduction to his tome to Benjamin Wade's aforementioned speech. "Mr. Wade, vice-president of the United States,
declared in public meetings that, after the abolition of slavery, a
radical change of the relations of capital and of property in land
is next upon the order of the day." Schurz recoiled at such
prospects just as he had two decades earlier in Germany's revolutionary theater. And just as had been true before, it looked like
it was Marx once again leading the charge to realize what Wade
envisioned. Hence the need to take preemptive action—the Liberal Republican campaign in 1872—and sacrificing Reconstruction if need be. My Marx-on-Schurz's-brain hypothesis as an
important factor in the overthrow of Reconstruction is admittedly speculative, but the available facts warrant such conjec-
ture. What is certain, as Richardson demonstrates, is that
everything Marx stood for figured significantly in the defeat of
America's most democratic opening prior to the Civil Rights
movement of the 1960s.

Though Marx and Engels offered no systematic explanation for Reconstruction's overthrow, others in their wake who were inspired by their project and/or spoke in their names did so to one degree or another. A few examples are instructive. In the former category W. E. B. DuBois's monumental *Black Reconstruction in America, 1860–1880,* published in 1935, is most outstanding— the first major challenge to received wisdom about that most misunderstood moment in U.S. history. His authoritative biographer does not exaggerate when he writes that the "book represented one of those genuine paradigm shifts periodically experienced in a field of knowledge."[84] The original subtitle that DuBois wanted was *An Essay toward a History of the Part which Black Folk Played in the Attempt to Reconstruct Democracy in America.*[85] Given the central thesis of my project, I'm tempted to say that the last words in DuBois's subtitle are not accidental. They are a deliberate allusion to Tocqueville's famous title. DuBois not only favorably cited a number of Marx's pronouncements discussed earlier in this chapter but was clearly influenced by their logic. A passage in the concluding pages of the book encapsulates a central thesis of the tome about the role of racial hatred in the demise of Reconstruction and its consequences.

> The racial element was emphasized in order that property holders could get the support of the majority of white laborers and make it more possible to exploit Negro labor. But the race philosophy came as a new and terrible thing to make labor unity or labor class consciousness impossible. So long as the southern white laborers could be induced to prefer poverty to equality with the Negro, just so long was a labor movement in the South made impossible.[86]

What's notable here, specifically the last sentence, is the similarity to Marx's famous passage from *Capital*: "Labour cannot emancipate itself in the white skin where in the black skin it is branded."[87] Much of DuBois's exposition is a detailed elaboration of this claim. More recently, David Roediger's *Wages of Whiteness* is in turn inspired by DuBois. His book is largely an effort to understand why white workers would "prefer poverty to equality with the Negro," or, what he and

DuBois call the "wage" that white status conferred. Roediger, not surprisingly, emphasizes white working-class racism in the defeat of Reconstruction.[88]

Revolutionary Marxist Farrell Dobbs also drew on DuBois's research and insights. The interests of the "property holders," the first part of DuBois's thesis, are prioritized along with their actions in promoting working-class racism. [Reconstruction's] defeat was engineered by the dominant sectors of the industrial ruling class, who were incapable of carrying through a radical land reform in the old Confederacy and rightly feared the rise of a united working class in which Black and white artisans and industrial workers would come together as a powerful oppositional force, allied with free working farmers.

> The rural poor and working class were forcibly divided along color lines. The value of labor power was driven down and class solidarity crippled. Jim Crow . . . was legalized. Racism was spread at an accelerated pace throughout the entire United States.[89]

Dobbs, like Roediger, recognizes the importance of working-class racism, but places the blame for it squarely on the property holders. Richardson's aforementioned findings lend credence to such a reading. For Roediger this is insufficient and a problem with "traditional Marxist analyses." He calls for an examination of the reasons why the property holders could and can still be effective with their racist appeals to the working class. To be clear, he states that "no answer to the 'white problem' can ignore the explanatory power of historical materialism, but neither does Marxism, as presently theorized, consistently help us focus on the central issue of why so many workers define themselves as white."[90] While this debate occurs outside the parameters of this book, it should be emphasized that there is nothing in the record to suggest that Marx and Engels were precluded from considering the phenomenon of the "wages" of privilege, that is, the psychological benefits of white racism to which DuBois and Roediger rightly call our attention. Marx not only recognized and offered an explanation for a similar phenomenon in Britain and drew parallels with the United States—that of English, working-class, anti-Irish racism—but also waged a fight against it. Furthermore, Marx, it may be recalled, suggested, in a letter to Lafargue, a kind of "wages of privilege" explanation for anti-Black white racism—the need for some to feel superior to others. It can also be argued that the "prerogative of the white-skinned labourer" that Marx employed in his letter to Lincoln is exactly what DuBois and others mean by the "wages of white skin privilege." But, for Marx and Engels, and Dobbs as well, such a factor, however important in and of itself, had to be considered within the larger sociopolitical economy of post–Civil War America—a matter to which we now return.

Were Marx and Engels Derelict?

I stated earlier that the appropriate criteria for evaluating Marx and Engels is how they voted with their political feet—their actions. It's for this reason that the charges that eminent labor historian Phillip Foner—by no means a gratuitous Marx basher—has leveled about their conduct after the Civil War should be taken seriously. Briefly, he argues that the two communists did not do enough (1) to encourage the U.S. sections of the IWMA to attract Black workers and (2) to resist the overthrow of Reconstruction.

Regarding the first charge, Foner acknowledges that in some instances IWMA sections did take initiatives to bring in Blacks as members, such as in Galveston, Texas, and, as already mentioned, Section I in New York City. The fact that the "reports of the International [to the GC] did not even mention" these steps, which were "*for the time*, an advanced position on the Negro question," was symptomatic of the problem.[91] That the IWMA leadership in the United States—Sorge in particular—failed to take sufficient initiatives in this area, in Foner's view, is attributable to Marx and Engels.

As for the second charge, Foner claims that as the counterrevolution was taking steps to overthrow Reconstruction, Sorge, the "most influential Marxist in the United States, and the one closest to Marx, had nothing to say about" what was underway.

Because Sorge and his comrades lacked "guidance from their theoretical leaders," that is, Marx and Engels, the latter, again, were ultimately to blame.[92] Rather than explicitly address the accusations about Sorge, the focus here is primarily on Marx since he was the effective head of the International; Sorge's strengths and limitations will be discussed in the appendix.

Foner offers as evidence for the first charge the apparent failure of the GC to extend invitations to IWMA congresses to the Colored National Labor Union (CNLU) while it solicited the white NLU to attend at "almost every convention." This is an odd charge, since as Foner points out, the CNLU—formed in 1869—agreed to send a delegate to the 1870 congress in Paris, which was cancelled owing to the breakout of the Franco-Prussian War. It can only be assumed—Foner doesn't offer contrary evidence—that the CNLU decided to participate because it was invited by the GC. The next IWMA congress was in 1872 in The Hague but, according to Foner, elsewhere, "the CNLU . . . never met again after 1871."[93] Hence, this charge is groundless.

Foner then argues that however insightful Marx was in making the comparison between English working-class anti-Irish racism and white southern racism, his "failure to make the analogy clear to his American correspondents is proof that the issue of black-white relations was a minor one in his mind at this time."[94] He should have, Foner insists, pressed the New York Section of the IWMA "to seek a coalition with the oppressed Negro in the South or to seek to educate the 'poor whites'" about their true class interests. This would have matched what he fought for in England. This charge, which has already been addressed indirectly, appears at first glance to have merit. But upon reflection it raises more questions than it answers. It assumes that the New York IWMA was in a position to carry out such a campaign and that Marx was aware of such readiness. Foner presents nothing to substantiate either assumption. If anything, he shows, again elsewhere, why this would have been impossible. Commenting on the CNLU's difficulty to expand into the South—noted earlier in this chapter—Foner details the near slavish conditions that most freedmen faced. "When they sought to change their conditions, they were set upon by the Klan and similar terrorist organizations. . . . The Colored National Labor Union was in no position to make strides in the South in the face of Klan opposition."[95]

If, in other words, a Black organization of far greater numbers couldn't make any headway in the South, why would the New York German American Section, with probably less than fifty members have been able to do so? What Marx did know is that the IWMA—save for a fledgling chapter or two in New Orleans—had virtually no presence in the Old South. He may have also known that the NLU likewise lacked any significant forces. There was, therefore, no vehicle through which the kind of campaign that Foner believes Marx and Engels failed to mount could actually be waged. What Marx knew about Section 1 is that it had some possibilities of influencing Irish workers. But even that hope proved to be futile. The evidence suggests that it would have been irresponsible for Marx from afar to urge them to launch an effort for which they had no capacity.

As for northern Black workers, the reports that Marx received had virtually nothing—except for the aforementioned strike in Washington, D.C.—to say about their potential as recruits to the labor movement. A report sent on the eve of the London conference in September 1871 commented on the composition of the U.S. working class: the "great majority . . . immigrants from Ireland, Germany, England etc (in California Coolies, imported under contract)." Blacks are conspicuously absent. Foner, again elsewhere, in discussing the demise of the CNLU by the end of 1871—after only two years in existence—says "it is difficult to see how [its] failure could have been avoided. It was operating against insurmountable obstacles." Unable to recruit in the South, it could only look to the North, where the Black workforce was simply "too few in numbers and too poor to create a viable labor movement by themselves."[96]

In Foner's view the "Marxists apparently believed that a vigorous independent working-class movement, prepared to do battle with capital, was emerging in the United States, and that it was not the time to divert that movement with other issues. The problem of black liberation would have to wait until after the successful organization of the independent working class." He convincingly and critically documents how this position unfortunately informed most of those who spoke in Marx's name in subsequent generations. One of the reasons, according to Foner, why "American Marxists" failed to wage "as consistent a struggle against racism in white working-class circles as they had waged in convincing the antebellum Northern workers to give priority to the abolition of Negro slavery," is that "they themselves were not entirely free of racism."[97]

Though Foner is careful not to attribute such a state of affairs to sins of commission on the part of Marx and Engels, he implicitly faults them for omission: their alleged failure in not being more vocal about Black rights in the post–Civil War period led their U.S. followers to adopt an abstentionist posture. Foner knows that this wasn't the first nor would it be the last time that those claiming to speak in Marx and Engels's names erred. The all too often nostrum of later U.S. Marxists that Black liberation would have to wait for the socialist society is reminiscent of the stance that Marx once held about Irish self-determination vis-á-vis the class struggle in England. But, as already discussed, he rejected that position in 1869 in favor of one that prioritized the Irish struggle. Though the extant record is uninstructive, there is nothing to suggest that he would not have arrived at a similar conclusion about the United States. What was determinant in Marx's change of opinion was the new upsurge in the Irish struggle for self-determination in the second half of the 1860s.

The abolition of slavery gave rise to unprecedented Black political mobilization. Unlike what was underway in Ireland, the effort was first and foremost for inclusion in the political order. It did not, therefore, represent a threat to the status quo as the Irish struggle did for Britain's ruling class. In that sense, there is an element of truth to Foner's charge about Marx and Engels's priorities but not for the reason he suggests. Marx, as noted earlier, told the New York reporter in 1871 about the IWMA's perspective on the United States: the "chief centres of our activity are for the present among the old societies of Europe" because the class struggle had yet to assume "an all-absorbing importance" in America. In other words, it was in Europe—and Britain in particular at that moment—that the possibilities for socialist revolution existed. This warranted the organization's highest priority. With far greater weight in the revolutionary process than U.S. developments as a whole, the Irish struggle obligated them to throw their limited resources in support of it. This was the real basis for the importance they attached to Irish workers in the North—something that Foner fails to acknowledge.

It's not clear how much Marx and Engels even knew about the initiatives the former slaves were taking. What they would have known is that virtually all Blacks were loyal to the Republican Party—symptomatic of their efforts to be included. How Marx and Engels regarded the Republicans during this period, specifically, whether the workers' movement should have continued to support it or not is a most interesting question but one that can't be answered here. The record indicates that they were pleased with its presidential victories in 1864 and 1868. Whether their opinion changed with the 1872 election is difficult to say. By 1876, it can be confidently conjectured that they would have ended their critical support for the party.

In a report to Marx in June 1871, Sorge expressed the hope that Blacks might break with the Republicans. That was not to be the case. As Eric Foner explains, "ordinary blacks reacted with extreme hostility to any political strategy that threatened to weaken the party of emancipation. . . . Thus, black political leaders had few options outside the party, since gestures toward political autonomy not only threatened their access to patronage, but undermined their credibility in their own community." This applied as well to Frederick Douglass who once said that Blacks like himself could only act as "field hands" for the GOP."[98] Only with the rise of an independent Black movement in the twentieth century would a new generation of those speaking in Marx's name in the United States take a stance on Black rights similar to that which he took on the Irish struggle in 1869.

If a credible case can be made that Foner's first charge—that Marx and Engels failed to do enough to win Black workers to the IWMA—is without merit because it ignores the reality of what was possible and what they actually understood to be possible, what about the other charge that the two insufficiently resisted the overthrow of Reconstruction? Foner's charge assumes that Marx and Engels were, in the years leading up to the Compromise of 1877, aware of the counterrevolution's ineluctable advance. But it's not certain that those who lived within the United States—let alone those afar, like Marx and Engels—comprehended the dynamics of the events in motion. As late as 1875 it appeared that the Grant administration would finally take a strong hand against the counterrevolution. Even Wendell Phillips, the leading critic of Washington's vacillation, took heart in Grant's actions. A year later, however, reality would begin to set in. Even then, it must be remembered that Reconstruction's final demise would take almost two decades. From Marx's comment about a possible Black reaction to the compromise one can infer that he thought of the deal as a setback for Reconstruction, but not the triumph of the counterrevolution.

Whatever Marx and Engels understood to be in progress, they didn't have the means to respond effectively even if they had wanted to. Though the IWMA officially disbanded in 1876, in reality it was moribund by 1873. A comment Marx made in 1874 about the American scene gives some sense of what they were up against: "our party has to fight against great difficulties, partly economic, partly political, but is making headway. The greatest obstacle there are the professional politicians, who immediately try to falsify every new movement and change it into a new 'floatation business.'"[99] His optimism wasn't unwarranted if he was speaking about the *longue durée*. But in the short run, the lack of an independent working-class alternative to bourgeois politics hampered any effective response to the growing counterrevolution. That would only be solved, in their view, once a hereditary U.S. working class came into existence.

The case of Frederick Douglass is more instructive. Closer to the scene, he knew what the compromise portended, but owing to his commitment to the Republicans and new President Hayes, he was not willing to wage a fight against what was underway. Hayes rewarded him for such abstention by appointing him to be marshall of Washington, D.C., a largely ceremonial post.[100]

More than anyone on the scene, Wendell Phillips knew what it would have taken to counter the counterrevolution. While pleased with Congress's decision in 1871 to authorize Grant to suspend habeas corpus in order to deal with the terror of the Klan, Phillips urged the president to do more: "I wanted him to go down to arrest some ex-general, who counts his acres by thousands, numbers his wealth by millions, and who stands enshrined in the loving admiration of half the South. I want to track him to his lair in this nest of assassins, and then arrest him at midnight, try him by sunrise, and shoot him before the sun is an hour high—and when it is done Georgia and South Carolina will learn unmistakably that they have a master."

For Phillips, this was the easiest solution in his opinion. "It does not need an army, it does not need a hundred men. You do not need five lives taken; but they must be lives of the topmost line; lives that stand out like the peaks of the Alps above society."[101] It was exactly the kind of stance—what Marx and Engels had once called "stern duties"—from which Liberal Republicans like Schurz recoiled. To them, it was a "Reign of Terror" against the old slavocracy, never mind the real juggernaut of violence against the former slaves.

This recalls the question raised in chapter 3 about the consequences of Lincoln's reluctance to employ dictatorial methods to defeat the confederacy. The same can be asked about the counterrevolution. The failure to institute just what Phillips advocated explains the daily horrors that the recently freed slaves encountered, and the eventual overthrow of Reconstruction. Not surprisingly, Phillips's prescription not only angered apologists for the plantocracy but also fair-weather abolitionists. There is little doubt with whom Marx and Engels would have sided in this debate. That Phillips joined the IWMA the same year he offered his solution is not coincidental.

It is understandable why Foner might question Marx and Engels's practice in the aftermath of the victory over the Confederacy. Given all they did to assist in that victory, their relative inattention to what transpired afterward warrants an explanation. What Foner offers is distilled by hindsight. Only if properly contextualized in the postwar U.S. reality and read within Marx and Engels's overall expectations about the American movement— along with their involvement and obligations in the international movement—can their actions or lack thereof begin to be understood. When Marx dropped everything in 1861, including the writing of *Capital*, to do what he could to affect the outcome of the Civil War, he did so because he correctly recognized that the center of the international democratic movement, or *world* revolutionary process, was at that moment on the other side of the Atlantic. By 1866, with the Austro-Prussian War, and certainly with the Paris Commune in 1871, the axis had shifted to Europe. That fact, more than anything, explains why, in the aftermath of the abolition of slavery, he and his partner relegated the U.S. theater to the back burner. Never, however, did they doubt that America would eventually take center stage.

The overthrow of Reconstruction confirmed a basic conclusion that the young Marx drew on the road to becoming a communist—the fundamental incompatibility between real democracy and private property relations. Frightened by the prospect of an alliance between labor in both "black" and "white skin," the newly triumphant U.S. industrial capitalist class willingly allowed the defeated slave owners to impose their rule over the former slaves—but this time under the domination of capitalist relations of production.

When "Conditions" Become "Ripe"

With the effective end of the IWMA, Marx and Engels's orientation toward the United States was both literary and scientific. They needed to get their writings published and circulated there and required ongoing research about the extension and deepening of the country's capitalist property relations.[102] Marx's research confirmed his earlier pronouncements in *Capital* about that process and its consequences for the working class. "The people will try in vain to get rid of the monopolising power and the . . . baneful influence of the great *compagnies* swaying industry, commerce, property in land, railroads, finance—at an accelerated rate since the outbreak of the Civil War. The best Yankee writers are loud in proclaiming the stubborn fact that, if the Anti-Slavery war has broken the chains of the black, it has on the other hand enslaved the white producers."[103] Three years before his death in 1883 he asked Sorge to send him "some sound stuff (meaty) on economic conditions in *California*. . . . California is of great moment to me because in no other place has revolution by capitalist centralisation been effected with such effrontery at such great speed."[104] Marx lived long enough to see the age of the robber barons and get a glimpse of the ravages left in their wake.

Though he wasn't able to elaborate on it, the phenomenon that Marx anticipated—monopoly capitalism—was consistent with his historical materialist analysis about the logic of capital. Hence, his reaction in 1881 to Henry George's *Progress and Poverty: An Inquiry into the Cause of Industrial Depressions and of Increase of Want with Increase of Wealth*. Widely popular, especially amongst working people, the work is an effort, as its subtitle suggests, to explain the economic crisis of 1873 that ruined millions, including George. The book was significant, in Marx's opinion, "in being a first, if unsuccessful, attempt at emancipation from orthodox [bourgeois] political economy." But George failed to take account of the real world in which he lived. To understand why a minority of society was enriching itself at the expense of the majority, George should have "asked himself the question: How comes it that in the UNITED STATES, where the land was relatively—i.e. by comparison with civilised Europe—accessible to the great mass of the people and TO A CERTAIN DEGREE (again relative) still is, the capitalist economy and the corresponding enslavement of the working class have developed more *rapidly* and *brazenly* than in any other country?" Marx wrote.[105] The outcome about which George complained was exactly presaged by capitalist relations of production, a phenomenon that Marx had long ago diagnosed.

George's book is significant for this study because it harkens to a line of analysis that was articulated by Tocqueville and then later by the U.S. economist Henry Cary, whom Marx had critiqued almost three decades earlier. All three assumed the inherent harmony of interests between capital and labor in America. As the first version of "American exceptionalism," their common claim was that the country had escaped the kind of class formation, inequality, and conflict that characterized the "old world." For Marx and Engels, however, "actually existing" capitalism revealed quite the contrary. What always struck them about the United States was the rapidity with which class formation took place in the absence of a feudal tradition—confirmation for them of basic theoretical premises. Almost forty years earlier, in their *Critique* of Kriege's "communist" approach to the Free-Soil movement, Marx and Engels accurately predicted that land reform under capitalism would not be a panacea for the working class because it would result in the maldistribution of land that George so bemoaned. In a new introduction to the *Manifesto* in 1882, they took note of this outcome. "Step by step the smaller and middle landownership of the farmers, the basis of the whole political constitution, is succumbing to the competition of giant farms; simultaneously, a numerous proletariat and a fabulous concentration of capital are developing for the first time in the industrial regions."[106] The realization of the Jeffersonian-Tocquevillian ideal—the self-employed farmer/small property owner, the "basis of the whole political constitution," that is, the "White Republic"—would be undermined by capital's logic, with its increasing concentration of land ownership and corresponding increase in the proletariat—a process that continues unabated through the present.

Eric Foner makes an insightful point about Reconstruction's significance despite its overthrow. "The policy of according black men a place in the political nation while denying them the benefits of land reform fortified the idea that the free citizen could be a dependent laborer. Thus, Reconstruction helped to solidify the separation of political and economic spheres, the juxtaposition of political equality and economic inequality, as the American way. Henceforth, it would be left to dissenters—labor radicals, populists, socialists, and the like—to resurrect the older idea of economic autonomy as the essence of freedom."[107] Hence, what happened to Black men through political means would begin, albeit more slowly, to transform whites, through the logic of capital. The breaking of the "chains of the black," Marx and Engels long argued, would unleash this process and bring about the painful but necessary birth of a hereditary U.S. working class. Only then would workers in Black and white skin have a chance to see their common class interests. As long as one component was enslaved as chattels, the other would see itself as more privileged and thus exempt from the sharpest edges of capitalist property relations—thinking that it had an escape route as small landowners.

The working-class political response to the forced march to proletarianization that Marx and Engels anticipated came, as Foner pointed out, in various incarnations. One of them, the populist movement, an effort by white producers to be included in the now more regional White Republic, was ultimately reactionary. Other initiatives, such as the Knights of Labor or the Socialist Party, were also handicapped by the pervasive influence of the racial order. As long as the Jim Crow system was in place, the branding of one segment of the working class, working-class radicalization would be limited and, in some instances, reactionary.

Following Marx's death in 1883, Engels kept close watch on developments in the United States. Mainly through correspondence, he actively sought to influence the thinking of close party members on the tactics of building an independent working-class party. Of particular significance—to be discussed in more detail in the appendix—was his effort, largely unsuccessful, to convince German American Marxists in the Socialist Labor Party to shed their sectarian habits. On more than one occasion he accused them of having "managed to reduce the Marxian theory of development to a rigid orthodoxy, which the workers are not to reach themselves by their own class feeling, but which they have to gulp down as an article of faith at once and without development."[108]

While Engels did what he could to rectify subjective or agential obstacles to the formation of a proletarian party in the United States, he recognized that the structural problems, "peculiar" to that country, required revolutionary patience as he frequently reminded his American comrades. Two years before his death, in a remarkably insightful letter to one close contact at the end of 1893, Engels outlined what he saw those obstacles to be. First, an electoral system inherited from England that employed the winner-take-all procedure, which was a disincentive to the protest vote. Second, divisions within the working class between the "native-born and the foreigners," between the European immigrants, "And then the Negroes." And lastly, "the workers . . . have been exposed to a prosperity no trace of which has been seen here in Europe for years."[109]

Regarding the "Negroes," Engels was no doubt referring to the consequence of Reconstruction's defeat. Its overthrow allowed the branding process, the institution of Jim Crow, to unfold with a vengeance. "Labor" could not "emancipate itself in the white skin where in the black it is branded." In 1888, Engels visited the United States for the first time. "It is a place one really must have seen with one's own eyes . . . the promised land of capitalist production."[110] Unfortunately, his trip was confined to the most northeast regions. He therefore didn't get to see Jim Crow in its lair. In spite of the "very great and peculiar difficulties," Engels was not pessimistic. "A country like America, when it is really ripe for a socialist workers' party cannot be hindered from having one by the couple of German socialist doctrinaires."[111] The sectarians could still hold forth because conditions were far from "ripe" for socialist revolution. By the end of 1893, the proletarianization process itself had yet, Engels believed, to run its full course.

Whatever one thinks of his opinion about the *longue durée*, Engels's concise overview of the objective obstacles to independent working-class political action in the United States continues to have currency. While Engels did not explicitly address the source of the branding process, he was clear that class consciousness and the political independence of the working class in the United States were intimately linked to its racial reality. Engels offered an answer to the second version of American "exceptionalism," that is, "why no socialism in America"—an issue to be revisited in the conclusion. To him, the fight to overcome the racial order could not be divorced from the other structural conditions "peculiar" to the United States.

It fell on the shoulders of subsequent generations of those who fought in the name of Marx and Engels to amplify on the bones of their insights about the U.S. race-class nexus conundrum. Until the Bolshevik revolution, those who acted in Marx's name in the United States treated the race question as a tertiary matter. Black liberation had to wait on the socialist revolution, a utopian position which in practice dissolved the fight against Jim Crow and racist discrimination into abstentionist platitudes—effectively capitulating to capital and the southern Bourbons. This was the stance of even the best socialists like Eugene Debs. It was the Bolsheviks who reclaimed Marx and Engels's real teachings on the national question.

Marx's prioritization of the Irish struggle for self-determination in 1869 was accurately understood by Lenin who in turn drew parallels with the situation of American Blacks. Lenin's conclusions on the national question were driven by the daunting and complex tasks of the Russian Revolution. Russia was both the "weak link in the imperialist chain" and "a prison house" of oppressed nations and nationalities. Fighting great nation chauvinism, defending the right of self-determination for oppressed nations and nationalities and forging worker-peasant unity in the battle against czarism and for a new society enabled Lenin to grasp with precision the "national question" in the United States. However, the Stalinization of the U.S. Communist Party in the 1930s—a process much too complex to treat adequately here—resulted in the subordination of the fight for Black rights to the state and diplomatic interests of Moscow's bureaucracy.

Leon Trotsky, the leading opponent of the Russian Revolution's degeneration, strove to ensure that Lenin's insights and the experiences of the Bolsheviks be faithfully transmitted to U.S. communists in the 1930s who no longer looked to Moscow for direction. In conversations with those who would later form the Socialist Workers Party, including the West Indian Marxist, C. L. R. James, Trotsky pulled no punches. Regarding white workers, "Ninety-nine percent . . . chauvinists; in relation to the Negroes they are hangmen as they are also toward the Chinese, etc. . . . The American worker is indescribably reactionary." Following Marx on the Irish question, he defended the right of self-determination for Blacks. "The argument that the slogan for self-determination leads away from the class point of view is an adaptation to the ideology of the white workers. . . . The Negro can be developed to a class point of view only when the white worker is educated."

Yet Trotsky was thoroughly convinced that like the Russians in relation to other Europeans, Blacks would "proceed through self-determination to the proletarian dictatorship in a couple of giant strides, ahead of the white workers. They will be in the vanguard. . . . That, however, can happen only provided the Communist Party carries on an uncompromising, merciless struggle not against the supposed national prepossessions of the Negroes but against the colossal prejudices of the white workers and makes no concession to them whatever."[112] Never had anyone speaking in Marx's name made clearer the implications of his prescient words: "Labour cannot emancipate itself in white skin where in the black it is branded."

Trotsky described the racially segregated American Federation of Labor, the country's leading union body, as one of the "organizations of the workers' aristocracy . . . the basis of opportunism, one of the sources of adaptation to capitalist society." Thus, the need to recruit to the party the most oppressed workers of which Blacks were the "most exploited. . . . If it happens that we in the SWP are not able to find the road to this stratum, then we are not worthy at all. The permanent revolution and all the rest would be only a lie."[113] His advice made it possible for revolutionary communists to respond positively to the rise of Black nationalism in the 1960s when it appeared in the person of Malcolm X. Albeit a minority of those who claimed to speak in Marx and Engels's names, they embraced Malcolm unconditionally, even before his break with the Nation of Islam.

Trotsky could justifiably charge in 1931 that the "American worker is indescribably reactionary" because of the consequences of the overthrow of Reconstruction. One way to grasp this is to consider a setting only ninety miles from U.S. shores— Cuba. Throughout most of its history, the Cuban working class has been relatively free of the kinds of racial divisions that hampered its counterpart to the north, even though it was the next to last country in the hemisphere to eliminate slavery. A vivid demonstration of this took place in New York City in December 1871 at a massive march sponsored by the local sections of the IWMA commemorating the martyrs of the Paris Commune. The procession included a Black contingent, something of significance given race relations in the city at that time. But more telling was the presence of a Cuban delegation.

What struck one reporter was that it included "quite a number not of the Caucasian race . . . but nevertheless placed in the ranks without the least distinction as to race or color, the Cuban mulatto and black being found in many files side by side with his fellow-countrymen of the fairer race, all in perfect concordance no doubt with the International's demand for 'liberty, equality, and fraternity,' particularly the two last."[114] The contrasting composition of the Cuban and U.S. contingents spoke volumes about the differences between the working classes of both countries.

This was the product forged in Cuba's two wars of independence, from 1868 to 1898. A new nation came into being in which Blacks saw themselves, owing to the character of their participation in the fight against the Spanish, as Cubans first and foremost.[115] In the United States, in contrast, and at virtually the same time, the overthrow of Reconstruction and the institution of Jim Crow destroyed the country's brief experiment with Black-white working-class unity. Marx and Engels's expectations proved to be premature. The result, certainly by 1931, was the creation of a Black identity separate and apart from the "American" one that was now synonymous with whiteness. This explains Lenin and Trotsky's characterization of Blacks as an oppressed nationality and their support for its right to self-determination. In Cuba, on the other hand, even Washington's best efforts during its official occupation of Cuba, from 1898 to 1934, failed to overturn what was forged three decades earlier.[116]

Cuba's working class never suffered the kind of historic defeat that Farrell Dobbs asserts the U.S. proletariat endured when Reconstruction was overthrown. When the revolutionary process erupted again in the 1950s and triumphed in 1959 it was able to move quickly from a radical democratic program to one that embraced socialist demands. If the latter could be on Cuba's agenda in 1959, only a democratic revolution—one to restore the rights that Blacks lost after 1877—could be on the American agenda that same year. The legacies of the past weighed heavy on both societies. Martin Luther King, Jr., the best that the Civil Rights movement had to offer in the way of leadership, was never able to embrace the Cuban revolution. That Malcolm X did, however, testifies to Trotsky's prescience about the revolutionary potential of the struggle for self-determination for an oppressed nationality.

Given what the Cuban revolution achieved at home for Black rights, it is no accident that it contributed mightily to the most important victory for the democratic process in the last quarter of the twentieth century—the overthrow of the racist apartheid regime in South Africa. This is what Nelson Mandela acknowledged when he visited Cuba after release from jail in February 1990. Referring to the victory of mainly Cuban troops over South African forces in Angola in 1988, he thanked the Cuban people and said that the "defeat of the racist army at Cuito Cuanavale [Angola] has made it possible for me to be here today!"[117]

Michael Goldfield enticingly suggests that what happened in Cuba after 1959 could have been a possibility in the United States had it not been for the liberal takeover of the struggle for Black rights. He argues convincingly that until about 1950 the leadership of the fight for Black rights had been in the hands of a coalition of the Black working class and the "labor left" in which the Congress of Industrial Organizations (CIO), born in 1936, played a major role.

Owing, however, to the CIO's default and the machinations of the pro-Moscow Communist Party, liberal elements such as the NAACP became hegemonic. What had been a "class-based approach to civil rights" gave way in the 1950s and 1960s to the perspective of individual and constitutional rights or what Goldfield calls "bourgeois or abstract rights." While he applauds what was won under the liberal leadership, those gains came with a price—the neglect of "those class issues that were at the root of problems faced by poor and working-class African-Americans" and the absence of the "organized labor movement." The result, he claims, explains "why a white racist political coalition was able to emerge and dominate U.S. politics for much of the post-civil rights period."[118]

Goldfield's thesis has merit but it tends to underestimate the severity of the defeat that came with Reconstruction's demise. As laudable as the achievements of the "labor-based civil rights" coalition had been in the 1930s and 1940s, the unavoidable fact is that as long as the Jim Crow system was in place that coalition was limited in what it could do. The labor movement could hardly lead a successful fight against Jim Crow when it couldn't end such practices within its own ranks. Segregated unions in the South also cast a long shadow over the entire labor movement. All that labor could realistically do was form a united front with bourgeois and petty bourgeois liberals to end Jim

Crow while maintaining programmatic independence. But it failed to be part of such a coalition with the consequences that Goldfield correctly underscores. He is also right to point out the wretched role of the Stalinists in all of this but however despicable, their actions in and of themselves weren't determinant.

The main problem with Goldfield's argument is that it fails to take into account what Engels recognized at the end of 1893 and what Marx had earlier addressed. However important the branding of labor in black skin in explaining the "reactionary" character of U.S. labor, it couldn't be divorced from another reality, the objective opportunities that existed for U.S. workers, specifically, those in white skin, to realize the American dream. Yes, it is true that the radicalization of the 1930s occurred in the depths of the worst economic crisis in half a century. But it is also the case that liberal hegemonic ascent in the Black rights movement occurred during the long wave of expansion of U.S. capitalism, the post–Second World War economic boom. As long as the real standard of living of most white workers continued to improve, as it in fact did, then the material basis for a working-class alternative was absent. Such a reality, both Marx and Engels argued, had to be considered in estimating the potential for independent working-class political action and, thus, the probability for a socialist alternative.

Goldfield rightly acknowledges the historical significance of what was achieved with the Second Reconstruction despite its liberal leadership. Not only did Blacks become full citizens for the first time but women as well, along with other oppressed nationalities and minorities. The Second Reconstruction, therefore, completed America's bourgeois democratic revolution. The question that remains, then—the subject of the conclusion—is whether, as Marx and Engels predicted, the victory set the stage for the struggle against class oppression, that is, the realization of "real democracy."

Notes

1. **20**, p. 99.
2. **42**, pp. 150-53.
3. Irving H. Bartlett, *Wendell Phillips: Brahmin Radical* (Boston: Beacon Press, 1961), p. 296.

4. **42**, p. 163. Phillips's brief infatuation with Johnson ended a month after his inauguration and for the same reasons.

5. **42**, p. 167–68.

6. Four months later, in October 1865, when Black squatters in Jamaica rebelled against English settlers, Marx reacted favorably and denounced the hypocrisy of Britain's ruling class and the atrocities committed by its colonial authorities to put down the revolt (**42**, pp. 199, 205).

7. It was read at a GC-sponsored soiree by one of its members. Marx, thirteen years later, seemed to confuse it with his Lincoln address of 1864 (**24**, p. 236).

8. Herman Schlüter, *Lincoln, Labor and Slavery* (New York: Socialist Literature Co., 1913), pp. 200-1. For details about the discussion that accompanied the address see *MEGA [New]* Band 20, Apparat, pp. 1524–27.

9. Philip S. Foner, *American Socialism and Black Americans: From the Age of Jackson to World War II* (Westport, Conn.: Greenwood Press,1977) p. 32.

10. Ibid., p. 36.

11. **42**, p. 269.

12. **42**, p. 334 Although a Republican, Johnson, in a losing cause, backed the Democratic candidates against the Radical Republicans. Technically, then, the *MECW* editors are in error in saying that Johnson belonged to the Democratic Party (p. 643). It's important to note that Marx's comment was to the father of his mulatto son-in-law—the significance of which will be discussed later.

13. Samuel Eliot Morrison, *The Oxford History of the American People* (New York: 1965), p. 715.

14. Eric Foner, *Reconstruction: America's Unfinished Revolution, 1863–1877* (New York: Harper & Row, 1988) p. 267.

15. Rogers Smith, *Civic Ideals: Conflicting Visions of Citizenship in U.S. History* (New Haven: Yale University Press, 1997) p. 305. The congress obviously included holdovers from previous elections; the newly elected congressmen made the difference.

16. *Capital*, vol. I., p. 10.

17. Quoted in Eric Foner, *Reconstruction*, p. 309.

18. Ibid., pp. 309–10.

19. **42**, p. 414. His emphasis was due to his fear that a IWMA-affiliated newspaper in France had illusions in Johnson and required clarification.

20. *Capital*, Vol. I, p. 940.

21. **20**, p. 146.

22. **22**, p. 587.

23. **43**, p. 123. Marx was overstating the case since *Capital*, unbeknownst to him perhaps, was now being serialized in some of the German American socialist press by 1868.

24. Karl Marx, *Grundrisse* (Middlesex, England: Penguin Books, 1973), p. 885.

25. **22**, p. 606.

26. Quoted in David Roediger, *The Wages of Whiteness: Race and the Making of the American Working Class*, rev. ed. (New York: Verso, 1999), p. 174. Roediger argues persuasively that "what made the eight-hour movement itself possible, was the spectacular emancipation of slaves between 1863 and 1865."

27. **20**, p. 187.

28. **42**, p. 326.

29. **42**, pp. 451–52.

30. Schlüter, p. 235

31. Ibid., p. 236. The advanced position the NLU had taken regarding woman workers prompted Marx to write in 1868 his well-known comment: "very great progress was demonstrated at the last (1868) congress of the American 'LABOR UNION,' inter alia, by the fact that it treated the women workers with full parity. . . . Everyone who knows anything of history also knows that great social revolutions are impossible without the feminine ferment. Social progress may be measured precisely by the social position of the fair sex (plain ones included)" (**43**, 184–85).

32. Quoted in Bernard Mandel, p. 213.

33. **43**, p. 351.

34. The events leading up to and the records of the founding meeting make clear that Black workers had not ruled out future cooperation with the NLU. The call for the meeting said, in fact, that delegates would be admitted "without regard to race or color." For details, see Philip Foner, *Organized Labor and the Black Worker, 1619–1981* (New York: International Publishers, 1981), pp. 23–26.

35. **43**, p. 97.

36. **21**, p. 54. In a letter to Engels a few months later Marx wrote: "the railway to California was built by the bourgeoisie *awarding* itself through Congress an enormous mass of 'public land,' that is to say, *expropriating* it from the workers; by importing Chinese rabble to depress wages; and finally by instituting a new off-shoot, the 'financial aristocracy'"(**43**, p. 343–44).

37. Philip Foner, *American Socialism*, p. 37.

38. Federal Council Correspondence: Letterbooks, Folder 7, Box 1. International Workingmen's Association Papers, State Historical Society

of Wisconsin. Section I took other initiatives of varying importance to collaborate with Black workers in New York City; some sections elsewhere did the same. See Philip Foner, ibid., pp. 37–39.

39. *The Hague Congress of the First International. Minutes and Documents.* (Moscow: Progress Publishers, 1972), p. 49.

40. In the introduction to Sorge's book, *Friedrich A. Sorge's Labor Movement in the United States: A History of the American Working Class from Colonial Times to 1890,* eds. Philip S. Foner and Brewster Chamberlin (Westport, Conn.: Greenwood Press, 1977), Foner writes about Sorge's comment: "Sorge appears to identify Americans with 'whites,' even though he here for the first time refers to Negroes as part of the working class"(p. 20). To reach this conclusion Foner relies on the transcript of the other minute taker that didn't include the comment about what constitutes "American-born." The context for Sorge's comment will be discussed in the appendix.

41. **43**, p. 392.

42. **43**, p. 398.

43. A similar adjustment was made in the case of India; see my "The Eurocentric Marx and Engels and Other Related Myths," in *Marxism, Modernity, and Postcolonial Studies,* Crystal Bartolovich and Neil Lazarus, eds. (Cambridge: Cambridge University Press, 2002). For any remaining doubts about their position regarding the anticolonial struggle in settings such as India, Algeria, and Egypt, see Engels's unqualified endorsement in 1882; **46**, p. 332.

44. **43**, pp. 474–76. On Marx's usage of the 'n-word' see chapter 3, p. 131 n. 35

45. On the constraints that confronted Black labor during this period see Philip Foner, *Organized Labor,* see chapter 3.

46. *The General Council of the First International Minutes, 1870–1871,* vol. 4, (Moscow: Progress Publishers, 1974), p. 258.

47. **46**, p. 77.

48. The circumstances surrounding the International's end in the United States will be addressed in part in the appendix.

49. **44**, p. 258.

50. In what may be the most tendentious of all the "marxological" endeavors, Nathaniel Weyl, *Karl Marxist: Racist* (New Rochelle, N.Y.: Arlington House, 1979), manages to read Marx's concerns as an effort to milk the Lafargue family (p. 73). Precisely because the real record fails to support his "Marx-as-racist" thesis, he is forced to invent "facts." That it took a most obscure publisher to bring this piece of drivel to the surface and, then, a laborious effort on my part to locate a copy is no accident.

51. Leslie Derfler, *Paul Lafargue and the Founding of French Marxism, 1842–1882* (Cambridge: Harvard University Press, 1991), p. 46.

52. Ibid., p. 15.

53. **42**, p. 334.

54. **43**, p. 9. The comment, according to the editors of the *MECW*, is "an allusion to J. G. Seume's poem 'Der Wilde,'" which I've not been able to locate.

55. Ibid., p. 271.

56. Derfler, p. 46. Regarding "nigger," see chapter 3, p. 131 n. 35. Why Marx put quotation marks around "black" is not clear since he occasionally used the word, as the above-mentioned quote from *Capital* shows.

57. The work in question was P. Trémeaux's *Origine et transformations de l'homme et des autres êtres* [The Origin and Transformations of Man and Other Beings](1865); see **42**, p. 324.

58. Ibid., p. 327.

59. **22**, p. 618.

60. Sorge to GC, August 6, 1871, Federal Council Correspondence: Letterbooks, Folder 7, Box 1, International Workingmen's Association Papers, State Historical Society of Wisconsin. On the circumstances of the events and the shadow of Paris, see Edwin G. Burrows and Mike Wallace, "Chapter 57: The New York Commune?," *Gotham: A History of New York City to 1898* (New York: Oxford University Press, 1999), pp. 1002–19.

61. The most detailed account of the reception of the Commune in the U.S. is Philip M. Katz's *From Appomattox to Monmartre: Americans and the Paris Commune* (Cambridge: Harvard University Press, 1998).

62. This is a central argument in Heather Cox Richardson's *The Death of Reconstruction: Race, Labor, and Politics in the Post-Civil War North, 1865–1901* (Cambridge: Harvard University Press, 2001). More about Richardson's findings later.

63. For details on how this unfolded, see Eric Foner, *Reconstruction*, especially the last three chapters, and Richardson.

64. Farrell Dobbs, *Revolutionary Continuity: The Early Years 1848–1917* (New York: Monad Press, 1980), p. 52.

65. Philip S. Foner, *The Great Labor Uprising of 1877* (New York: Monad Press, 1977), p. 9.

66. **45**, p. 251.

67. Ibid., p. 255. Six months later in an article for an Italian publication, Engels wrote: "The worker question has been put on the agenda in America with the bloody strike of the employees of the big railways. This will turn out to have been an epoch-making event in American history: the formation of a *working-class party* is thereby making great

strides in the United States. It is advancing rapidly in that country, and we must follow its progress, to avoid being taken by surprise by the important successes which will soon be produced" (**24**, p. 204).

68. Again, see Richardson.

69. Eric Foner, *Reconstruction*, p. 491.

70. Marx's *Civil War in France* "first appeared in the United States in pamphlet form as *Defence of the Paris Commune* (Washington, 1871)" but was "soon reprinted in various places under Marx's original title" (Katz, p. 98).

71. **10**, p. 372. For details on the differences within the democratic movement and how the Marx party responded, see my *Marx and Engels*, chapters 3 and 4.

72. **11**, p. 257.

73. Carl Schurz, *The Reminiscences of Carl Schurz, Vol. 1, 1829–1852* (New York: The McClure Company, 1907), pp. 139–40. Though it's not clear when Schurz actually wrote his autobiography, it can be assumed to have been many decades after the events he described.

74. Ibid., p. 138. What Schurz remembered was probably the meeting of the Cologne Democratic Association in August 1848 that Marx chaired. Schurz lost most of his personal things, including letters, diaries, etc., in a fire in 1866. So he was forced to rely on his memory for much of what he recalled in the autobiography. What he failed to remember, whether intentionally or not, is that Marx had good reason to be opinionated at the meeting even if it meant alienating some in attendance. According to a newspaper report, Marx denounced the proposal of Wilhelm Weitling to institute a "dictatorship . . . of a single class," namely, the proletariat. The "intention to carry on a dictatorship in accordance with a system devised by a single brain, deserves to be called nonsensical." (**7**, p. 556.)

75. Frederic Bancroft, ed., *Speeches, Correspondence and Political Papers of Carl Schurz* (New York: G.P. Putnam, 1913), pp. 286–87.

76. Quoted in Michael Les Benedict, "Reform Republicans and the Retreat from Reconstruction," in Perman, p. 427.

77. Bancroft, p. 437.

78. Eric Foner, *Reconstruction*, p. 500.

79. See my *Marx and Engels: Their Contribution to the Democratic Breakthrough* (Albany: State University Press of New York, 2000), chapter 5 for details.

80. "Foreign birth barred Schurz," from challenging Grant himself (Eric Foner, *Reconstruction*, p. 510).

81. About the campaign, see Sorge's letter to the GC, August 6, 1871. Federal Council Correspondence, Letterbooks, Folder 7. Papers of the

International Workingmen's Association, State Historical Society of Wisconsin.

82. Unfortunately, his autobiography ends a couple of years before the Commune. His *Speeches, Correspondence and Political Papers* are only selected, again, unfortunately.

83. Richardson, pp. 244–45. Ruling class efforts to undermine the right of suffrage for working-class whites in this period lends support to Richardson's class analytic take on Reconstruction's demise. See Alexander Keyssar, *The Right to Vote: The Contested History of Democracy in the United States* (New York: Basic Books, 2000), chapters 4 and 5.

84. David Levering Lewis, *W. E. B. DuBois: The Fight for Equality and the American Century, 1919–1963* (New York: Henry Holt, 2000), p. 367. Regarding Marx's influence, Lewis, betraying his own persuasion, says he "both inspires and deforms the book." Nevertheless, Lewis provides rich detail about DuBois's history in relation to Marxism and how it actually impacted the book; see especially chapters 7 and 10.

85. Lewis, p. 361.

86. W. E. B. DuBois, *Black Reconstruction in America* (New York: Athenum, 1962), p. 680.

87. Though this particular passage isn't cited by DuBois, Lewis reveals that he was very familiar with *Capital* (p. 361).

88. Roediger, chapter 8.

89. Dobbs, p. 52.

90. Roediger, p. 6.

91. Philip Foner, *American Socialism*, p. 39.

92. Ibid., pp. 42–44.

93. Philip Foner, *Organized Labor*, p. 43.

94. Foner, *American Socialism*, p. 41.

95. Foner, *Organized Labor*, p. 42.

96. Ibid., p. 44.

97. Foner, *American Socialism*, pp. 41–42.

98. Foner, *Reconstruction*, pp. 544–45.

99. **45**, p. 18.

100. For details see David Blight, *Frederick Douglass' Civil War: Keeping Faith in Jubilee* (Baton Rouge: Louisiana State University Press, 1989), pp. 208–18.

101. Quoted in Bartlett, pp. 318–19.

102. Marx, as already mentioned, devoted his remaining years to detailed research on developments in two countries—the United States and Russia. For the former, for example, he had an arrangement with the head of the labor office of Massachusetts to send directly to him their annual

publications. He also read in great detail on the indigenous peoples of North America, particularly, Bancroft's five-volume work, *The Native Races of the Pacific States of North America*. It was just this research, along with that on Russia, that held up, in Engels's opinion, the completion of Volume II of *Capital*.

103. **45**, p. 344.

104. **46**, p. 46.

105. **46**, p. 101.

106. **24**, pp. 425–26.

107. Eric Foner, *The Story of American Freedom* (New York: W. W. Norton, 1998), p. 113.

108. Karl Marx and Frederick Engels, *Letters to Americans, 1848–1895* (New York: International Publishers, 1969), p. 263.

109. Ibid., p. 258.

110. **48**, p. 221.

111. Ibid.

112. George Breitman, ed., *Leon Trotsky on Black Nationalism and Self-Determination* (New York: Pathfinder Press, 1978), pp. 29–30. Trotsky employed "Communist Party" only in a generic sense and clearly didn't mean the Stalinist U.S. Communist Party.

113. Ibid., p. 62.

114. Philip Foner, *American Socialism*, p. 37.

115. The best accounts of this process are Ada Ferrer, *Insurgent Cuba: Race, Nation, and Revolution, 1868–1898* (Chapel Hill: University of North Carolina Press, 1999), and Alejandro de la Fuente, *A Nation for All: Race, Inequality, and Politics in Twentieth-Century Cuba* (Chapel Hill: University of North Carolina Press, 2001).

116. Though the historical record isn't clear, it's very possible that events in Cuba beginning in 1868, with Blacks in arms, frightened the southern oligarchy, especially in places like New Orleans. That Black leaders like Douglass praised the Cuban struggle was also, no doubt, disconcerting. Later, when Antonio Maceo became a hero not only in Cuba but among U.S. Blacks, such worries were given added credence. This explains, according to independent historian David Riehle, why Maceo became a popular first name for boys in Black America at the turn of the century (private communication). The U.S. occupation, therefore, may also be read as an effort to prevent Cuban notions of racial equality from finding their way to American shores.

117. Fidel Castro and Nelson Mandela, *How Far We Slaves Have Come* (New York: Pathfinder Books, 1991), p. 20. For details on the advances of Blacks in Cuba since the 1959 revolution see, Fuente, Part IV.

118. Michael Goldfield, *The Color of Politics: Race and the Mainspring of American Politics* (New York: The New Press, 1997) pp. 285, 295, 353.

Conclusion

Even the most die-hard admirers of the Tocquevillian portrait of American democracy have likely felt some unease in the aftermath of that supposedly defining moment in modern politics—"9/11." The broad assault on civil liberties in the name of fighting "terrorism," and especially what this has meant for "communities of color," must certainly put in question for the faithful the claim of America as the "absolute democracy."

Before that fateful day, though, there was much to indicate that the portrait was a flawed one. Modern scholarship, as I discuss in chapter 1, reveals that Tocqueville missed the most significant feature of Jacksonian America—the gigantic class struggle in all of its varied forms between those who resisted and those who promoted the "market revolution" then underway. The steady advance of the latter brought to a head the fundamental incompatibility of two modes of production, capitalist and slave, in the same social formation. Little, if anything, in Tocqueville's portrait prepared its reader for the great conflagration and its outcome that laid ahead—the means for resolving this contradiction. It's true that he saw the possibility of "sectional conflict" but not what it would lead to. Since the "absolute democracy" was already in place, he couldn't envision that it would take a confrontation of unprecedented proportions—the Civil War, and not "providence"—to make liberal democracy in America a reality for the first time.

Neither does the literature sustain many of Tocqueville's assertions about what he did limit his account to. Myopia about the big picture explains his central but mistaken claim about the "equality of condition" in Jacksonian America. The evidence is unambiguous about the significant inequalities in wealth that translated into unequal access to political power and governance. His claim about the institution of universal suffrage in every state was patently false not only for women and Blacks but for much of the white male working class. Just as important, as I show in chapter 2, his attitude and actions in relation to the end of slavery in the French Caribbean, France's conquest of Algeria and, finally, the workers' upheavals of 1848–1849, cast doubts on his own democratic credentials. That he failed to publicly identify with the abolitionists, the real democrats in America at that time, or offer any assistance to them should therefore come as no surprise.

On the eve of 9/11 there were signs that Tocqueville's democratic portrait was beginning to wear thin in some intellectual circles. Two recent major works—cited earlier—appeared within four years of one another and may have forever depreciated Tocqueville's stock. The most recent, Sheldon Wolin's *Tocqueville: Between Two Worlds*, is primarily a textual analysis. It dissects both his literary and political career. Looking not only at *Democracy in America* but also, to a lesser degree, his two later books, *Souvenirs* and *Old Regime*, Wolin admits that Tocqueville's treatment of democracy denies—its fatal flaw in my opinion—"sovereignty" to the masses; he wishes for a democracy without the revolutionary intervention of the "demos." Though Wolin doesn't say so—admittedly his treatment is on balance sympathetic to Tocqueville—this is why *Democracy* fails to anticipate the most important democratic development of the nineteenth century, the overthrow of slavery in America. Had Wolin looked beyond the main texts and in more detail at Tocqueville's own practice, again, as I do in chapter 2 and elsewhere, he could have enriched this most instructive insight about Tocqueville's visceral distaste for the "demos" in motion.[1]

Wolin is unable to offer a solution to what he and Tocqueville correctly recognize as the Achilles' heel of liberal or bourgeois democracy—the inherently atomizing/privatizing character of bourgeois society itself. Those who, like Robert Putnam, thought that 9/11 could provide a solution to this dilemma have no doubt come back to their senses as the reality of bourgeois society asserts itself once again.[2] The despair, Wolin argues, that haunted Tocqueville at the end of his life about such a society seems to have also afflicted him. In the very last paragraphs of his weighty tome, Wolin, having utilized Tocqueville to explain current politics in the United States, sounds despondent.

> Far from being valued as symbolizing an aspiration toward the democratization of power and a participatory society of political equals—democracy as subject—democracy would come to be regarded by late-modern power elites as object, an indispensable yet malleable myth for promoting American political and economic interests among premodern and post-totalitarian societies. At home, democracy is touted not as self-government by an involved citizenry but as economic opportunity. . . . Democracy is perpetuated as philanthropic gesture, contemptuously institutionalized as welfare, and denigrated as populism.[3]

This is how Wolin ends, without any suggestion of an alternative scenario and, hence, on a note of implicit inevitability. At the same time, he implies that the bourgeoisie and its political agents should behave differently—probably because he mainly employs the more optimistic Tocqueville of *Democracy*—that somehow they would have it in their interest to promote a "participatory" democracy.

An even weightier tome, Rogers Smith's 1997 *Civic Ideals* takes, as discussed in chapter 1, Tocqueville and his modern day followers to task for ignoring the ascriptive reality of U.S. democracy for most of its history, that is, the White Republic. Smith's method—unlike Wolin's textual approach—is to marshal massive empirical evidence, mainly from the legal arena, in order to paint a very different portrait of Jacksonian America from that of the author of *Democracy*. He concludes that the hierarchically ascriptive agenda that reached its zenith in that period, especially in regard to race and nationality, remains in place until today. Smith, unfortunately, ends his presentation of evidence long before the Second Reconstruction and therefore denies his reader the opportunity to learn about the politics of that struggle and to see what was and remains achieved.

As formidable and cogently argued as they are, Wolin and Smith's critiques of Tocqueville, respectively implicit and explicit, are only the beginning of wisdom. What is missing in both is precisely what Marx and Engels supplied—a thoroughgoing critique of bourgeois society that concluded that only the working class has it in its interest and capability to bring about real democracy. Marx and Engels saw the limitations of the bourgeoisie quite early in their collaboration. The revolutions of 1848–1849—their baptisms of fire—convincingly demonstrated in theory and practice that the bourgeoisie had decreasing interest in advancing the democratic struggle. More fearful of its own small but growing proletariat than the feudal aristocracy, its traditional adversary, ascendant capital, including its liberal wing, was now willing to settle for and even encourage an antidemocratic outcome: the "man on the horseback," what Marx called "bonapartism." No one exemplified this orientation more than Tocqueville himself. Faced with the realization that only the revolutionary intervention of the French masses could salvage bourgeois democracy, he held his nose and helped to enable the coup in 1851 that ushered in Louis Bonaparte's two-decade-long dictatorship.

Marx and Engels understood that the ability of the working class to carry out its historic mission depended on it being able to overcome the divisions that capital promoted among the toilers. In the U.S. setting this meant first and foremost, the racial divide. Because of their perspective, they were disposed to see what Tocqueville denied—that racial slavery was the greatest obstacle to democracy in America. The "branding" of labor in black skin undermined the ability of the nascent working class to clearly appreciate its interests. It was also an obstacle to the emergence of a real, hereditary proletariat. The two Germans, living in Europe, also saw something else that Tocqueville missed despite his sojourn to the United States: that the democratic movement was global, and a breakthrough in America would have positive results for the process in Europe and elsewhere. Thus, they encouraged and worked closely with their comrades in America, especially Weydemeyer, to get German American workers to understand that slavery was an obstacle to their own advancement. While Tocqueville grew despondent over the prospects of civil war, its approach heartened Marx and Engels. When it finally erupted they became active partisans for the Union, mobilizing all resources and energies from afar to aid and abet its cause. As I argue in chapter 3 their contribution was not inconsequential.

Although Radical Reconstruction was finally overthrown with the Compromise of 1877, their prediction of the eventual emergence of a majority of dispossessed producers who could only sell their labor power in order to survive—a hereditary proletariat—was fulfilled.

Even though Marx and Engels vastly outdistanced Tocqueville in understanding *and* acting on behalf of the democratic process in nineteenth-century America, does their perspective still retain validity in today's America? I answer in the affirmative, especially if compared to what Tocqueville has to offer. The Tocquevillian alternative, based fundamentally on providential intervention and seriously at odds with the real history of the United States, does not, contrary to what Wolin suggests, equip us for understanding the world in which we live and the requisites for the struggle to defend democratic conquests.

Jacksonian America taught the young Marx about the reality of bourgeois society; Tocqueville's *Democracy*, I argue, was particularly instructive. He and Engels would have easily understood, unlike Putnam, that it would take something far more significant than 9/11 to overcome the privatizing and, hence, inherently undemocratic features of such a society. If the twenty-five-year-old Marx was able to see more than a century and half ago what the thirty-year-old Tocqueville failed to grasp—and what modern scholarship has now verified—that democracy in the "most progressive nation" was still very much a work in progress, perhaps there is something in that insight that bears a revisit today. Most importantly, there is nothing in the record to suggest that Tocqueville was prepared to act as Marx and Engels did—to put in the requisite time and effort to actually advance the democratic quest in America. That fact alone affirms the objectively superior heritage of Marx and Engels—for those to whom history and social progress are living challenges and seek to be protagonists in their making.

Arguably the most glaring feature of U.S. society today—the world as well—is the increasing inequality in the distribution of wealth, possibly the greatest it's been since the founding of the country. Every arena of society reflects this tendency from the corporate world to the academy. For Marx, this would not have been surprising. It was the inevitable result of the market system based on private ownership of the means of production. His insight in 1843 about how "private property," as well as "education, occupation . . . act in *their* way . . . to exert the influence of their *special* nature" was a crucial point of departure for the communist conclusions he later reached. The United States in which we live today verifies the validity of this insight on a continual basis, again, in virtually every arena. In the political sphere in particular the disproportionate influence in the political process for those with wealth is continually confirmed. Does anyone really believe that the most recent version of campaign finance reform will alter in any fundamental way this reality? But for Marx, the existence of class society itself—not the degree of class inequality—was the structural impediment to real democracy. Only with the abolition of class society could real democracy be instituted.

The most important question about class society for Marx and Engels was whether it made possible the growth and political development of the proletariat. In fact, it was the most conscious layers of the working class in this country, as I have tried to demonstrate, allied with the abolitionists, who composed the plebian vanguard in the signal battle for democracy in the nineteenth century; their coworkers in Britain, through the anti-interventionist actions during the Civil War, proved to be just as heroic. The victory in 1865 inspired the fight for an eight-hour workday—a connection duly ignored in standard accounts of the period. This critical struggle was an elementary aspect of self-defense for those toiling at the mercy of rapacious capital. Its achievement was likewise a necessary requirement for labor to be able to participate fully in politics and a key to pioneer efforts to organize trade unions. To delegates at the International Workingman's Association congress in 1866, Marx praised the workers' movement in the United States for their fight: "[the eight-hour workday] is needed to restore the health and physical energies of the working class, that is, the great body of every nation, as well as to secure them the possibility of intellectual development, sociable intercourse, social and political action."[4] As capital seeks unrelentingly to lengthen the workday of labor, those, like Putnam, who seek a remedy to the increasingly low rates of political and civic participation in the United States might consider Marx's advice.

The support that Europe's working classes, especially in England, gave to the abolitionists and the Union cause in the Civil War laid the basis for independent working-class political action for the first time. Modern scholarship has verified that the liberal democratic breakthrough at the end of the nineteenth and beginning of the twentieth centuries was due first and foremost to this development. I have argued elsewhere that no two individuals did more to promote the political "self-organization of the working class" than Marx and Engels making them, thus, the leading protagonists in the nineteenth-century democratic movement. Their contribution was not inadvertent but conscious, consistent with earlier theoretical conclusions about the unique role of the proletariat in the realization of real democracy.[5]

Marx and Engels shared the Tocquevillian optimism about democracy in the United States but for quite different reasons. The growth of capitalism in the United States, they held, brought into existence the true and efficacious democrats—the proletariat. They understood that optimism alone about the future of democracy in America, or simply asserting that the historical trajectory is positive, would not bring about democracy and progressive social change. The important question is why. They posed the necessity of appropriate leadership for the necessary social forces—the proletariat in alliance with farmers—an approach that was true then, and remains so. Lack of clarity on such questions can be fatal for the democratic quest.

The historical record is unambiguous: any discussion about the working class in the United States being a force for advancing the democratic struggle has to address the question of race. Efforts by today's ruling elites—and not only in this country—to play the "illegal alien" card, challenges not only white workers, or white male workers but all toilers regardless of skin color, gender, national origin, or sexual orientation to reject modern branding. Hence, the question for the democratic struggle is whether race today plays as effective a role in undermining class consciousness as it has at key moments in U.S. history—what Du Bois, Goldfield as well, saw as the answer to the age-old query, "Why is there no socialism in America?"

Posed in the framework of this book: to what extent has the Second Reconstruction—embodied in the gains of the Civil Rights movement—succeeded in accomplishing the tasks that Marx hoped that the First Reconstruction would complete, above all, end the "branding of labor in black skin," and, therefore, put the "social" question on the agenda?

Though Rogers Smith's *Civic Ideals* argues that the ascriptive hierarchy, i.e., the White Republic, remains basically in place, the analysis ends long before the Civil Rights movement. His more recent book, *Unsteady March: The Rise and Decline of Racial Equality in America*, coauthored with Philip Klinkner, does focus on that historic moment and developments until 1998. As the subtitle suggests, the authors acknowledge that while significant gains were made by Blacks—owing largely, according to them, to Washington's concerns, in the context of the Cold War about America's image abroad—those advances are now being threatened. The situation, they allege, looks increasingly similar to the circumstances in which the First Reconstruction was overthrown. This can only be avoided, they argue, if the government takes appropriate measures, which they spell out at the end of the book.[6]

There is no denying that the branding process persists—the evidence is all too available as in the case of education. The disenfranchisement of Black voters in Florida in the 2000 presidential election is an obvious example and not just because of the more blatant tactics used by electoral officials—reminiscent of the Jim Crow era—but also the less visible and just as insidious methods. Late Reconstruction era laws still in effect today that forever barred felons from voting effectively meant, when coupled with current drug laws that disproportionately criminalize Blacks, that about a fourth of Black Floridians were unable to vote. The now acknowledged and widespread practice of "racial profiling" is another example. The so-called "war against terror" after 9/11 has given the bourgeois state the excuse to be more inclusive— branding those who look "middle eastern."

What's so striking about the picture that Klinkner and Smith paint is its utter incompleteness. The discussion, for example, of the overthrow of the First Reconstruction—as is also true in Smith's *Civic Ideals*—is amazingly undertheorized given their central claim about the similarity between then and now. The basic problem with their analysis, however, is that they cannot— owing to the liberal terrain upon which they travel—face the fact that racial equality can't be achieved under capitalism, for the same reason that "human emancipation," as the young Marx called it, can't be realized in a social system based on private ownership of the means of production. That's the lesson Marx drew, in large part, on the basis of what he learned about the best that liberal democracy had to offer—Jacksonian America.

Klinkner and Smith, on the other hand, think otherwise. This is expressed in the naive claim that "Few can doubt that private markets must generate most economic opportunities in America."[7] Given Black America's overwhelmingly proletarian character—a development that was largely completed by the end of the Second World War—the end of Jim Crow and acquisition of full political citizenship for the first time, represents the fruition of what is attainable under bourgeois social relations. These were enormously significant victories not only for Blacks but the entire U.S. working class. Yet workers in black skin like all workers can never achieve real equality and freedom via "private markets." Exactly because Klinkner and Smith can't envision an alternative to capitalist America and, hence, a state that serves first and foremost the interests of that class, they betray a pessimism about the long-term prospects for racial equality. They are right to be concerned that the gains of the Civil Rights movement are under real threat. But they are incapable of explaining why.

Capitalism, because of the private property relations upon which it rests, is inherently incompatible with democracy and, thus, all reforms for political and social justice under it can only be temporary. This is why, as I discuss in chapter 4, the First Reconstruction was overthrown. The specter of Marx and what he represented help explain the triumphant bourgeoisie's eventual hostility to the fortunes of the former slaves. Though not deter-minant, the counterrevolution's success was enabled by the Black leadership's decision, exemplified by Frederick Douglass, to wed Black America to the party of Abraham Lincoln, the party of the victorious industrial capitalists. Since the Republicans never had a real interest in the marriage, the decision undermined what un-til then had been the driving force in the Reconstruction effort, in-dependent Black political action. This futile effort to embrace the Republicans also figures in the failure to construct an inclusive, that is, real working-class political party—independent working-class political action—for the first time in the United States.

Not until the middle of the twentieth century would Blacks, in their majority, transfer their allegiances to the Democratic Party. The main reason why it, the party of the slave owners and their like-minded descendants, "saw the light," that is, took steps to grant full political citizenship for Blacks, is because it, the party in power, felt the heat of the mass movement for Black rights. John F. Kennedy admitted as much in explaining why he would be the first U.S. president after the Compromise of 1877 to seek meaningful civil rights legislation. The flames and mass actions in Birmingham and elsewhere in the spring of 1963 helped concentrate ruling-class minds unlike ever before. Con-trary to what Klinkner and Smith argue, the decisive factor that led to the Second Reconstruction was not the actions of the rul-ing class in its effort to win friends and influence in the Cold War but rather the mass mobilizations at home. These were objec-tively an expression of independent working-class political ac-tion. Also determinant were the struggles abroad in the so-called Third World for political rights and self-determination. It's al-ways instructive to remember the racial and gender composition of the Congress and the White House that enacted the key legis-lation for the Second Reconstruction (as well the Supreme Court for the key *Brown* decision)—far from the more "diverse" crowd that populate them today—in order to appreciate the power of mass movements.

Combined with the onset of the historic downturn in the U.S. economy, the demobilization of the Civil Rights movement as a mass protest movement at the end of the 1960s, and the decision of its leaders to wed it to the Democratic Party, explains in large part the successes of today's counterrevolution—not unlike the circumstances surrounding the overthrow of the First Reconstruction. It's no accident that on many domestic issues such as social welfare and affirmative action the Clinton White House was to the right of the Nixon administration. Since, again, reforms under capitalism are always tenuous, their defense requires the continuous independent mobilization of their beneficiaries and supporters. Hence, the inefficacy and compromised character of the Black Democratic Party establishment, the other side of the counterrevolution's successes—not unlike, again, what happened to the Black Republican leadership a century earlier. The mantra, "out of the streets, into the suites," came to be the swan song for these leaders of the Civil Rights movement.

Klinkner and Smith must of necessity look to an enlightened government and the Democratic Party—both capitalist institutions—for a hopeful answer to the counterrevolution, since like Tocqueville they relegate the mass movement to a minor role in understanding progressive social change. They are not alone, as U.S. political scientists, in failing to appreciate the power of the Civil Rights movement. It speaks volumes about the discipline that virtually only one book-length analysis of that monumental development has ever been written by a U.S. political scientist—Dennis Chong's 1991 book *Collective Action and the Civil Rights Movement*. Even then, the movement for Chong served only as a case to test his particular brand of rational choice analysis.[8] Again, it's not surprising that Tocqueville commands such a following among this community of scholars.

Marx and Engels held that the working class—not the capitalists, their state or parties—was the only social layer that has it in its interest and capacity to bring about human and, hence, racial equality. They asserted, unlike those who saw workers as passive observers, that to realize such equality the proletariat would have to *overthrow* capitalism by means of a social revolution. The important question for Marx and Engels, specifically in the U.S. setting, was whether the branding of labor in black skin had ceased enough to allow the necessary unity for the working class to carry out its historical task.

I argue that the central gains of the Second Reconstruction remain in spite of the successes of its enemies. Those advances have attenuated the historical racial divide in the working class to such an extent that opportunities exist today for forging the kind of unity that Marx and Engels envisioned. I contend that this is what Malcolm X was alluding to in an oft-quoted but under appreciated comment made after he had left the Nation of Islam and shortly before his assassination in 1965. "I believe that there will ultimately be a clash between the oppressed and those that do the oppressing. I believe there will be a clash between those who want freedom, justice and equality for everyone, and those who want to continue the systems of exploitation. I believe there will be that kind of clash, but I don't think that it will be based upon the color of the skin."[9]

The best evidence, I think, for my claim comes from today's workplace, which by historical standards is more racially integrated than it has ever been. This is especially true if looking from the bottom rather than from the top of the workforce. Workers of different skin colors—and genders, also owing to the legacy of the Civil Rights movement—find themselves in increasingly similar structural situations and, hence, are forced to act collectively. It's important to point out that this phenomenon also exists increasingly at the global level since developments in the U.S. can't be divorced from working-class struggles elsewhere.

Having been subjected to the Jim Crow system in New Orleans until I was a teenager and raised in a trade union household where both parents once served as heads of their respective Black-only locals, I shall forever remember three experiences that exemplify for me the very profound changes that came in the wake of the Second Reconstruction. All three occurred in the course of carrying out political activity.

The first was in Pittsburgh in 1984 at a meeting of unemployed and dislocated industrial workers. As the mostly male and all-white audience of about seventy began to gather, I remember feeling conspicuous as the lone Black in the church that night. A young unemployed man began the meeting and said that the first thing on the agenda was a film on the Civil Rights movement. There was much, he said, to be learned from the movement for Black rights for those facing the reality of what was then called—falsely—the "deindustrialization of America." The marginalization that those in the room were experiencing was not unlike, he said, what Blacks had once endured. Then, he asked, "How many niggers are there in the room? I want all the niggers to raise their hands." I could feel myself tensing up until everyone's hand in the room, slowly, went up, including my own belatedly. "Yes," he exclaimed, "we're all niggers! And I'm proud to be a nigger!" Only at that moment, I must admit, did I began to relax and finally feel part of the meeting.

The second experience occurred about a year later in Minneapolis. The context was the rural counterpart to the crisis that cities in the "rust belt" like Pittsburgh were undergoing. As farmers were losing their land they began to look outward for allies. For many, the Civil Rights movement was the only successful struggle of the oppressed that they knew about. A group of local farmers who belonged to the North American Farm Association contacted the short-lived but important national Black formation in which I was active in the city, the National Black Independent Political Party (NBIPP). The group, composed of farmers from the area who were white, had heard about the Black Panther Party's once famous free-breakfast program and wanted to do something similar in an impoverished section of the Black community—not on a continuous basis as the Panthers had—but as a onetime gesture of solidarity. In exchange, they wanted an opportunity to explain and win support for their efforts to defend their farms from foreclosure.

Without much fanfare but lots of goodwill and cooperation, about ten farmers and their families provided and prepared meals, together with NBIPP activists, for about fifty Black children and their families. The latter got a chance to hear about the harsh reality of small family farmers that few in the neighborhood were aware of. For the farmers, their families, and those in the Black community who took part in the event, its most memorable aspect was the experience of working together, a first for both groups, from beginning to end to make it a success.

The last example also took place in Minnesota, about a year and a half later in the town of Austin, site of one of the most important labor battles of the 1980s, the meatpackers strike against the Hormel Corporation. Rather than downsizing, the problem that these workers faced was the concerted effort of the bosses to drastically cut their wages. In the spring of 1986 meatpackers organized in the P-9 local of the United Food and Commercial Workers union at the Hormel plant in Austin decided to resist. One of the leaders of the now defunct NBIPP quickly embraced their struggle. Her prior dismissals of the "white working class" fell by the wayside as she saw them stand up to the bosses, and battle the police and national guard on the picket lines. Equally as important was the transformation in consciousness among the workers in this virtually all-white southern Minnesota town whose claim to fame until then was "Home of the Miss Minnesota Pageant."

As the strike wore on, the worldview of the strikers began to broaden. They proudly appropriated with pride the label that the local press hurled disparagingly at their president, the "Ayatollah." Indicative of their growth in consciousness was their decision to dedicate to Nelson Mandela the mural they had painted on the union hall about the strike and history of the local. They had only recently learned about him and were particularly impressed with his refusal after twenty-five years in jail to be freed in exchange for agreeing to call an end to the armed struggle against the apartheid regime. He was a model of principled behavior that they wanted to emulate. Because the strikers knew that I was active in the anti-apartheid movement in the Twin Cities, they asked me to bring to the official dedication event any Black South Africans who could accept their gesture on behalf of Mandela—a request that I was only too happy to accommodate.

To be clear, I make no claims about the current consciousness of the individuals, specifically, the white workers and farmers, who I encountered in those three settings—though I believe those experiences forever changed the thinking of many who went through them. All I can testify to is what occurred in those particular moments. The strike in Austin, it must be admitted, was later broken and a more conservative union regime took office that soon painted over the very powerful and, in its eyes, strident mural. Nonetheless it could not erase what had taken place. Clearly the crisis that these groups of producers faced explains why they were open to making connections with Blacks. In hindsight, they were some of the early victims of the end of the post–Second World War U.S. capitalist expansion, a secular downturn that continues unabated in spite of the ups and downs of the regular business cycles. Unless one is willing to make the untenable argument that what they faced was aberrant then there is no reason to believe that such responses were unique or confined to the dustbin of history.

Downsizing, layoffs, wage reductions, and loss of family farms have all characterized the capitalist mode of production from its inception, with all the consequences that afflict the producing classes. What these three experiences reflected was the willingness of labor in white skin to reach out and make alliances with those in black skin to confront the lawful realities of capitalism. And therein lies the difference with the past. I submit that only as a product of the Second Reconstruction could this change have been possible. It must also be noted that in the two cases I was more intimate with, Minneapolis and Austin, the connections were not spontaneous. Conscious political intervention was necessary to bring all the parties together. Thus, while I argue that there are more opportunities to realize such connections owing to the gains of the Civil Rights movement, I make no claim that they are automatic.

The last decade of the twentieth century provides ample evidence that the laws of capitalism with all their daily terror for workers, above all uncertainty and insecurity, continue to reign. As Marx so accurately explained more than a hundred and fifty years ago in the *Manifesto*: "Constant revolutionising of production, uninterrupted disturbance of all social conditions, everlasting uncertainty and agitation distinguish the bourgeois epoch from all earlier ones. All fixed, fast-frozen relations, with their chain of ancient and venerable prejudices and opinions, are swept away, all new-formed ones become antiquated before they can ossify. All that is solid melts into air, all that is holy is profaned, and man is at last compelled to face with sober senses, his real conditions of life, and his relations with his kind."[10] Marx's prescience is almost uncanny.

Touted as the longest expansion in the history of U.S. capitalism, the decade of the 1990s witnessed an increase in the wealth gap and either deterioration or stagnation of the standard of living for most workers. Owing to the profit crunch and competition at the global level—what brought the post–World War II boom to an end in the 1970s—all capitalists are obligated to squeeze as much labor out of their work forces as they can get away with without increasing wages and salaries. As capital penetrates every pore of society, all workers, that is, anyone who has to sell his or her labor power to survive, be they academics, doctors, lawyers—their self-image as members of the "middle class" notwithstanding—or meatpackers are subjected to this grinding reality. The growing attractiveness of unions for "middle class" workers is an inevitable by-product of capital's drive to solve its profit problem.

This was the context for one of the most visible acts of resistance to this trend in the period, the 1997 United Parcel Service (UPS) strike. Like the developments I witnessed a decade earlier, it too registered what had been achieved in the aftermath of the Second Reconstruction. As one of the strikers, a Black woman, explained after the successful action: " 'We now feel more like brothers and sisters than co-workers,' she said, noting the diversity of the strikers, who until the walkout, had often kept to their own racial or ethnic group. 'We all learned something about color. It comes down to green.'"[11] The Civil Rights movement battles and achievements made such consciousness possible. The increasingly common reality in which workers of all skin colors and genders find themselves makes it possible—and here I stress the word possible—for them to see that they indeed have mutual, common class interests. And nothing advances that process as well as the consciousness forged on the picket line, that is, in struggle. This new reality is unprecedented for the U.S. working class. Thus, I argue, the potential for U.S. workers achieving class consciousness that is far more inclusive than in the past, real class consciousness and acting collectively, is greater today than at any time in history.

Probably the most representative set of events about the potential for real class consciousness for the first time in the United States occurred in the first month of the new millennium in South Carolina. A march on the state capitol in opposition to the continued hoisting of the slavocracy's flag—larger than any demonstration during the civil rights struggle in the state—was followed within three days by a multiracial militant trade union action of longshoremen in Charleston protesting shipping bosses use of nonunion labor to unload ships—a first in that part of the old confederacy. That many had participated in the march three days earlier is not insignificant. Both actions tellingly illustrate what has changed and what remains to be done. The changes are real. The now dethroned and possibly chastened Trent Lott learned this the hard way.

Undoubtedly, the most important change has been in the consciousness of Blacks that came with the successful overthrow of the Jim Crow system. This was soon reflected in the confidence and fighting spirit of Black workers to challenge the day-to-day racism that most have had to face on the job. More than anything it engendered respect on the part of white coworkers (grudgingly on the part of the backward elements). It's no accident that the aforementioned P-9 strikers consciously looked to the tactics of the Civil Rights movement as an inspiration for many of their actions. In a number of union locals, where Blacks have disproportionately been elected to leadership positions, this has often resulted in more representative and militant organizations.

I distinctly remember the comment of a white Soo Line railroad worker on a picket line in Minneapolis in 1994. Looking at one of his coworkers on the line, a young Black woman, he said: "Boy, I'm glad we have more Blacks in the union because they sure know how to fight!" It was that fighting spirit that made it possible for the young worker to be in the union—the fight for affirmative action. In fact, the most effective defense of affirmative action I've heard came from a striking white male worker at Bridgestone-Firestone Company in Des Moines, Iowa, in 1995. The strikers were very much on the ropes then because the company had successfully brought in "replacement" workers who were mainly Black and Latino. "Now," he said with regret, "I wish we had supported affirmative action." The failure of the virtually all-white male union to do so had isolated it from the Black and Latino communities in the city, thus facilitating the company's ability to hire workers who were willing to cross their picket line.

The changes, both materially and in consciousness, have also, not surprisingly, been accompanied by increasing class polarization within U.S. racial groups. Exactly because of the gains of the Civil Rights movement the class differences within the Black population are more stark than they've ever been, making the notion of "the Black community" less and less viable. Nothing testifies better to the growing class cleavage among Blacks than the deafening silence of Black Clinton supporters in the face of the unprecedented incarceration of Blacks during his eight-year tenure. Clinton was not just disingenuous when he justified this on the grounds that he was simply "following the will of the public" in making this possible. Much of that "public" was the Black petit bourgeoisie who, as a result of the Second Reconstruction, has enough of a material stake in U.S. capitalism to now feel threatened by the so-called "underclass."[12]

After three decades in the classroom and mass movement politics, most of it in the Black struggle, never has it been easier to make the case for the primacy of class analysis to young people of every hue and background. The likes of the Condoleeza Rices and Colin Powells at all levels of government, and other kindred sorts in the so-called private sector—products of the Second Reconstruction—have been enormously helpful. As long as Jim Crow was in place, class differences amongst Blacks as well as whites tended to be obscured. The potential for clarity is greater now than at any time in history. Those, for example, who mistakenly thought that U.S. imperialism would be kinder and gentler in the hands of a Black secretary of state—or, in the previous administration, a woman—will now be more open to looking at Washington's foreign policy through the lens of class. All of this depends, of course, if there are those so willing to make the case for class.

These changes take place, again, in the context of the continuing crisis of late capitalism, which manifests itself not only in the growing wealth gap and job insecurity but also in the cuts to the already inadequate so-called social safety nets, i.e., social wages. Because the attack on the standard of living of workers is not only bipartisan but literally business as usual for the capitalist mode of production, the crisis is a global one, characteristic of all social formations where the capitalist market is allowed to do its thing. It's not a question whether the real terror—recession and depression—that most of the world's producing classes is subjected to today will come to the shores of the United States, but only when.

I cannot emphasize enough that I make no claims about the inevitability of independent working-class political action and proletarian victories in the class struggle in the United States. I argue only that the conditions propitious for such outcomes currently exist. Clearly, the social catastrophes being gestated by the crisis have the potential for undermining working-class solidarity should effective leadership not emerge to counter ideas and perspectives alien to the interests of workers—not the least of which is fascism. This is why the fight for democracy, especially for the working class, must always include militant opposition to any manifestations of racial, gender, sexual preference, and national oppression and any attacks against the gains previously won; thus, the fight to maintain and extend affirmative action is a decisive battle in post–Second Reconstruction America. Finally, no issue is as salient as that of workers without papers—in many ways the new civil rights agenda. This is a challenge for the entire working class in all of its skin colors.

One must also be leery of political nostrums that are peddled today in progressive garb. Antiglobalization à la Ralph Nader or the trade union bureaucracy is as dangerous as that of the Patrick Buchanan variety. They all assume, falsely, that the crisis that afflicts workers in the United States can be solved separate and apart from that of workers elsewhere. What's fascinating about Nader's perspective, in the context of this book, is how much it resembles the view Tocqueville held and repeated by the economist Henry Carey and the populist Henry George—the claim that America had escaped the kinds of class conflict that characterized the old world, that is, American exceptionalism. To hear Nader, one would think that there was some "golden era" in America's past in which capital and labor lived in harmony and that the behavior of today's "greedy corporations" is a violation of that norm. U.S.

workers, like their counterparts elsewhere, are experiencing just what Marx and Engels foresaw. Like Tocqueville, Nader's false portrait of America's past ignores the centrality of racial subordination in that era. Because his is fundamentally a retrospective view—an effort to return to the "good old days" of precorporate capitalism—racial equality is marginal to his vision of democracy.

Marx and Engels certainly recognized what distinguished America and how that benefitted working people everywhere. I know of no more insightful tribute to what was achieved on the western shores of the North Atlantic than Marx's praise of Lincoln when he issued the Emancipation Proclamation. "The new world," to repeat, "has never achieved a greater triumph than by this demonstration that, given its political and social organisation, ordinary people of good will can accomplish feats which only heroes could accomplish in the old world." From the characterization of America as the "most progressive nation" by the young Marx to his and Engels's later judgements, they often noted its more thoroughgoing bourgeois democratic character and how that provided more political space for the producing classes to organize and resist.

It is just for this reason that Washington's response to 9/11 must be fully grasped. First and foremost, and contrary to all the Osama bin Laden/al Qaeda/Saddam Hussein-bashing, it is an effort to reduce the political space by actually executing laws that had already been on the books—many promulgated during the Clinton administration—as well as adding new ones. In other words, this has been a campaign to make it more difficult for working people in the United States to do what they had been able with relative freedom to do throughout history—organize themselves for the resistance. As the American dream vanishes and becomes the American nightmare for increasing numbers of workers—again, because of the historical crisis of late capitalism—this is a necessary task for capital and its political agents. Given the history of the U.S. working class, capital knows full well that the most effective way to do this is to play upon the divisions within the class. With the victory of the Civil Rights movement no cleavage is now more potentially divisive than that between workers who have citizenship papers and those who do not. It's no coincidence that this offensive takes aim initially at the foreign born, though its eventual target is all workers.

Less than two years before his death in 1895, Engels, as noted in chapter 4, acknowledged other peculiarities about the United States, specifically, the structural obstacles to the emergence of a real worker's political party. In effect, he anticipated Werner Sombart's question a decade later and alluded to earlier, "Why is there no socialism in America?" and its most recent formulation by Seymour Lipset.[13] He pointed to three factors: the winner-take-all electoral system; U.S. economic expansion and the resulting gains for workers—the "American dream"; and the divisions within the working class, especially, the Black-white and native-foreign born distinctions.

Had Engels lived long enough he would have added another obstacle—imperialism. It was just this factor, as he argued in 1883, that explained why the English working class lagged far behind its counterparts on the continent in forming its own political party. "Participation in the domination of the world market was and is the economic basis of the English workers' political nullity. As the appendage of the bourgeois in the economic exploitation of this monopoly, though nevertheless participating in the advantages that accrue from the said exploitation, they are, in the nature of things, a political appendage of the 'Great Liberal Party.'" Crumbs from the booty of imperialism made it more difficult for English workers to pursue independent working-class political action. "But," Engels predicted, "once America and the combined competition of the other industrial nations have made a sizeable breach in this monopoly . . . just wait and see what happens here."[14] Indeed, as the spoils began to diminish because of sharpened international capitalist competition in the last quarter of the nineteenth century, English workers—especially the most deprived—began to mobilize, leading to the birth in 1893 of what became the Labour Party, Britain's first working-class party.

Three years after Engels's death, U.S. rulers commenced their global imperial project with the Spanish-Cuban-American War (as the Cubans refer to it). The consequences were not unlike what Engels described for English workers. The conservatizing impact of the benefits of economic expansion on the consciousness of American workers came to have an international as well as a domestic dimension.[15] The overthrow of Reconstruction paved the road to U.S. imperialism in that it provided the ideological justification for the subjugation of those in the world on its receiving end—racial superiority. In so doing it globalized the domestic branding that hindered working-class political consciousness. When that movement, however, materialized in an unprecedented way in the 1930s, as the American dream shattered for millions of workers, it was quickly undermined by the imperial project of the Second World War.

Indispensable to this subversion was the enlistment of both the AFL and CIO bureaucracy in the war effort, and the common cause made by the "radical" CIO officialdom and the 100,000 member Communist Party to block any independent break with the Roosevelt administration. Support to Roosevelt's procapitalist "New Deal" program was the U.S. variant of Moscow's class-collaborationist "popular front" schemas in Europe. The decision of the labor bureaucrats to embrace the Roosevelt administration enabled the subsequent incorporation of the Civil Rights movement into the Democratic Party. Therein lies, as Engels would have predicted, the "political nullity" of the U.S. labor movement. It's no wonder that so many mouthpieces for the ruling class began conjuring up images of Pearl Harbor after 9/11. That was, for them, *the* event that undermined what was and remains the most significant expression of independent working-class political action in American history. In the context of late capitalism, and increasing working-class resistance to its predictable consequences, the need to play the patriotic card becomes even more pressing for the ruling class and its sycophants.

Though Engels recognized that the "foreign" versus "native" divide among U.S. toilers hampered working-class consciousness, he also knew, on the basis of firsthand experience, about the positive side of immigrant labor. Germans, particularly those who migrated in the aftermath of the revolutions of 1848–1849, made a major contribution to the democratic and social revolution that came with the overthrow of slavery. Their revolutionary experiences and traditions prepared them to assume leadership positions in that struggle, out of proportion to their numbers. Marx and Engels's closest comrade, Weydemeyer, epitomized what the second American revolution gained with the arrival of these proletarian emigrants. In subsequent generations, such workers would continue to play a decisive role in the labor movement as was demonstrated in the case on the eve of and in the aftermath of the First World War.

What's so striking about the U.S. proletariat today is the breadth and depth of its multiracial, multigendered and, above all, multinational character. That the U.S. government ended its preferential quota policy on immigration from Europe in 1965, at the crest of the Civil Rights movement, is not coincidental. The classic image of the American worker as a white male was bypassed by reality at least a quarter century ago. The combination of the gains of the Civil Rights movement and its offshoot, the second wave of feminism, and the end of the post–World War II boom brought women into the workforce as never before. The increasing inability of working-class families to survive on the wages of one wage earner enabled this development and guaranteed the institution of a hereditary proletariat. The proletarianization process that Marx and Engels had foreseen took this particular form after the Second Reconstruction.

The multinational composition of the working class is due in large part to "the empire strikes back" syndrome—"blow back" from the imperial project. As early as 1853, Marx grasped the reality of the project better than anyone in his characterization of British rule in India. "The profound hypocrisy and inherent barbarism of bourgeois civilization lies unveiled before our eyes, turning from its home, where it assumes respectable forms, to the colonies, where it goes naked."[16] Because of imperialist superexploitation in the periphery, the producing classes there radicalize at a greater rate than those in the center, who are still relatively more protected from capital's worse excesses. But increasing numbers of the Third World toilers are forced to migrate to the center, owing to imperialism's nakedness, with consciousness and traditions that they gained in struggle—not unlike what the German "'48ers" brought with them in the decade before the Civil War. The reality of late capitalism means that these migrants, unlike those who came in earlier waves, arrive at a time when the realization of the American dream is an increasingly fleeting possibility for all workers. Already they have begun to engage in and lead resistance to what capital is forced to do.

One of my most vivid memories in recent years is the strike of members of the Hotel Employees and Restaurant Employees union in Minneapolis in the summer of 2000. Notwithstanding the challenge of forging unity among hotel workers who represented at least seventeen distinct languages, the union triumphed. It won most of its demands. I was especially struck by the solidarity expressed by union members with more seniority, mainly white. This was not automatic, since they had been contractually grandfathered in and provided with better wages and benefits as a result of the two-tiered contract to which many unions in the 1970s and 1980s submitted—decades of capitulation and concessions to the employers. Such solidarity is another example of what was achieved with the victory of the Second Reconstruction. My favorite image was that of Somali women strikers on the picket line—in veil and with their signs raised high. This occurred deep in the "American heartland" and was as significant as the multiracial, multinational demonstration/parade in New York City in 1871 in honor of the martyr's of the Paris Commune—an indication of the degree to which the U.S. proletariat has changed in composition.

Engels's accurate prediction that a weakened imperialism would open up possibilities for the English working class has lessons today for America's proletariat. The triple whammy of the mid-70s, recession, Watergate, and Vietnam, brought the American Century to a premature end. The recession, as already noted, signaled the end to the post–World War II quarter-century expansion. U.S. economic hegemony was challenged by competitors, especially Germany and Japan, putting greater pressure on U.S. capital to lower its wage costs—a major reason why real wages are less than what they were in 1973. Watergate undermined working-class trust in government, which has never recovered in spite of ruling class hopes that 9/11 would be the remedy. But it was Vietnam more than anything that weakened U.S. imperialism. For the first time since the project got off the ground at the end of the nineteenth century, it suffered a defeat at the hands of the peripheral subjects. The outcome resulted in what Henry Kissinger bemoaned as the "Vietnam syndrome," the reluctance of the working class to send its sons and daughters to be maimed and killed for the project.

It is doubtful, at the time of this writing, that Saddam Hussein, who politically outlived George Bush I, will have better luck with his scion. Yet, I can confidently predict that it will be easier to overthrow Hussein than to turn the region into a bed of stability in which U.S. capital will reap untold bounty. Capitalist world disorder places real limits on the ability of U.S. capital to extract the kind of surplus value abroad as it was able to do for much of the twentieth century. The hope that the collapse of the Stalinist regimes in Russia and Eastern Europe would open up unlimited markets remains just that—a hope. All of this means that the benefits that trickled down to the U.S. working class from the plunder of U.S. capital abroad have diminished. If anything, U.S. workers find themselves having to compete more and more with wage rates abroad—the effects of capital's unprecedented mobility. American exceptionalism, the belief that workers here could escape the laws of capital, is under constant challenge. This is the basis for the appeal to some workers of a nationalistic solution to the crisis, be it that of the variety of Ralph Nader, the trade union bureaucracy, or Patrick Buchanan.

Most importantly, Washington's inability to wage war as it would like limits its ability to promote patriotic/nationalistic consciousness as an alternative to that of class. This is why the strike of Minnesota state workers (I apologize for another Minnesota example, but this is obviously the terrain that I know best)—the largest such strike by state workers anywhere in decades—six weeks after 9/11 was so significant. They were subjected to a tremendous amount of guilt-baiting from the governor and other state officials, both of the Republican and Democratic Farmer Labor Parties (as the Democratic Party is known in Minnesota), and the corporate media. The charge that their strike undermined the war effort that had just begun failed to deter them. After two weeks on the picket lines they settled on fairly favorable terms. However they may have seen what they were doing, they engaged, successfully, in class struggle in the midst of the most concerted ideological campaign in support of patriotism since Pearl Harbor. This too registers the limits of Washington's ability to make war.

My main argument is that for those who are prepared to emulate Marx and Engels—to act to advance the democratic struggle and to bring about "real democracy"—the opportunities today are unlike any in the past. No set of events did more to plant the seeds of such opportunities than the Second Reconstruction.

Germany in the 1920s and 1930s teaches what happens if such opportunities are not taken fully advantage of. The world we live in today begins to have an uncanny resemblance to what preceded the horrors that eventually unfolded there. Increasingly the question becomes not whether we can provide an alternative but what happens if we do not. Today's world demands action. It's not as if we can abstain from struggle without consequences. The unavoidable and reassuring fact is that in the face of deepening capitalist crises the most immediately affected will search for answers and solutions; inaction, temporizing and paralysis of action due to angst is the luxury of those who can find temporary respite from those horrors. As the most oppressed search for answers they will inevitably encounter those who'll promise answers of the kind that the fascists in the 1930s offered. For every progressive pessimist, there is at least one follower of Patrick Buchanan who understands all too well how the crisis produces a growing audience to hear the "solutions" their side proposes. And it is exactly that fact that should move any handwringers to act; otherwise the space will be filled in ways that will make the horrors of the 1930s and 1940s pale in comparison.

The case I've tried to make is the necessity and utility of knowing the ideas and deeds of Marx and Engels, specifically in the American theater, to study, evaluate, and build upon them on the basis of the real record of the two communists and the actuality of the class struggle. One lesson, above all, from this exposition is that the best of theoretical perspectives and political programs are for naught unless fought for. The record of Marx and Engels makes this clear. One can speculate, as I did in chapter 3 on the Civil War, whether or not Marx and Engels made a decisive contribution to the democratic struggle in the United States. The evidence is admittedly inconclusive. But the central conclusion to be drawn from their record is that they acted in the belief that they could make such a contribution to human emancipation on U.S. soil. That legacy should inspire all who seek to do likewise in the face of the immense challenges on the horizon and, hence, opportunities to make history.

I would be derelict if I didn't acknowledge all the crimes done in the name of Marx and Engels throughout the twentieth century and the understandable reluctance it might generate to what I propose. Hasn't history discredited what they were about? Exactly because of this widespread assumption, I have consciously employed language about their project that hopefully resonates with sincere democrats who might be leery of their argument about what it would take to realize "real democracy," that is, the conquest and defense of political power by the proletariat—the much maligned and misunderstood "dictatorship of the proletariat"—the necessary step to a socialist and eventually a communist society.

This is not the place to take up the question of Stalinism in any detail.[17] Suffice it to say that little that was done in the name of Marx and Engels in the twentieth century—and Lenin as well, I'm prepared to argue—resembled what they were actually about. Why should we believe Stalin, the inveterate liar, when he said that socialism had been achieved in the Soviet Union in 1936—a claim that would be parroted by not only the apparatchik and fellow travelers elsewhere, but all too happily by enemies of the real project of Marx and Engels? One of the purposes of this book is precisely to reclaim the true history/practice of Marx and Engels (I am prepared also to argue that no one in their aftermath had a better grasp of their project than Lenin). What is especially advantageous about doing political work today is that the deadly weight of Stalinism exercises less influence than at any time in its history.

The collapse of the Stalinist apparatchik has done more to advance the socialist project than anything since the Cuban revolution of 1959—the only post–Russian Revolution overturn that did not have roots in Stalinism; hence its healthy birth and why it can continually renew itself in spite of all the obstacles in its course.

Always mindful of the difficulties in achieving independent working-class political action, Engels remained optimistic about America. He anticipated, as he wrote in 1893, a time "when it is really ripe for a socialist workers' party." To some eyes and ears the claim I make that the time Engels foresaw has arrived owing to the victory of the Civil Rights movement, the secular crisis of late capitalism, and a weakened U.S. imperial project looks and sounds encouraging but seems premature. Aren't working people still smitten by the virus of racism? Isn't it the case that the majority of working people in the United States are still taking it on the chin from capital and still have yet to go on the offensive? Isn't Washington flexing its muscles in the aftermath of 9/11? All of this is indeed true.

It was Lenin who absorbed the lessons that Marx and Engels codified better than anyone of his generation and advised "what is to be done" before the masses would go into revolutionary action. It was just the kind of advice, discussed in chapter 4, that Marx gave to cothinkers in the United States in 1871 about the need and creation of "previous organization" before workers could conquer political power that Lenin drew upon to reach perhaps his most important insight. To try to accumulate the forces and forge a working-class revolutionary leadership—yes, the also much maligned and misunderstood vanguard party (which means no more and no less than the obvious fact that in politics some individuals achieve clarity and act sooner than others)—when the proverbial "shit hits the fan," or when all the conditions are ripe, would be too late. This is why every excuse to delay this necessary step, such as the "lesser of two evils" thinking that keeps many a well-meaning progressive from breaking with the Democratic Party entails, in today's world, increasingly prohibitive opportunity costs. Unless steps are taken today to begin the process of putting together such a leadership, the revolutionary opportunities that the lawful operations of capital will inevitably create will be lost and those masking in the garb of democracy and socialism will get a hearing for their "solution" if a real working-class alternative is not in place.

While the working class in its majority is still taking it on the chin, a growing minority is beginning to resist in varied forms. Very much in the vanguard is the resistance of workers without papers since these efforts often combine economic, political, and social questions. But wherever and however they manifest themselves, today's struggles are what fight-minded activists should immediately gravitate to in order to learn through successes as well as defeats how to begin the process of constructing what history has made clear—both gloriously and tragically—will be needed when "it" really does "hit the fan," a revolutionary workers' party.

In response to the question posed by Sombart in 1906, "Why is there no socialism in America?" the argument here is that the two necessary ingredients for the demise of U.S. capital are in place for the first time—the overthrow of Jim Crow and the existence of a hereditary proletariat. The crisis of late capitalism that commenced in the 1970s takes place, therefore, in a context that is completely different from what existed in earlier crises. Nothing will do more to accelerate that crisis than the war drive that the current administration in Washington launched after 9/11. In a desperate move to solve the long-term crisis—in part, to restore U.S. capital to its preeminent position coming out of the Second World War—those leading this charge will actually exacerbate their own problems. Imperialist aggression against the people of Iraq is but a prelude to a series of wars that open the twentieth-first century. Combined with the war at home already in progress for almost two decades—the drive to reduce the standard of living of workers for the sake of capitalist profitability—this offensive will concentrate working-class minds unlike anything else. U.S. workers will be forced to come to grips with the real character of bourgeois democracy. The bipartisan character of the offensive will enable them to see that workers have neither their own foreign policy nor political party and that the government they think is "theirs" is really one of the rich, for the rich, and by the rich. The kinds of conclusions they reach about this cold reality

will depend on the existence of that crucial factor—the sufficient ingredient—a revolutionary workers' party.

As the crisis of late capitalism inevitably polarizes politics
and promotes war, the question becomes not whether we should
embark on the path for which Marx and Engels advocated but,
again, what happens if we do not. This is the real lesson about the
gains that rightist parties have made in European elections in recent years. Particularly instructive was the first round of the 2002
French presidential elections which saw the incipient fascist Jean-
Marie Le Pen finish second and ahead of the socialist candidate
Lionel Jospin. The election also reaffirmed one of the major political lessons of the twentieth century. If the record of Stalinism
teaches that socialism cannot be constructed on the backs of the
working class, that of Social Democracy makes clear that the market and the capitalist state cannot be employed to overcome the
inherent contradictions of capitalism. That was the basic reason
for Jospin's defeat. The inability of his social democratic-led government to provide real solutions for workers opened the door
to the false solutions of Le Pen. His U.S. counterpart, Patrick
Buchanan, who works untiringly to accumulate like-minded
cadres, hopes to follow in his path. "Socialism or barbarism" begins to have currency unlike ever before.

If capitalist crises and the political polarization they breed,
including their drive toward war, are inevitable, the successful
forging of a socialist alternative is not. This is why, contrary to all
the many misreadings of Marx, party building was always at the
center of his project. This book, therefore, constitutes a conscious
intervention in the assistance of that effort.

François Furet, the eminent historian of the French Revolution who died in 1997, was one of Tocqueville's most ardent admirers. In his final work, a critical review of twentieth-century
"communism," he revealed that he had been a member of the
French Communist Party until Moscow crushed in blood the
1956 Hungarian uprising. His disillusionment with Stalinism
forced him, as this and other writings suggest, to reevaluate
"Marxism" and eventually adopt Tocqueville as an alternative.
Though he applauded the "end of communism," Furet, the democrat, looked forward to "a world beyond the bourgeoisie and

beyond Capital, a world in which a genuine human community can flourish."[18]

I think the greatest crime of Stalinism, all of its many horrors notwithstanding, is that it mis-educated entire generations of young people like Furet—not just about the real communist project of Marx and Engels but politics as well. Rather than a means to advance the interests of the majority, politics came to be seen as the grease for the skids of an opportunistic and cynical minority of careerists. What's to be celebrated about the "end of communism"—read the demise of Stalinist hegemony—is that radicalizing youth today, unlike those of Furet's generation, have a better chance of entering politics without Stalinism's demoralizing and deadly embrace and finding the real Marx and Engels. For Furet to adopt Tocqueville as an alternative to Marx was also a tragedy. While it is doubtful that Tocqueville ever wanted a "world beyond the bourgeoisie and beyond Capital," it is certainly clear that he was not about to act to bring it about. His greatest disservice was to suggest, if not claim, that real democracy could be achieved without the revolutionary intervention of the "demos." More than anyone, Marx knew that only in the "world" Furet longed for could real democracy, that is, "human emancipation," be realized. And no one did more to make such a "world" a reality.

Notes

1. Again, in chapter 5 of my *Marx and Engels: Their Contribution to the Democratic Breakthrough* (Albany: State University Press of New York, 2000) I discuss how Tocqueville, in contrast to Marx and Engels, behaved in the 1848–1849 upheavals and show how his democratic credentials are far less deserved than theirs. Even when Wolin examines Tocqueville's main text on those events, *Souvenirs*, he ignores what may have been his most consequential action, his role in crushing the Parisian working-class uprising in June 1848—the defeat that prepared the ground for Louis Bonaparte's dictatorship. For an analysis that explains in part Wolin's myopia, see Steven Holmes's critical review, "Both Sides Now," *The New Republic*, March 4 and 11, 2002.

2. Robert Putnam, "A Better Society in a Time of War," Op-Ed, *New York Times*, 19 October 2001.

3. Sheldon Wolin, *Toqueville between Two Worlds: The Making of a Political and Theoretical Life* (Priceton, N.J.: Princeton University Press, 2001), pp. 571–72.

4. **20**, p. 187.

5. Nimtz, *Marx and Engels*. For an abbreviated version of the argument see my article, "Marx and Engels–The Unsung Heroes of the Democratic Breakthrough," *Science and Society* (Summer, 1999).

6. Philip A. Klinkner with Rogers Smith, *The Unsteady March: The Rise and Decline of Racial Equality in America* (Chicago: The University of Chicago Press, 1999).

7. Ibid., p. 332.

8. Dennis Chong, *Collective Action and the Civil Rights Movement* (Chicago: University of Chicago Press, 1991). I leave aside—here—the question whether Chong's analysis adequately explained the dynamics of the movement.

9. George Breitman, *Malcolm X Speaks* (New York: Grove Press, 1966), p. 216.

10. **6**, p. 487.

11. "Rank and File's Verdict: A Walkout Well Waged," *New York Times*, 20 August 1997, p. 15.

12. As informative as Loïc Wacquant's article is about this development, "From Slavery to Mass Incarceration," *New Left Review*, no. 13 (January–February 2002), he fails to explain how this came about, particularly the acquiescence of the Black middle class.

13. Seymour Lipset, *American Exceptionalism: A Double-Edged Sword* (New York: W. W. Norton & Co., 1996).

14. **47**, p. 55.

15. One could argue, correctly I think, that the antecedent to this was the subjugation of the Plains Indians in the aftermath of the Civil War. A portion of their confiscated lands ended up in the hands of white workers seeking to be self-employed producers who, therefore, benefitted from the booty of the domestic imperial project.

16. **12**, p. 221.

17. Leon Trotsky's *The Revolution Betrayed: What Is the Soviet Union and Where Is It Going?* (New York: Pathfinder Press, 1972), remains the best explanation of Stalinism. See also my "Marxism," in *The Oxford Companion to Politics of the World*, ed. Joel Krieger (New York: Oxford University Press, 1993 and 2001), the first and second editions, for a brief overview of Trotsky's thesis.

18. François Furet, *The Passing of an Illusion: The Idea of Communism in the Twentieth Century* (Chicago: University of Chicago Press, 1999), p. 502..

Appendix

Thomas Messer-Kruse's, *The Yankee International*
Recent Adventures in Gratuitous Marx-Bashing

> Where the working class is not yet far enough advanced in its organization to undertake a decisive campaign against the collective power, i.e. the political power, of the ruling classes, it must at any rate be trained for this by continual agitation against, and a hostile attitude towards, the policies of the ruling classes. Otherwise it remains a plaything in their hands.
>
> —Marx to Bolte in New York, 1871

Is it true that the failure of the U.S. labor movement to take up the cause of racial equality after the overthrow of the slavocracy was due largely to the "machinations" of Karl Marx and his co-thinkers in America? This is the most important of the charges that Thomas Messer-Kruse makes in his book, *The Yankee International: Marxism and the American Reform Tradition, 1848–1876*, (1998). As such, it's of major relevance for this book and, thus, necessary to address in a serious and detailed manner.[1] Messer-Kruse's claims are not just of historical significance. The charges he raises speak to one of the central questions in the fight for racial equality and, therefore, real democracy today: to what extent should that struggle prioritize the role of the working class and their organizations, specifically, trade unions? His book is also an example of why it is so important to understand the depth of Marx's understanding of the U.S. reality.

227

As part of his central thesis, Messer-Kruse argues that in the immediate aftermath of the Civil War the "possibility of a true union between those whose long fight against slavery had instilled in them the most egalitarian view of race and sex of their time and those whose resistance to the coming industrial order had shaped a native radical labor ideology promised to create a new powerful synthesis of reform ideas."[2] For a brief moment this promise embodied itself in a section of the U.S. branch of the International Workingmen's Association (IWMA), or, First International. The highest expression of that "possibility," he argues, was Section 12 in New York City or what he calls the "Yankee International," exactly because it more than any other local embraced these two "native" traditions, the egalitarians and radical labor activists. This promise came, however, to a premature end after about only a year and for reasons that have to do with the perspective and actions of Marx and his comrades, especially the German Americans in New York.

According to Messer-Kruse, Marx never understood or was really interested in the liberal republican tradition of America and, thus, didn't appreciate what the Yankee Internationalists brought with them to the IWMA. "Unlike their Internationalist immigrant Marxist comrades, who, because they had complete faith in the efficacy of Marxist theory to comprehend and analyze any given social-political-economic moment, tended to believe that there was but one true line of socialist progress, these descendants of the native radical tradition believed that all reform proposals represented different means to similar ends."[3] Marx, on the other hand, Messer-Kruse claims, was driven by his historical materialist method that required him to fit the U.S. reality into a preconceived global schema and it was that view that he imparted to his German American comrades in the U.S. branch of the international led by Frederick Sorge. Anything that weakened British imperialism and assisted the proletarian revolution in England was for Marx an advance in the worldwide class struggle of producers and no development to this end was as important as that of the Irish movement for self-determination.

In urging the German Americans to reach out to the Irish workers in New York, who were more conservative on race and gender issues, but a potential thorn in London's side across the Atlantic, Marx, alleges Messer-Kruse, objectively undermined the promise represented by the Yankee Section 12. The latter, as inheritors of the progressive native tradition on race and sexual equality, were increasingly seen as an obstacle to attracting the Irish workers. "Marx's Irish strategy led to great mischief in America. Because of the rivalries and racial hatreds that had grown up between the Irish and African American communities in New York, Marx's approach encouraged Sorge and his comrades to turn their backs on their own internationalist principles of human brotherhood and ignore the needs of their potential black constituency. . . . Marx's Irish strategy further deepened the divisions between Sorge's Marxists and the libertarian Yankees."[4]

That Section 12 was quite middle class and professional in composition and headed by Victoria Woodhull, the well-known proponent of women's rights, was also, according to Messer-Kruse, problematic in forging the "promising" alliance. The great emphasis that the Sorgean leadership placed on trade union work, also at Marx's urging, reinforced the orientation to Irish workers who tended to be disproportionately trade union activists. The conservative position of the trade unions on women's equality once again led the Sorgeans to distant themselves from Section 12. Marx's followers, informed by his alleged depreciation of liberal republicanism and his Irish strategy, increasingly saw the Yankee Internationalists as incompatible with what they understood was his vision of the International in America and, hence, carried out a successful campaign to exclude them from the organization. Messer-Kruse accuses Marx of complicity in this effort in both New York in the fall of 1871 and the later congress of the International at the Hague in September 1872.

Thus, the ouster of the Yankee Internationalists deprived the future labor movement of the benefits of a native tradition that combined the struggle for both economic and social rights. Because, in Messer-Kruse's view, of what Marx and his followers had done, "the goals of civil rights and political liberty were loosened from those of economic equality and social justice" in the subsequent trajectory of the U.S. reform movement. For labor specifically, the orientation of the Sorgeans resulted in an

apolitical labor movement that began with the American Federation of Labor (AF of L) and continues until today. The "father"
of this outcome, Samuel Gompers, was, according to Messer-
Kruse, a direct product of the Sorgean perspective. This also explains, in his opinion, the failure of the labor movement to
embrace the Civil Rights and Women's Rights movements of the
1960s and 1970s. "In the long run, the institutional absence of the
Yankee International's focus on the principles of republican liberty, civil rights, and human equality made it possible for the
early American left to abandon racial minorities and women."[5]

Sorge's actions, therefore, go a long way in answering the
age old question, "Why is there no socialism in America?" A
"truly American version of socialism," Messer-Kruse argues,
would have to figure out how to combine republican traditions
and social equality. "Marx and Sorge had no interest in the question and chose to cynically dismiss such concerns as so much
petty bourgeois humbug . . . Had . . . Yankee socialist ideology
been allowed to become the face of American socialism, it would
have . . . perhaps even made American socialism far less excep-
tional than it once seemed."[6] Not only then did Marx and Sorge's
actions undermine the emergence of a progressive American labor movement but they, "ironically," obstructed a solution to
American exceptionalism.

For reasons obvious to anyone who understands the claims I
make in the preceding chapters of this book, Messer-Kruse's
charges are indeed serious and require careful and thoughtful
response. There is not sufficient space here to take up the other
charges that he levels at Marx and his partner Engels. None of
those are new, including such hoary allegations that Marx operated in a manipulative and undemocratic fashion within the
IWMA; that he mistreated his onetime comrade Georg Eccarius
who figured significantly in the events of his book; that his
alleged "eurocentrism" predisposed him to disdain Asian peoples; or that he "sprinkled his original German texts with the
English words 'poor whites' and 'niggers.'" I have in fact either
addressed and/or disputed all of these in other places—including this book—or pointed to where a convincing response can be
found.[7] The task here is to respond to the above-listed charges,

specifically as they relate to the central claims of my book. To do so it is necessary to distinguish between those that speak explicitly to Marx and those directed to Sorge; responding to the accusations against the former has priority. On occasion, when appropriate, Engels will be brought into the conversation. Rather than take up every detailed claim, the intent here is to focus on the most significant charges.

Marx, the Suspect Democrat

For Messer-Kruse, any suggestion that Marx was a democrat is "silliness."[8] His basic charge that Marx had little or no interest in or even depreciated the liberal democratic-republican tradition is exactly what this book disputes. The young Marx, as I argue in chapter 1, was very much aware of and appreciated—as other Europeans of his generation, including Tocqueville—the importance of what was achieved on the other shores of the Atlantic. At the same time he recognized, unlike Tocqueville, the limitations of those gains. If America was the best that liberal democracy had to offer then clearly it was not sufficient for human emancipation. This led Marx, as I document, to his communist worldview. The crucial insight that made him a communist, based on his reading of history and current reality, was that the working class was the only social layer that had both the thoroughgoing interest *and* capacity in instituting real democracy. This and the related insight that the bourgeoisie and petit bourgeoisie no longer had the political will to advance the fight for democracy was strikingly confirmed in the revolutions of 1848.

Contrary to what Messer-Kruse asserts, Marx never dismissed or rejected liberal or, as he began to call it, bourgeois democracy as unimportant. Had he made an effort to look at Marx's Civil War writings and activities, as I do in chapter 3, he would have found how deeply Marx understood—at times better than his comrade Engels—both the strengths and weaknesses of the U.S. political reality. It is worth repeating Engels's retort in 1892 to a similar charge about his and his partner's alleged democratic deficit. "Marx and I, for forty years, repeated ad nauseam that for us the democratic republic is the only political form in which the struggle between the working class and the capitalist class can first be universalised and then culminate in the decisive victory of the proletariat."[9] If the charge is that they didn't regard liberal democracy as an end in itself, they would plead guilty precisely because they realized very early, as slaveholding America visibly demonstrated, that its presence was no guarantee for human emancipation. This is constantly confirmed in daily life in all bourgeois democracies. But that position shouldn't be confused, as Messer-Kruse does, with a disregard for bourgeois democracy. As I have shown elsewhere, they never stood on the sidelines whenever liberal democratic rights were threatened and always recognized that in the end it was the working class that had the greatest interest in defending democratic conquests and the political space it opened for all oppressed layers.[10]

Messer-Kruse's failure to acknowledge the contribution of Marx and his co-thinkers in the United States to the overthrow of slavery is revealing, not the least because of the method employed throughout the book—the selective usage of the facts to support his thesis. It betrays a nativist tendency in that it suggests that the only real fighters against the slavocracy were "home grown," thus earning them the franchise on the struggle for racial equality. As both chapters 2 and 3 of this book make clear, the partisans of Marx and veterans of Europe's 1848 revolutions threw themselves wholeheartedly into the Northern armies, making contributions all out of proportion to their numbers, while Marx did all he could on the other side of the Atlantic to advance the cause of abolition.

The "native" crowd that Messer-Kruse feels more at home with certainly helped to prepare the ground for the fight. But in the decisive moment for realizing the fruit of that work, the Civil War, the partisans of Marx and like-minded German American immigrants made an equally outstanding contribution. This was recognized by the most prominent abolitionist, Frederick Douglass, both before and after the war. To argue as Messer-Kruse does, that in the postwar period that the "natives" would be more vigilant in defending Black rights than the "immigrants" isn't consistent with the facts. He rests his case on what the former did both before and apparently during the war, but presents nothing to demonstrate that their reaction to the overthrow of Reconstruction was qualitatively different from the supposedly less racially egalitarian supporters of Marx. Had such evidence been available there is no doubt that he would have gladly offered it to drive home his thesis. Progressive native origins were no guarantee for the defense of racial equality after the abolition of slavery. There is no more obvious example than a wing of women's rights supporters, once fervent abolitionists but which opposed the extension of voting rights to Black males because it wasn't granted to white women. Messer-Kruse is noticeably silent about this well-known development.

A related problem is Messer-Kruse's tendency to glorify the "native liberal-republican tradition" in comparison to the non-republican origins of the immigrants. This buys into the notion of American exceptionalism that Tocqueville first propagated. The veterans of the German revolution of 1848, especially Marx's co-thinkers, brought with them—exactly because of the experiences they had just gone through—a more demanding conception of republicanism. America may have indeed been the best example of existent republican rule but it was the "White Republic," the republic of the slave owners and those who collaborated with or capitulated to them. Messer-Kruse comes close to sounding like Tocqueville and those nativists who thought the United States had written the last word on the subject of democracy and thus felt threatened by what these new immigrants envisioned. Historian Bruce Levine notes that "Anglo-American critics," in Tocqueville-like fashion, "responded to German-American labor and other radical reform efforts by declaring the newcomers and their doctrines to be beyond the pale of American tradition. 'Theirs is a democracy eminently European,' warned nativist author John P. Sanderson. 'No one can mistake its paternity. . . . It is not the republicanism of Washington, Adams, Jefferson, Hamilton, Jay, Madison, and their illustrious compeers.' Rather it was 'the democracy of the leaders of the revolutionary movements in Europe, whose ultra, wild, and visionary schemes and theories have brought obloquy upon the very name of republicanism in Europe.'"[11] It's probably no accident that Messer-Kruse, who praises the racial egalitarian values of progressive "natives," can ignore how in the heartland of that crowd—Massachusetts—anti-immigrant sentiments could be as at home as in the less-enlightened frontier lands of Illinois or Indiana.

The Irish Turn

The centerpiece of Messer-Kruse's allegations is the charge that it was Marx's "Irish strategy," coupled with his encouragement of trade union work, that set into motion the events that led to the ouster of Section 12—an example of what he calls Marx's "reductionist analysis" and the "hubris" it engendered. "What supreme confidence he must have had in the scope of his social vision, his grasp of the direction of political economic variables, and the firmness of his final calculations to make such a demand of his little clique. The sophistication of Marx's social analysis towered above his contemporaries and yet paled beside the sheer unbounded possibilities of social being and historical development."[12]

Marx, unlike Messer-Kruse, approached politics from a global perspective. He did so because the real movement of history had revealed that the struggle of the oppressed was globally intertwined. These were conclusions drawn on the basis of the living class struggle and not, contrary to what Messer-Kruse implies, Marx's intellectual arrogance. His prescience has been overwhelmingly verified by a succeeding century and a half of events. Implicit in Messer-Kruse's criticism is the epistemological assumption of the "unbounded possibilities of social being," the giddy notion that social reality has no inherent logic nor is it comprehensible. Marx thought otherwise and that is why he dropped everything, including writing *Capital*, to work on behalf of the Union cause when the Civil War began in April 1861. The overthrow of slavery in the United States, he foresaw, would be an advance for the struggle of the producing classes everywhere. History proved his "reductionist" assumption to be correct, giving further credence to his "materialist conception of history." Those of us who are conscious beneficiaries of his actions are inspired by his confidence and apply his methodology, including necessary adjustments and improvements.

If Washington had been the capital of the global slavocracy until the outbreak of the Civil War, London was now, at the end of the 1860s, the headquarters of global capitalism in the beginnings of its imperialist phase. A blow from anywhere against that empire but especially from Ireland opened up political space not only for its subjects but for the English working class itself. Since Messer-Kruse asserts that Marx's "reductionism" blinded him to the struggles of anyone but the working class, it's useful to remember that in 1869 Marx decided that the initiative for England's proletarian revolution would come from the Irish struggle for national self-determination and not, as he had previously thought, England's workers. Marx's changed position recognized an interdependency between working-class struggles and other democratic contests, primarily those for the self-determination of oppressed peoples. This is why when the Black upsurge came forward in an unprecedented fashion in the 1930s, Marxists who had grasped Marx's Irish strategy and its logic could give it their unconditional support.

Unlike an academic observer of history, Marx, the communist political activist and leader of the IWMA, had every obligation to raise with and urge his comrades in New York to make an effort to reach out to the Irish working class. Abolitionists tried as much in the 1840s. Marx's efforts were, in however modest the form, the organization and mobilization of the agential or subjective factor in history—conscious, organized individuals intervening in events to effect the outcome. Opportune political moments, according to the historical materialist method, are just that—momentary. Failing to act in a timely manner is to default on political responsibility. Collective discussion afterward in an appropriate venue, such as a congress, could draw a balance sheet on what had transpired in order to learn what to do better the next time.

I have discussed earlier in the book the context necessary for understanding Marx's Irish initiative.[13] He specifically urged, in his official capacity as a General Council (GC) member of the IWMA, Sigfrid Meyer and August Vogt in April 1870—the two corresponding secretaries for the German affiliate in New York—to reach out to the Irish workers. *"A coalition of the German workers with the Irish workers* (naturally, also, with the English and

American workers who wish to join in) is the greatest thing you could undertake now. This must be done in the name of the 'International.' The social significance of the Irish question must be made clear."[14] Note that he said "naturally" American workers should also be invited to take part; Messer-Kruse asserts that "according to [Marx's] own theories, Yankees were the least important element of the American working class while the Germans and the Irish were its vanguard."[15] Marx raised another reason for taking this initiative—which Messer-Kruse fails to mention. It would help counter efforts by England to play the patriotic card in its ongoing war threats against the United States. Support by U.S. workers for the Irish struggle would go a long way in overcoming London's campaign to play "its" workers off against those on the other side of the Atlantic.

It is noteworthy that this was the only time that Marx made this proposal in his communications with the German Americans. He never broached the subject with Sorge after he became, in 1871, the official correspondent to the General Council of the IWMA (GC) for the umbrella body of the American sections, the Central Committee (CC). The letter to Meyer and Vogt suggests in fact that at the time it was sent they were neither in contact with nor part of the same organization that Sorge was in, the General German Workers' Association Labor Union No. 5, the soon to be Section 1. This apparently escapes Messer-Kruse's otherwise observant eyes. That there had been "personal hostility between Sorge on the one hand, and Sigfrid Meyer and August Vogt on the other" also seems to escape his attention.[16]

It is true, as Messer-Kruse points out, that in his report to the GC in August 1871, sixteen months after Marx's proposal, Sorge stated that efforts to recruit Irish workers to the IWMA had not been successful but that the section would continue to try to do so.[17] He also asked Engels to recommend some books for him to read about the Irish question from a historical materialist point of view.[18] And finally, in the debate at the Hague congress Sorge did say that, "to win over America we absolutely need the Irish and they will never be on our side if we do not break off all connections with Section 12 and the 'free lovers.' The working class in America consists of 1) Irishmen, 2) Germans, 3) Negroes and 4)

Americans."[19] But that is the entire written record from which Messer-Kruse infers what might have been Sorge's response to the "Irish strategy." I say "might" because in order to prove his thesis about Marx creating "mischief in America," he has the admittedly difficult task of proving that Sorge and his comrades only made the effort to recruit Irish workers because of what Marx wrote to Meyer and Vogt. The record of Sorge's monthly reports over the course of a couple of years makes clear that IWMA sections in New York and elsewhere cast their nets widely in recruiting the foreign-born, at least those of European origin. The correspondence reveals that in May 1871, Marx complained that there were no branches of "U.S. workmen" but only those formed by "foreigners residing in the United States"—a charge with which Sorge, on behalf of the CC, took issue.[20]

  · Yet, on the basis of the three aforementioned facts about Sorge and the "Irish strategy" Messer-Kruse defends his thesis that Marx's proposal "encouraged Sorge and his comrades to turn their backs on their own internationalist principles of human brotherhood and ignore the needs of their potential black constituency."[21] This is an awfully thin database upon which to rest such weighty allegations.[22]

"Narrow Trade Unionism"

"In Sorge's determinedly instrumentalist vision of social change," according to Messer-Kruse, "his concept of the working class was shrunk to the point where it encompassed little more than the trade union movement."[23] The "Irish strategy" "mightily reinforced" his "narrow trade unionism" with its exclusive focus on "bread and butter issues." Sorge, infected with "cynical economism," viewed trade union work as the be-all and end-all of political work. Marx, Messer-Kruse claims, encouraged this failing when "on the eve of the splitting of the American International [December 1871], he wrote a confidential letter [November 10] to Carl Speyer and Friedrich Sorge, telling then that "you must strive to win the support of the Trade Unions at all costs."[24] By "confidential" Messer-Kruse is apparently alluding to the fact that the letter was not an official communication of the GC and that Marx specifically requested that Speyer, to whom it was written and a contact he had known from London, share it only with Sorge.

To understand what Marx may have meant—since this came at the very end of the letter and without elaboration—it is necessary to know what Messer-Kruse ignores: his overall approach to trade union work. That requires a broader context.

The bottom line for Marx in the IWMA and the lesson he had drawn on the experiences of the 1848 revolutions, was the stance of independent working-class political action—the emancipation of the working class could only be achieved by workers *themselves*. Be they Messer-Kruse's Yankee Internationalists or any similar grouping, well-intentioned liberals and progressive petit bourgeois forces could in no way liberate workers. Marx wrote the documents, the preamble and rules, that embodied this idea, which were approved at the founding of the IWMA. The fight for independent working-class political action was the training ground and precondition for the rule of the proletariat and its allies. Independent working-class political action required that workers needed to have their own political party. They could not look to or depend on any other class, including the best-intentioned middle-class liberal forces and their parties. To do so would mean they were still not yet prepared to take state power and rule in their own name and that their authentic interests, irreconcilable with bourgeois rule, would be subordinated to capital by the mediating agency of middle-class reform.

Since the working class, given its history and situation, was born into the role of subjects, not of rulers, it would have to prepare itself for such a historical transition. While 1848 had taught that workers could only depend on themselves, it did not mean that workers should never enter into coalitions with liberal petit bourgeois forces. To the contrary, they were obligated to do so as part of the process of workers eventually taking state power in what Marx called the "people's alliance."[25] But that could only be achieved from a position of strength if—and only if—workers had their own organizations, independent of other social layers.

There is nothing more pedagogical by Marx or Engels about the process of workers taking state power than the letter Marx wrote to Friedrich Bolte, one of the leaders in the German section in New York, about ten days before the expulsion of Section 12 (the context for the letter was discussed in chapter 4). The epigraph that begins this appendix, an excerpt from the letter, is especially relevant for this discussion. What Marx said is that in those settings, such as the United States, where the working class is not yet politically mature, that is, doesn't yet have its own political party, it can nevertheless take steps toward that end through the daily struggles between workers and bosses.

Within the larger global view, Marx took into account—again, contrary to what Messer-Kruse would have us believe—the particular reality of the United States. It should be remembered that in the aftermath of the overthrow of slavery he was under no illusion that socialist revolution was on the agenda, that workers were set to take state power. Slavery's demise meant rather that the United States had now entered into a prolonged state of capitalist expansion with all the consequences this implied in the process of proletarianization. Marx recognized that while America had been at the center of the worldwide revolutionary process during its Civil War and immediately afterwards, the pendulum had now swung back to Europe, especially in Britain with the beginning of the upsurge in the Irish struggle in 1867. Only after extended capitalist development would political momentum swing back across the ocean. Political work in the United States would have to adjust to this new reality—specifically, the slow but inevitable process of creating an hereditary working class for the first time in America. And the fate of Black America would be intimately tied to those developments, as indeed history would verify.

In the daily struggles between capital and labor, trade unions figured significantly. Marx's resolution, entitled "Trade Unions, Their Past, Present, and Future"—which he wrote for the 1866 IWMA congress, and approved by the delegates, more explicitly than ever laid out his views on trade unions. Historically, unions had been the necessary means by which workers defended themselves through the daily "guerilla fights" around "everyday necessities"—what Messer-Kruse calls the "bread and butter issues." But in so doing, unions, consciously or not, became the vehicles for organizing workers *as a class*. Currently, however, unions had yet to "fully understand their power of acting against the system of wage slavery itself. They therefore kept too much aloof from the general social and political movements," Marx stated. An exception was the fight for the eight-hour workday in the United States. As for the future, Marx elaborated on his criticism and preempted—as well as anticipated Lenin's critique of economism—any subsequent claim that he was infected with "narrow trade unionism."

> Apart from their original purposes, [the unions] must now learn to act deliberately as organising centres of the working class in the broad interest of its complete emancipation. They must aid every social and political movement tending in that direction. Considering themselves and acting as the champions and representatives of the whole working class, they cannot fail to enlist the non-society men into their ranks. They must look carefully after the interests of the worst paid trades, such as the agricultural labourers. . . . They must convince the world at large that their efforts, far from being narrow and selfish, aim at the emancipation of the downtrodden millions.[26]

Marx understood in the marrow of his bones what constituted "narrow and selfish trade unionism" and he unambiguously fought against it.

Contrary to what Messer-Kruse alleges, Marx's conflict with the British trade union heads on the GC was due just to such a mentality *on their* part. It prevented them from embracing the Irish struggle and defending the Communards of the Paris insurgency in 1871—exactly the kinds of social and political movements that Marx enthusiastically embraced and promoted. The other political compliment to the economist outlook of the British labor officialdom was their support of Gladstone's Liberal Party and opposition to forming an independent workers' party.

At the London conference of the IWMA in September 1871, attended by a representative of the New York sections, Marx lambasted them. "The TRADE UNIONS . . . are an aristocratic minority—the poor workers cannot belong to them . . . peasants, day labourers never belong to these societies. The TRADE UNIONS can do nothing by themselves—they will remain a minority—they have no power over the mass of proletarians . . ."[27]

In the midst of the fight within the American section, Marx, in the same letter to Bolte—and what Messer-Kruse ignores—advised him and the other German Americans to be more tolerant of the Section 12 forces. The reasons he gave are most instructive. The GC, he said, included a couple of individuals who "belong to the sect of the late Bronterre O'Brien [1804–1864], and are full of follies and CROTCHETS, such as CURRENCY quackery, false emancipation of women, and the like."[28] Bronterre had been a left Chartist and later an advocate of a utopian monetary scheme that Marx dismissed. Then, he wrote: "They are thus BY NATURE allies of Section 12 in New York and its kindred souls." That the two GC members, he suggests, may have been in touch with Section 12 was not forbidden by the body's norms. Only if they did so in an official capacity or compromised in some way the integrity of the GC would "necessary measures . . . be taken to prevent such mischief." In spite of their "follies," however, "these O'Brienites . . . constitute an often necessary counterweight to TRADE UNIONISTS in the COUNCIL. They are more revolutionary, firmer on the LAND QUESTION, less NATIONALISTIC, and not susceptible to bourgeois bribery in one form or another. Otherwise they would have been kicked out long ago."[29] Messer-Kruse's lawyer's brief against Marx conveniently ignores this advice, since it impeaches the credibility of his thesis.

Marx emphasized that when it came to "narrow trade unionism" he was willing to ally with forces that resembled in many ways the very types that Messer-Kruse claims he and his comrades in New York didn't want in the International—in order to negate the influence of economism. Marx's reference to "bourgeois bribery" alluded to the political component of "narrow trade unionism," the class-collaborationist course in which the trade union heads on the GC had engaged with Gladstone's Liberal Party. Contrary to what Messer-Kruse insinuates, "non-Marxism" was not incompatible—at least in Marx's view—with membership in the International and its ruling bodies. Having "revolutionary" positions and acting in a principled manner was far more important to him than trade union credentials. Less than a year later at the Hague congress—after most of the British trade union officials had completely severed their ties with the International—Marx left little doubt about what he thought of them. When one of their sympathizers questioned the credentials of Maltman Barry, a journalist and chair of the new British section of the IWMA, with the charge that he didn't represent English workers, Marx retorted: "[I]t does credit to Barry that he is not one of the so-called leaders of the English workers, since these men are more or less bribed by the bourgeoisie and the government."[30] Although his widely publicized remarks led to a complete break with the trade union heads, Marx was unapologetic two years later: "I knew that I was letting myself in for unpopularity, slander, etc., but such consequences have always been a matter of indifference to me. Here and there people are beginning to see that in making that denunciation I was only doing my duty."[31]

To argue, therefore, as Messer-Kruse does, that Marx "reinforced" Sorge's "narrow trade unionism" because his approach supposedly denied any room for the kind of broader social justice issues that the Yankee Internationalists favored is not only bogus but dishonest. There is nothing in his record from which Sorge could have drawn a conclusion contrary to Marx's explicitly revolutionary approach on this question.

"False Emancipation of Women"[?]

This may be the best place to take up a recurring charge in Messer-Kruse's account—Marx's alleged opposition to women's emancipation. As with his specious claim against Marx on the trade union issue, the indictment is tissue thin—a couple of sentences in a letter. Since neither he nor the source he's quoting from provides the full statement, a little hygiene is in order.[32] Marx's comment is directed to a close political contact in Germany in December 1868, Ludwig Kugelmann. The "smoking gun" comes at the very end as a postscript: "Is your wife also active in the German ladies' great emancipation campaign? I think that German women should begin by driving their husbands to self-emancipation."[33] Anyone who knows or takes the time to read the correspondence between

Marx and Kugelmann will find it studded with jocular commentary. It's clear that Marx also had a joking relation with the latter's wife, Gertrud, often in regard to women's equality issues. (I quote below one such comment made two years earlier, which must be read alongside the nugget mined by Messer-Kruse.) On the basis of these two sentences both Messer-Kruse and Mari Jo Buhle claim that Marx either "treated the subject ["woman suffrage"] with derision," or was "susceptible to . . . beliefs" that were hostile to women's equality.[34] So few words taken out of context do not, fortunately, make a serious case, let alone a verdict in the court of historical inquiry.

What about the previously quoted comment Marx made to Bolte in which he upbraided the O'Brienites for their advocacy of what he calls the "false emancipation of women"? Does this lend credence to the charge? But as with the "narrow trade unionism" accusation, historical context and facts are more useful than pseudo-scholarship.

The best place to begin is with Marx's work within the IWMA since this is the objective setting that frames Messer-Kruse's charges.[35] Related to his approach to trade unions was his systematic attention to the inclusion of women in the workers' movement in general and the International in particular. From the very beginning Marx was the most conscious of all the GC members in putting the issue of women on the agenda. To do so meant having to oppose in the International the followers of Joseph Proudhon, the so-called "father" of anarchism, especially its French section. They were "resolutely hostile to women working" and the "participation of women in industry."[36]

In London in September 1865, the first annual meeting of the International took place. It had the responsibility of drawing up the agenda for the IWMA's first congress in Geneva a year later. Marx proposed that "Female and Child Labour" should be one of the questions for discussion at the congress. [37] Along with the proposal to the Geneva meeting on "Trade Unions," referred to earlier, Marx submitted various others, two of which referred explicitly to girls and women. The "Limitation of the Working-Day," called for an eight-hour day and significant restrictions on "nightwork." This proposal "refers only to adult persons, male or female, the latter, however, to be rigorously excluded from all *nightwork whatever*, and all sort of work harmful to the delicacy of the sex, or exposing their bodies to poisonous and otherwise deleterious agencies."

The other proposal, "Juvenile and Children's Labour (Both Sexes)" began with an unmistakably clear materialist premise: "We consider the tendency of modern industry to make children and juvenile persons of both sexes co-operate in the great work of social production, as a progressive, sound and legitimate tendency, although under capital it was distorted into an abomination."[38] It then went on to outline a series of concrete proposals to counter the "abomination" through public education for all young people between nine and seventeen years of age. However, unlike the previous proposal this one made no distinction between the sexes. While this isn't the place to discuss the merits of these proposals it should be noted that in the context of 1866 these measures embodied progressive ideas on the advancement of women's rights.

In June 1867 the GC voted to bring on Harriet Law (1831–1897) as a member, the only woman to ever serve on it. Law was a well-known secular activist. Although Marx was absent for the decision—he was busy with the final preparations for *Capital*'s publication in September of that year—it is noteworthy that Frederick Lessner (1825–1910) seconded the motion in spite of the fact that it had been moved by a sometime opponent. Lessner was Marx's most loyal supporter on the GC before Engels came on board in 1870. Marx, in preparing the agenda for the upcoming congress in Lausanne for the approval of the GC, which now included Law, proposed two resolutions for debate. The first was "On the practical means by which to enable the [IWMA] to fulfil its function of a common centre of action for the working classes, female and male, in the struggle tending to their complete emancipation from the domination of capital."[39] Whether Law's presence made a difference, this appears to be the first instance of Marx explicitly signaling in an IWMA document that the organization, in spite of its name, was not exclusively male. From then on, almost every subsequent address or declaration issued in the name of the organization or an affiliate that Marx either wrote or edited no longer addressed only "working men" but "working women" as well.[40]

For the upcoming congress in Geneva, Marx unsuccessfully sought to have Law be elected by the GC as one of its three delegates; she was defeated by one vote.[41] Marx, nevertheless, was proud of the fact that the International had "appointed a lady, Madame Law, as a member of the [GC]" as he boasted in a letter to the aforementioned Ludwig Kugelmann. While that comment was made somewhat jokingly, to be shared with his wife Gertrud, Marx was nonetheless serious about the issue of women in the workers' movement:

> Joking aside, very great progress was demonstrated at the last congress of the American 'LABOR UNION' . . . by the fact that it treated women workers with full parity; by contrast, the English, and to an even greater extent the gallant French, are displaying a marked narrowness of spirit in this respect. Everyone who knows anything of history also knows that great social revolutions are impossible without the feminine ferment. Social progress may be measured precisely by the social position of the fair sex (plain ones included).[42]

This comment reveals Marx's advocacy of women's "full parity" in the workers' movement as well as a sober and honest assessment of reality at that time; only in the United States—where the IWMA affiliate, the National Labor Union, formed in 1866, advocated equal pay for equal work for women and men—was real progress being made. If Messer-Kruse is to be believed, such praise by Marx for advances on the woman question in the United States should be treated as fiction, not fact.

On the eve of and after the Basel congress in 1869—which Marx didn't attend—he also took the lead in putting women workers on the GC's agenda. His proposal, seconded by Hermann Jung (1830–1901), another close supporter and agreed to by the GC, stated the "female president Philomène Rozan" of the Lyons silk-workers union be given "special credentials" to attend the upcoming congress.[43] At his first GC meeting after the congress, Marx, in an optimistic report about developments in the German movement, drew his colleagues attention to the fact that the bookbinders union in Leipzig had just agreed for the first time to admit women members.[44] Finally, about a year and a half before the IWMA's effective end and in the aftermath of the Paris Commune—where women Communards had played a vanguard role, an accomplishment duly noted by Marx in his *Civil War in France*—he raised another proposal in the GC. It was later adopted by the London conference in September 1871: "The Conference recommends the formation of female branches among the working class. It is, however, understood that this resolution does not at all interfere with the existence or formation of branches composed of both sexes."[45] The basis for this proposal was, as Marx noted, the increasing number, in some countries, of women in industrial jobs. His main concern was that these women workers become union members. If single-sex unions facilitated that process, then so be it. Such a tactic, however, was not meant to rule out what the bookbinders were doing in Leipzig.

With the IWMA closing down shop—effectively in 1873—Marx no longer had an organization in which to concretize his views on women as workers. Yet the perspective that he put forward within the International during its eight-year existence was far more advanced than anything that had been done on this matter until then and for some time afterward.[46] For this reason, as suggested above, it is of utmost importance to put Marx's advocacy of women's rights, or more correctly, working women's rights—from his class perspective the distinction was crucial—in context. He was not the first voice in the nineteenth century to recognize the relation between social revolution and the advancement of women. Others, like the utopian socialist Charles Fourier (1772–1837) and his feminist co-thinker Flora Tristan (1803–1844) had said as much decades earlier. Moreover, there were contemporary petit bourgeois forces and opponents like J. Stuart Mill who were also active in advancing women's rights, particularly the acquisition of the vote. But only Marx led the fight for a working-class perspective on the advancement of women.[47] While Tristan may have been the first to see the need to make the connections between the workers' and women's movements, Marx was unique in his revolutionary approach to the question.[48] With hindsight it is clear just how prescient his views were. Had they been implemented the proletarian movement would have been on firmer footing—not to mention the growing women's rights movement as well.

While Marx was in the vanguard on the woman question in the GC, others more directly and singularly focused on this issue made major contributions in the United States at the time; I leave aside for a moment figures inside Section 12. The distinction Marx made, as noted earlier, between working-class and bourgeois women might suggest—and I stress "might" since the written record isn't transparent—that he failed to see that democratic rights for all women would be an advance for working-class women and thus the proletariat as a whole. Like his approach to race (see chapter 4) Marx's position on women must be seen in the larger context of the world in which he lived and worked, specifically, the particular periods in which he did political work such as the one now under discussion. Messer-Kruse's method of indicting him on the basis of snippets taken out of context is exactly how not to proceed.

Returning to Marx's disdain for the "false emancipation of women," there is a hint about what he may have meant. It comes in the notes he prepared for a report to the GC about the split in the American section. He excerpted a position paper in which Section 12 stated its disagreements with the German Americans in Section 1. Most interesting is what Marx highlighted in a sentence about what it called the "necessary precursors of the more radical reforms demanded by the International"—views it regarded as counterposed to those of Section 1. The sentence states: *"The extension of equal citizenship to women, the world over, must **precede** any general change in the subsisting relations of capital and labour."* The highlighting of "precede" appears to be Marx's doing. That the sentence was selected from the rest of the statement is certain and in itself telling. I suspect that it means that he disagreed with the claim, especially if he read "equal citizenship" to mean full equality for women.

Nothing Marx ever wrote suggested that he held equality for women to be the precondition for the working class coming to power. Rather, his position was that the liberation of women would only come with the overthrow of capital and the proletariat becoming the ruling class. Evidence for this interpretation came seven months later at the Hague congress when Marx argued against seating William West, a leader of Section 12. Referring to the above statement, he said Section 12, "place[s] the women's question before the workers' question."[49] West said, in response, that "the emancipation of women must precede the emancipation of the workers."[50] It is with this understanding of the position of Section 12 that he probably used the phrase "false emancipation of women," actually, the chimera of freedom supposedly achievable prior to the post-capitalist regime.

Again, this interpretation hinges on Marx's understanding of "equal citizenship" and does not address the issue of suffrage. There is nothing to suggest that he opposed woman's suffrage; the evidence indicates that he supported it, as will be seen shortly. His overall position on suffrage, like other democratic rights, was that it was only a means to real democracy or human emancipation. To the extent that proponents of suffrage for women also assumed that it would bring equality for women, Marx qualified this too as an example of the "false emancipation of women," with great weight I should add.

There is no doubt that Marx prioritized the struggle of working-class women. As his praise for the aforementioned "full parity" position of the NLU indicates, he indeed viewed advances for women through the lens of class. What is less clear is how he viewed the efforts of bourgeois feminists. Was he principally opposed to their demands or entering into coalitions with them to fight for women's equality? There is, again, nothing in the record or program to say that he wasn't.

If the litmus test is, as Messer-Kruse seems to believe, Marx's attitude toward Victoria Woodhull, the most visible leader of Section 12 and well-known proponent of woman suffrage, for her sister Tennessee it merits rejection. To try to reduce, as he does, the struggle for women's rights to the activities of Woodhull is to belittle the significance of a movement that was far more important than her individual contributions, however spectacular they may have been for the two years of her participation.

A word or two about the Claflin sisters is in order. For Marx to call them "bourgeois" was not to hurl, as Messer-Kruse seems to believe, an epithet but to accurately describe who they were—at least in this chapter of their colorful lives.

They were raised as hustlers and self-promoters. The Al Sharpton of her generation, Victoria, especially, had the ability to glom on to individuals and real social movements—as diverse as Cornelius Vanderbilt and Marx himself, woman suffrage, spiritualism, free love, and radical labor politics—to realize her personal ambitions. In 1871 she discovered Marx and labor and decided, as one of her most recent biographers notes, that "her new constituency of workers would be a symbolic army to protect her against attack from the privileged class that continued to heap scorn upon her."[51] This drove her to the cause of the IWMA—which was growing in popularity—and the individual most associated with it. She was financially able to do so because of she and her sister's very intimate ties to the wealthiest capitalist in New York, Vanderbilt. He made it possible for her to become a brokerage banker—a bourgeois enough profession—as well as underwriting her political activities, including her run for president in 1872.

Woodhull's advocacy of "free love," while perhaps an advance in puritanical America, momentary support for woman suffrage, or seeking Frederick Douglass as her vice-presidential candidate in her bid for the presidency in 1872—though Messer-Kruse ignores that he declined the nomination—could not, however, transcend her bourgeois moorings. She violated the spirit, if not the letter, of independent working-class political action, a basic norm of the IWMA. Sorge and other leaders of the German section, whatever their possible shortcomings on women's equality and discomforts about "free love," had every right from the beginning to be suspicious of Woodhull and her crew in Section 12. The fact, as Messer-Kruse admits, that "none were ultimately more central to the meteoric rise and fall of the Yankee International" than the two sisters speaks volumes about the real intellectual, social, and political substance of this current.[52]

Employing his and Marx's historical materialist method, Engels put the actions of the Claflin sisters in the International in perspective. Unlike Europe, the bourgeoisie in America was not as frightened by the appearance of the IWMA as were their counterparts across the ocean. Because they had been in power from the beginning—due to the absence of a monarchial land-owning feudal tradition—they were more confident about their rule and could actually flirt with radical ideas. America's more progressive character was revealed in another way.

> The extent to which American society is ahead of European is strikingly exemplified by the fact that it was two American *ladies* who first discovered this and attempted to set up a business on the basis of it. Whilst the men of the European bourgeoisie trembled in fear of the International, two female members of the American bourgeoisie [the Claflin sisters] conceived the plan of exploiting this society of horrors—and they almost got away with it.[53]

So exactly at the moment when, according to Messer-Kruse, Marx and Engels did not appreciate or understand what had been achieved in the United States, Engels, in 1872, not only recognized it but argued that it was "strikingly" confirmed by what women could do in America—regardless of the fact that they were bourgeois. The thesis, quoted above, that Marx put to Kugelmann in 1866—"Social progress may be measured precisely by the social position of the fair sex (plain ones included)"—is exactly what Engels drew on for his claim. What Messer-Kruse cannot or will not understand is that for Marx and Engels those advances were most advantageous in the process of making real democracy a reality for the first time in the United States.

Just as was true for the national question—on Ireland—there is evidence that Marx's views on women's equality likewise evolved. From his earliest comments on patriarchy (see chapter 1), marriage, and the family in his *Economic and Philosophical Manuscripts*, to his research in the decade before the IWMA on the origins of women's oppression—which became Engels's *The Origins of the Family, Private Property, and State*, the first attempt at a rational/scientific explanation—it can be assumed that they certainly deepened with theoretical and programmatic consequences.[54] If there is uncertainty about his stance on the question of woman suffrage in the period that Messer-Kruse has as his focus, a comment by Engels—whose views can be assumed to reflect those of Marx—in 1877 to a woman friend in Germany should dispel such doubts. Aware that she could not take part in the elections there because of her gender, he said, "When we take over the helm, not only will women be given the vote, they will be elected and make speeches." He proudly told her also that he had recently voted in the local school board elections in London and "gave all my 7 votes to a lady who, as a result, had more votes than any of the other 7 candidates in the election."[55]

Three years later Marx and Engels helped to draft the electoral program for what was in Engels's opinion the *"first real worker's movement* in France." In the preamble, which he wrote, Marx began with the premise "That the emancipation of the producing class ["or proletariat"] is that all human beings without distinction of sex or race."[56] In the founding documents of the IWMA, sixteen years earlier, Marx mentioned only race. Perhaps this change in wording reflected the growing consciousness at a global level about women's equality. On the other hand, it could be argued, given what Marx once said about the IWMA—the forces that brought it into existence would not adhere together around a communist program—that he had to refrain from mentioning "sex" in order to win approval for what he wrote. But that choice reflects a more basic assumption and strategy—the priority of being a part of the "real movement," that is, the working class and the real process of elaborating a program and organization through trial and error, especially in the pioneering stage in which Marx and Engels led.

The contributions of middle-class advocates for women's equality deserve recognition. But what Messer-Kruse misses, and what Marx understood—correctly, in my opinion—is that the fight for women's equality, as was true with that of race, had to be waged *inside* the workers' movement if it was to succeed and advance. I only state the principle and leave aside the question of how to carry this out and whether those who claimed to function in Marx's name actually did so. All reforms, he understood, even the most far-reaching of them, would be temporary under capitalism. Only the working class had the objective motivation and social capability to bring about full human equality. It was no accident that Russian women got the right to vote, as a result of the Bolshevik revolution, before women in the United States and that the revolutionary government legalized homosexual relations in 1917. (Post–Lenin Russia also confirms—long before 1989—what happens to women when the working class ceases to directly exercise political hegemony.)

That most American workers in 1871 had little idea of their worth or capacity did not make their potential power any less real. This underscores why patient work and explanation was required on the part of those armed with such visionary knowledge and meant being organically linked to the working class to get a hearing for these ideas. Anything that got in the way of this—proletarian pedagogy and propaganda—including the false posturing of the Woodhull leadership, had to be opposed and rejected. It may have been easier for a middle-class women's rights advocate to work with the Section 12 crowd—though it should not be forgotten, as Messer-Kruse seems to do, that almost all of the national leaders of the woman suffrage movement parted ways with the Claflin sisters by the fall of 1872, the same time that the IWMA officially bid them adieu.[57] But as history showed, that milieu lacked the fortitude for the long haul. Marx's basic premise, with which Messer-Kruse fundamentally disagrees, was that only the proletariat would go all the way.

Marx's "Machinations"

Since politics is almost always the basis for organizational disputes, only after exploring the former in depth is it appropriate to assess the latter. On December 3, 1871, the New York-based Central Committee of the American branch of the IWMA, headed by Sorge, voted to expel Section 12 and three others in New York from the organization. The dismissed sections then formed a separate federation. Two such bodies thus came into existence. This development came to be known in the International as the "American split." In March, four months later, the London-based GC, on the basis of recommendations Marx made, upheld the Central Committee decision and voted to suspend Section 12 until the IWMA congress in the Hague in September could make a final determination. At the same time, it recommended that the two federations unite. In May, the GC voted to recognize only the original body—the old Central Committee under Sorge's leadership. The Hague congress upheld the GC decision and the IWMA officially ended its relation with Section 12. At every stage, according to Messer-Kruse, the expulsion of Section 12 was done with Marx's connivance and "machinations."

Before getting into Messer-Kruse's specific charges about Marx, it should be understood that though Marx exercised more influence than anyone else in GC, it was only of a "moral" nature, as he once explained. He had no authority above and beyond what the other members ceded to him. His ability to lead the GC was due to the enormous respect Marx garnered as a result of his tireless efforts, his willingness to put in the requisite time and energy at the level of programmatic and day-to-day organizational tasks, including the so-called shit work. Precisely because the GC lacked any real enforcement power, Marx was discreet about intervening in local affairs.[58]

Messer-Kruse is hard-pressed to find a shred of evidence that Marx had a hand in the expulsion of Section 12 in December 1871. The best that he can do is to convict by innuendo. If there's no Marx smoking gun, it's only because, unlike Sorge, "he did not perceive Section 12 as a viable alternative or threat to the well-organized, disciplined Section 1" of the German Americans.[59] The obvious implication is that Marx would have indeed acted in some kind of dictatorial, undemocratic manner if he thought it was necessary.

Once the GC had to respond to the expulsion, this is when the diabolical Marx—who had no "rival" on the GC "at the game of party politics"—went to work. Messer-Kruse issues a three-count indictment. The first is that Marx "bypassed the subcommittee" of the GC headed by Georg Eccarius that was "instructed to prepare a report on the matter" and presented it himself because he was "suspicious of Eccarius's sympathy toward the Yankees."[60] In fact, the GC minutes state only that "Citizen Engels proposed that the whole matter be referred to the Sub-Committee"—a motion that was "carried unanimously." Messer-Kruse's creative rewriting of the minutes notwithstanding, there were no such instructions. But more important, Messer-Kruse reinvents the organization of the GC. "The *Standing Committee*, or *Sub-Committee*," as the editors of the GC minutes book point out, "included Corresponding Secretaries for different countries, the General Council's Secretary and Treasurer. *Headed by Marx* [my italics], it exercised daily leadership of the International's activities, prepared documents which were then submitted for consideration to the General Council."[61] Eccarius, in other words, was not the head of the subcommittee—Marx was. As corresponding secretary for America, which he became in October, 1871 at Marx's suggestion, Eccarius was only a member of the subcommittee.[62]

Eccarius, who disagreed with one of Marx's recommendations, was upset with the fact that Marx submitted his report without presenting it to the subcommittee first. We know this from one of two letters Marx sent to Sorge about his report and the votes of the GC. But there was nothing in the bylaws of the GC that said that subcommittee reports had to be presented to it before going to the GC. As Marx explained to Sorge in his letters, he presented his report directly to the GC "in order to save time"—because of other pressing matters before the GC the issue had been postponed on a number of occasions. The GC "fully approved this proceeding, after my statement of the reasons which had induced me to act as I have done." Since Eccarius approved of this procedure he "ought to have dropped his personal spleen."[63] In other words, Eccarius voted with the rest of the GC to have the report come directly to it. His anger stemmed from the reports's recommendations—a concrete example of how organizational disputes are dictated by political differences. Only if one begins with the premise of a conspiracy is it possible to read what happened with Messer-Kruse's spin. The tone of Marx's letters to Sorge makes clear that there was no prior understanding between them about what Marx would report to the GC.

Messer-Kruse's second charge is directed to the report itself—that Marx manipulated the evidence against the Section 12. He "determined the 'facts' with which the rest of the General Council would debate the fate of the Yankees." What Messer-Kruse is actually referring to are the rough notes and excerpts from Section 12's positions published in its semi-official organ, *Woodhull & Claflin's Weekly*, that Marx drew on for his report.[64] Since the minutes do not quote any of this, there is no way that he can know with certainty what Marx actually presented to the GC to motivate his proposals. Rather than engage in speculation and invention, honesty and accuracy dictate the need to refer to the actual proposals that Marx presented to the GC members for their vote. They contain the motivations he employed.

Messer-Kruse disputes why the GC sustained the expulsion of Section 12. He alleges, his third charge, that Marx argued for it on the basis of "fraudulent" evidence—Section 12's supposed violation of IWMA rules. Specifically, Marx framed his proposal as follows: "Considering, that Section No. 12 . . . has not only passed a formal resolution by virtue of which 'each section' possesses 'the independent right' to construe, according to its fancy, 'the proceedings of the several congresses' and the 'General Rules and Regulations,' but moreover has fully acted up to this doctrine."[65] Thus, the charge was that Section 12 claimed the right to freely interpret IWMA rules. Messer-Kruse says this was bogus because "Marx failed to mention that this resolution, proposed by a lone member of Section 12, had been resoundingly voted down."[66] His proof, however, is buried in an unclear footnote.[67]

Why relegate to a footnote such supposed evidence given the seriousness of the charge? Messer-Kruse appears to suggest that the "independent right" proposal was mistakenly published by Section 12 as if it had been actually adopted. Not until after the GC decision in May, however, was what the section "ultimately said" published. On the other hand, at the Hague congress, Section 12 leader William West said the section "never took such a decision, but only discussed it." Thus, Messer-Kruse has a different reading from West about the reality of the "independent right" proposal. Confusion may have existed about the proposal. Messer-Kruse is obligated to provide evidence, given his charge, that Marx knew this to be the case and, therefore, acted in bad faith. Instead, he only spreads insinuation.

Since, according to Messer-Kruse, Marx manipulated the evidence in his report it was no surprise that his proposals "were passed by a lopsided vote." This Marx-baiting allows

Messer-Kruse to avoid the actuality of the vote. Eccarius, whom he applauds for being more sympathetic to the Yankees—he "had developed a keener understanding of America's social realities"—voted with everyone else on the GC for suspension of Section 12.

Eccarius, in fact, wrote a letter to Marx—which apparently eluded Messer-Kruse's scholarship—"dated December 20, 1871" in which he stated that "it is necessary to expel Section No. 12 from" the International—three months prior to Marx's proposal.[68] Where Eccarius and three other GC members differed with Marx—the only nonunanimous vote—was on the proposal "that in the future there be admitted no new American section of which two-thirds at least do no consist of wage-labourers."[69] The GC in its overwhelming majority—the vote was 16 to 3—reaffirmed what was Marx's fundamental principle for an IWMA that was proletarian in composition, one which fought for independent working-class political action, thereby rejecting the petit bourgeois orientation of Section 12. There were other significant aspects to Marx's proposals but for space and subject-matter considerations I refrain from discussing them. The case of Eccarius, however, should be mentioned in this context. As noted earlier, Messer-Kruse charges that Marx mistreated his longtime comrade through all of this, which led to a permanent break between them. Suffice it to say that this charge has long existed in the marxological arsenal. There is no better refutation of it than Hal Draper's very authoritative note, "Poor Eccarius and the Marx-Monster."[70]

Messer-Kruse's next set of charges focus on the Hague congress of the International in September 1872. Referring to what was clearly the central issue at the congress—the showdown between those who agreed with Marx's perspective on the International and those who agreed with that of the anarchist Mikhail Bakunin—"Marx and Engels," according to Messer-Kruse, "used every weapon and trick they could to slant the battlefield of the upcoming congress to their favor."[71] Thus, there's no reason for the reader to wonder about the fate of the GC's decision to expel Section 12. This is not the place to address all the charges and countercharges about Marx's fight with the Bakunin forces.

I have addressed elsewhere the high stakes in this fight, and others have provided more detail.[72] As was true with the "American split," the fight was first and foremost about political differences that were reflected in organizational disputes. There were a number of parallels between the two disputes.

"Marx and Engels," Messer-Kruse alleges, "knew that the single most important task at the convention was to dominate the committee on credentials. Whoever controlled that committee would carry the day."[73] The crux of this claim is that Marx and Engels packed the congress in their struggle against Bakunin, thus stacking the cards against the appeal of Section 12. Anyone familiar with delegated political meetings knows that credential issues can only be fully assessed by looking at the larger context and the actions of all parties.

Marx and Engels's vigilance and deliberate actions around credentials were perfectly justified when it is understood what they were up against. As Hal Draper has persuasively argued and documented, "Bakunin's was the first leftist movement to apply its conspiratorial patterns of subversion not to assail society at large or to defend itself against the police, but to destroy other socialists' organizations."[74] The operation against the International was carried out under the banner "against authority," the GC under Marx's leadership. This was a variant of the "independent right" espoused by Section 12. Given Bakunin's track record—let alone what is now public knowledge that Marx and Engels didn't know at the time—they would have been not only naive but politically irresponsible to not take action to prevent Bakunin from packing the congress with shell affiliates. It was not unreasonable for them to assume, as Engels told a comrade in Geneva, that Bakunin's operation would resort to "forged mandates," i.e., bogus delegate credentials, including some "from America (from the Woodhull people)."[75]

Marx spoke against the seating of William West of Section 12. Messer-Kruse claims that his opposition "revolved around his association with Section 12 and Victoria Woodhull."[76] More accurately, Marx opposed his being seated "because he 1) is a member of the suspended Section No. 12; 2) was a member of the Philadephia Congress, and 3) was a member of the Prince

Street Council. . . . Section No. 12 did not recognize the General Council's decision. West was also a member of the Philadelphia Congress and the Prince Street Council, which refused to recognize the General Council and maintained connections with the Jura Federation; the latter, according to newspaper reports, advised it not to pay subscriptions to the General Council"[77]

The Jura Federation in Switzerland was a stronghold of Bakunin supporters. Though Marx rested his case on these charges, he also accused Section 12 of being composed in the "beginning almost entirely of bourgeois [elements]," and agitating "mainly for women's franchise." As discussed earlier, he charged that they "place the women's question before the worker's question" and that they refused "to recognise that the I.W.[M].A. is a workers' organisation."[78]

West was granted an hour and a half to defend not only his credentials but to reply to the charges by the GC about Section 12 that Marx reiterated. As for the "independent right" proposal, he offered that the section never really adopted such a stance but "only discussed it." West might have won some sympathy from the delegates had he decided not to offer a defense of the *politics* of Section 12. Regarding Marx's charge about the "women's question," West retorted: "the workers' question is also a woman question and"—what Messer-Kruse again conveniently ignores—"the emancipation of women must precede the emancipation of workers." Sorge, the official minute taker wrote in parentheses, "Great animation." Feeling he had nothing to lose after riling the delegates West gave himself free reign. Messer-Kruse omits this outpouring. "The development and solution of the social question is as follows: first man is a slave, then he becomes a wage-worker, then a middle-class man, and finally, through the higher intelligence of man who has raised himself to be a bourgeois, he enters into universal cooperation, i.e., there is a substitution of society for individual labour. The bourgeoisie have and acquire the necessary experience and intelligence which we require in our movement."[79] At this point, I suspect that Marx said to himself, "I rest my case."

Contrary to all of Messer-Kruse's protests that there were no fundamental programmatic differences between his Yankee internationalists and the aims of the IWMA, West's perspective and the reaction it engendered spoke volumes about the deep political gulf between the two factions. In the final analysis, it was this reality that explains their parting of ways, not Marx's "machinations." Lawyer to the end, Messer-Kruse writes that "nine delegates abstained and none voted against expelling the Yankees from the International."[80] Less convoluted and more transparent, the minutes state that "West's mandate [to be seated] is rejected by 49 votes with 9 abstentions." This officially ended the brief flirtation of Woodhull and company with the revolutionary workers' movement.

About Sorge

This is the appropriate place to take up Sorge and his relationship with Marx. Since there is an unambiguously extant record, Messer-Kruse is compelled to admit that Marx and Engels were not always in accord with how Sorge and other German American leaders conducted themselves in the fight with Section 12 in particular, and the Yankee Internationalists in general. In response to their complaints, Marx frequently pointed out to Sorge and his allies that sections enjoyed autonomy as long as its exercise did not violate IWMA rules. He noted that the Central Committee should be more open to working with forces with whom they were not in complete agreement—like those in Section 12—as was Marx's practice in the GC from the beginning. He and Engels criticized Sorge for leading the expulsion of Section 12 in December 1871. Describing Sorge as a "busybody," Engels wrote that had "they only waited 1 day before staging their coup d'état they would have had the answer from here, which would have rendered it superfluous."[81] He was referring to a resolution the GC passed in early November—which didn't arrive in New York until apparently a day after the expulsion—that reaffirmed the authority of the Central Committee regarding Section 12.

Once Marx began reading all the documents about the politics of Section 12 in order to prepare his report to the GC in March 1872, his criticism ceased. His comment to Sorge about the report suggests why: "I have carefully gone through all the correspondence from New York together with everything that appeared in the papers and have discovered that we were by no means duly informed in time about the elements that brought about the breach."[82] While mildly rebuking Sorge for failing to clarify the gravity of the situation, he suggested that Sorge was justified in taking actions against Section 12. A few months later Engels explained to a comrade in Germany that "Sorge and Co. have . . . made a number of formal blunders but if the International in America is not to degenerate into a bourgeois tricksters' society pure and simple, they must have our full support."[83] If Marx and Engels were critical of the way Sorge conducted the struggle, they nevertheless were in basic political agreement with his decision and his leadership, given the forces they had to work with and what they sought to achieve.

Marx first communicated with Sorge in September 1870. Almost all of the six letters he wrote to him before the expulsion of Section 12 dealt with administrative matters regarding the New York branch of the International. Compared to the other German Americans he wrote to, the letters are typically absent of in-depth political discussions. There is little sense, contrary to what Messer-Kruse assumes, that Marx thought he was writing to an experienced comrade who shared his political framework. That would change dramatically in a few years, when Sorge became Marx and Engels's most trusted comrade in America. Sorge came to the Marxist movement in the United States and not Germany, unlike the other Germans Marx was in touch with. Like a number of others who founded Section 1, Sorge had been a partisan of Marx's opponent, Ferdinand Lassalle. Essential to Lassalleanism was the claim that both petit bourgeois and bourgeois liberalism were the main enemies of the working class. In Germany this translated into a search for an enlightened wing of the feudal class with which workers could block to introduce socialism from above. A related tendency was the deprecation of bourgeois democratic rights. To what extent Sorge continued to adhere to such views—if he ever had—is difficult to say, Messer-Kruse's opinions of him notwithstanding.[84]

Although Lassalle was a staunch opponent of trade unions, it might also be argued that in the context of the United States, where a feudal class was absent, knee-jerk opposition to bourgeois liberalism—latent Lassalleanism—could lead to a kind of workerism that elevated trade unions to a status inconsistent with how Marx saw them. Thus, there might be some truth to Messer-Kruse's accusations about Sorge's supposed "narrow trade unionism" and sectarianism toward the Yankees. Yet, in his presentation to the meeting to dissolve the IWMA in Philadelphia in 1876 Sorge "emphasized the need to avoid foreign models, especially the German, and for the Marxists to achieve closer relations with the trade unions."[85] If he still retained, in Messer-Kruse's opinion, his "narrow" trade union focus four years after the "American split," he did not uphold—if he ever had—the German experience as the way to bring the working class into power. It could also be argued that perhaps he had changed his opinions in the aftermath of the fight four years earlier. Another and very likely possibility is simply that his so-called sectarianism toward Section 12 was justified given the reality of Woodhull and company.

As for the charge that Sorge blindly tried to implement Marx's "Irish strategy" without due consideration for the actual situation in New York, Messer-Kruse ignores the city's political landscape after the Civil War and the centrality of the Irish masses in many parts of it.[86] If it was really the case that he was responding to Marx's urging—which Messer-Kruse fails to prove—Sorge was right to take up the challenge. Whether he and his comrades did so effectively is another question, beyond the purview of this book.

Communists had an unavoidable obligation to engage in debate, events, and struggle to see if they could shape results. What Messer-Kruse fails to appreciate is that Sorge, as an aspiring communist, did not require advice from London on the importance of relating to the Irish struggle.

Another example of Sorge being so aware—which apparently escapes Messer-Kruse's attention—was his comment to the GC following the massacre of scores of Irish working people on July

12, 1871, what the bourgeois press likened to the Paris Commune. It was possible that "an agitation will spring from it having for its object the discarding of the old political parties [i.e., Democrats and Republicans]."[87] This and other instances that Messer-Kruse cites as proof for his thesis that Sorge was carrying out Marx's line may likely have had nothing to do with London but what was actually taking place in New York.

In other words, it was the class struggle in New York and not the struggle for self-determination in Ireland that explains Sorge's action. He and his comrades may have understandably and rightly concluded, given the city's politics in that era, that appealing to Irish workers should be their priority. Any possibility of breaking the grip of Tammany Hall and the Democratic Party on the Irish working class would have been an advance not only for it, but for Blacks and women as well.[88]

Whether Sorge was a latent Lassallean or not, it is a fact that a decade after the split Engels began to severely criticize the behavior of the German Americans who spoke in his and Marx's names. Messer-Kruse finds this "ironic" only because he doesn't understand what Marx and Engels were about. By this time Sorge also had begun to denounce the German American sectarians.[89] In a series of very educational letters written to Sorge and another American contact, Engels left little doubt about the Marxist position on the charges Messer-Kruse makes. The occasion was the trade union-backed New York mayoral campaign of Henry George in 1886—discussed in chapter 4—and how the German American–led Socialist Labor Party responded. A few excerpts are revealing.

> The Germans simply have not realised how they can use their theory as a lever that will set the American masses in motion; they . . . treat [theory] in doctrinaire and dogmatic fashion as something which, having once been learnt by rote, is sufficient as it stands for any and every need. To them it is a credo, not a guide to action. Besides which, they refuse to learn English on principle. . . . But just now it is doubly necessary to have a few chaps on our side who are thoroughly versed in theory and in well-tried tactics and who can also speak and write English. . . . it must be done in English, the specifically German character must be sloughed off. . . .[90]

It is far more important that the movement should spread, proceed harmoniously, take root and embrace as much as possible the whole American proletariat, than that it should start and proceed, from the beginning, on theoretically perfect correct lines. There is no better road to theoretical clearness of comprehension than to learn by one's own mistakes. . . . And for a whole large class, there is no other road, especially for a nation so eminently practical and so contemptuous of theory as the Americans.[91]

Engels simply elaborates on Marx's letter to Bolte in September 1871—the epigram that opens this appendix. His advice makes clear that he not only understood the United States and its traditions but also how to bring independent working-class politics to the fore.

Whither Yankee Internationalism?

There is an overriding problem with Messer-Kruse's general argument. If Yankee Internationalism was the embodiment of such a well-trodden American political tradition, then how does Messer-Kruse explain what he terms its "brief independent existence"? Why couldn't it assume another organizational form and continue the tradition? Why did Yankee Internationalism dribble into the twentieth century as "distantly echoing voices" on the "winds of history"? (I refrain from posing what is implicit in his other admission—why did the Marxist alternative triumph?—since it should be clear by now that he does not really understand what that project was about and, thus, what was it that actually triumphed.) Yankee Internationalism gave up the ghost almost immediately after the expulsion of Section 12 from the International. It passed away ignominiously. Sorge reports that the remnants of Section 12, in search of a new sponsor following the Claflin sisters' financial collapse, sought and got the support of a well-known anti-Black Democratic Party politician. This soon destroyed what remaining credibility they retained with progressive forces and Blacks—evidence of the basically flawed character of Section 12.

Nothing is more telling about the substance of Yankee Internationalism than its passive response to the overthrow of Reconstruction. Key to Messer-Kruse's polemic against Marx is the claim that the Yankee Internationalists—owing to their abolitionist roots—had better racial equality credentials than those of his New York opponents. Since I raised the same question about Marx and Engels and those who spoke in their names in the United States in chapter 4, it's fair to subject the Yankee Internationalists to the same standard. Messer-Kruse's claim is weak enough on the basis of the two pieces of evidence he musters to make his case. These items are the decision by a Black military regiment to choose Tennessee Claflin for their honorary commander and the nomination by the Equal Rights Party of Frederick Douglass as Woodhull's vice-presidential running mate. Douglass, as previously noted, declined the nomination. But Messer-Kruse's silence about the impending counterrevolution that became official with the Compromise of 1877 is deafening. Why? As capable a researcher as he is, there is no doubt that if such evidence exists he would have gladly presented it.

One problem in answering the question about the significance of the fate of Yankee Internationalism is that it accepts Messer-Kruse's premise, one that unwarrantedly reduces, just as he did with the woman suffrage movement, the antebellum reform tradition to the fate of Woodhull and company in Section 12. There were in fact outstanding figures in that tradition. One who is glaringly absent in Messer-Kruse's account—except for a brief treatment in the antebellum period—is Wendell Phillips. Not only was he the best-known proponent of the abolitionist cause but for purposes here, more importantly, the most outstanding critic of the impending counterrevolution.

If anyone embodied the Yankee reform tradition, it was Phillips—far beyond anyone associated with Section 12. Significantly, he became a public supporter of the International, though its not clear if he actually joined a section. Phillips thus provides support for Messer-Kruse's argument that following the overthrow of chattel slavery the most conscious reformers took up the cause of wage slavery—labor. As one of his biographers writes, once Phillips came to that cause he began "making speeches that would have done justice to a convinced Marxist."[92] Whether that's true is another question but it registers how far he had moved.

If Phillips represented the best of that tradition and its trajectory, he also embodied its limitations. While willing to totally embrace the newly emerging labor movement after the Civil War, he felt that its destiny lay in "politics rather than as an economic force in competition with capital. The remedy for the exploited classes lay not in strikes and picket lines but in the ballot. "'When a laborer in Massachusetts wants his rights recognized, he disdains to strike. That is not American. . . . His remedy is the orderly operation of the focus of society.'"[93] The great railroad strike of 1877 forced him to reconsider the value of such combative actions. But he still retained the essence of his earlier views. "[H]e was always careful to distinguish Europe from America. Communism might be a good thing for Europe, but it was too doctrinaire for America. . . . Phillips was doing everything he could to prevent the development of class struggle in America. . . . His ideal was . . . the relatively classless society that flourished in Jefferson's day."[94] As radical as he was Phillips, like Messer-Kruse's Yankee Internationalists, was infected with American exceptionalism—not unlike that of Tocqueville. Therein lies the Achilles' heel of the Yankee reform tradition.

Most Yankee reformers in postbellum America became demoralized as the Jeffersonian ideal and the egalitarian hopes of abolitionism gave way to the ruthless logic of the market and capitalist relations of production. Unlike those who grasped Marx's *longue durée* perspective, nothing in the Yankee reform tradition prepared them for what was under way. Marx, on the other hand, had expected just what was taking place. American exceptionalism was being undermined. A hereditary American proletariat, the effective force for bringing about real democracy, was slowly coming into existence for the first time. The demise of the Yankee reform tradition was due fundamentally to basic changes in America's social reality flowing from the institutionalization of industrial capitalism. These and not the "machinations" of Marx were decisive. However significant the Yankee reform tradition's contribution in overthrowing the old order and ushering in the new one, it was now a spent force.

Another striking absence in Messer-Kruse's account is the great railroad strike in 1877, the closest approximation of a national general strike in U.S. history. This explosive labor battle brought together significant numbers of Black and white strikers for the first time. As noted in chapter 4, while Marx and Engels were heartened by the strike they were sober about its fate. More than anything it was confirmation for them about what was now on the agenda in the United States—the working class coming slowly to center stage. Theirs was a prescient glimpse into the future despite the fact that they would not live long enough to see it. It's no accident that Messer-Kruse ignores the strike because it challenges his assertion of the irrelevancy of Marx's perspective about long-term developments in America.

As I noted earlier, Messer-Kruse fundamentally and repeatedly disagrees with Marx and Engels. His clear preference for the politics of the Yankee Internationalists is not just of historical interest. Their "pragmatism . . . was a needed but absent counterbalance to the hubristic faith in political strategizing that became endemic in the American Left after the Yankee elements were purged from the IWA in 1872. Indeed much of the infighting, the circular firing squads that have been the sad and constant plague of the American Left, has been fueled by the persistence of this unreasonable faith in the proscriptive power of abstract social analysis."[95] His target isn't just the "historical" Marx and Engels, but all those subsequently who claim to speak in their names or, what he confesses at the end, the "Old Left." His mission is to defend the authenticity of the "New Left," "homegrown American radicalism," and the "counterculture," by claiming that they are the legitimate, modern descendants of the Yankee Internationalists of Section 12. What an honor!

It's no surprise, then, that Messer-Kruse's critique of Marx's "Irish strategy" has such a contemporary ring to it. In many ways this is a variation on an old New Left theme. The working class, especially its unionized "white" sectors, are politically and socially conservative and therefore, should not be a priority for progressive political work. Besides, as the mantra goes, these toilers are racists and sexists![96] This disdain for the working classes—rendered usually in a self-serving, fallacious caricature—is in some ways reminiscent of the Lassalleans of the nineteenth century who dismissed petit bourgeois and bourgeois liberals in quest of an alternative ally in the feudal junkerdom. Having written off the working class, their New Left counterparts today are in constant quest for some enlightened wing of the bourgeoisie, specifically, inside the Democratic Party or its Green tail. And as was true for the Lassalleans, they have little to show for their utopian efforts—let alone the opportunity costs incurred in this futile quest. Just as Yankee Internationalism was incapable of stemming the tide against Reconstruction, its modern day counterpart has dramatically demonstrated its inability to respond in struggle to the assaults on the gains of the Second Reconstruction.

To write off the working class because of alleged racism or sexism is the luxury of those who have found a niche of temporary comfort within the capitalist nightmare. Such a dismissive approach ignores the dramatic changes in the composition of the U.S. working class, which is more racially integrated and diverse, international and female than ever. It's exactly because of these changes that any nod to nativism, that "homegrown American radicalism" is somehow superior to what exists elsewhere, risks dangers and leads ineluctably to missed opportunities. Workers migrating to the United States from the so-called Third World, where there is less room to escape from the ravages of capitalism, bring with them more advanced revolutionary ideas and traditions, just as the refugees to the United States from Germany's 1848 revolution did. They should be warmly embraced as fellow fighters. Any hint of a nativist response must be completely rejected. Anything less emboldens those forces which seek to overturn the Second Reconstruction and, more broadly, impose the staggering social and economic costs of the actual and coming crisis on the working class as a whole.

Real democrats have opportunities today beyond the most farsighted hopes of their forebears in postbellum America, who lacked the social force of a hereditary proletariat. But that's a potential that can only be realized if recognized and acted on.

Notes

1. Thomas Messer-Kruse, *The Yankee International: Maxism and the American Reform Tradition, 1848–1876* (Chapel Hill and London: University of North Carolina Press, 1998). His book is in a number of important ways an elaboration of the central thesis of Mark A. Lause's "The American Radicals & Organized Marxism: The Initial Experience, 1869–1874" *Labor History*, 33, no. 1 (Fall 1992). Many of the criticisms made here of Messer-Kruse's book apply as well to Lause's article.
2. Ibid., p. 31.
3. Ibid., p. 43.
4. Ibid., p. 151.
5. Ibid., p. 255.
6. Ibid., p. 258.
7. See my *Marx and Engels: Their Contribution to the Democratic Breakthrough* (Albany: State University of New York Press, 2000), specifically, chapters 7, 8, and 9 which, detail Marx's practice in the IWMA. As for the Eccarius charge, see Hal Draper's most informative "Special Note H" in *Karl Marx's Theory of Revolution*, vol. II (New York: Monthly Review Press, 1978). About the "eurocentric" charge, see the discussions on Algeria and Mexico in chapters 2 and 3 in this book and my "The Eurocentric Marx and Engels and Other Related Myths," in Crystal Bartolovich and Neil Lazarus, eds. *Marxism, Modernity and Postcolonial Studies* (Cambridge: Cambridge University Press, 2002).
8. Messer-Kruse, pp. 278–79 fn. 45.
9. **27**, p. 227.
10. See my *Marx and Engels* for details.
11. Bruce Levine, *The Migration of Ideology and the Contested Meaning of Freedom: German-Americans in the Mid-Nineteenth Century*. Occasional Paper no. 7. (Washington, D.C.: German Historical Institute, 1992), pp. 13–15.
12. Meser-Kruse, p. 150.
13. See chapter 4, pp. 154–56.
14. **43**, p. 476.
15. Messer-Kruse, p. 167.
16. **43**, p. 586 fn. 145. See also, Hal Draper, *Marx-Engels Glossary* (New York: Schocken Books, 1986), p. 141.
17. Federal Council Correspondence: Letterbooks, Folder 7, Box 1, International Workingmen's Association Papers, State Historical Society of Wisconsin, August 20, 1871 [hereafter IWAP]. Messer-Kruse gives August 23 as the date.
18. **44**, p. 329.

19. *The Hague Congress of the First International. Minutes and Documents* (Moscow: Progress Publishers, 1972), p. 136. As part of his campaign to slander Marx and his supporters, Messer-Kruse chooses the version of this comment that contains the word "niggers"—from a newspaper article written by Eccarius. In the two other versions—one of which is quoted here—the official minutes of the congress, "Negroes" is employed. Elsewhere when he quotes from the proceedings of the congress Messer-Kruse uses those minutes rather than secondary sources such as newspaper accounts.

20. IWAP, May 21, 1871. He argued that in the United States, unlike Europe, workers from abroad—he no doubt was referring to those from Europe—didn't see themselves as temporary and were in fact called "citizens" or "adopted citizens" and constituted the major and sometimes overwhelming members of trade unions. If space permitted, this would be worth exploring because it has some bearing on Messer-Kruse's assumptions about postbellum working-class politics.

21. Messer-Kruse, p. 151.

22. There is one other comment Sorge made about the Irish of which Messer-Kruse may or may not be aware; its significance will be discussed later.

23. Ibid., p. 146.

24. Messer-Kruse, 151.

25. See my *Marx and Engels*, chapters 3 and 4 for details.

26. **20**, pp. 191–92.

27. **22**, p. 614.

28. **44**, pp. 251–52. As for the "false emancipation of women," this will be revisited shortly.

29. Ibid.

30. *The Hague Congress of the First International. Minutes and Documents* (Moscow: Progress Publishers, 1972), p. 124.

31. **45**, p. 18.

32. Messer-Kruse, pp. 152–53. The cited source is Mari Jo Buhle, *Women and American Socialism, 1870–1920* (Urbana: University of Illinois Press, 1981), pp. 11–12.

33. **43**, p. 175.

34. Messer-Kruse, pp. 152–53, and Buhle, ibid. Buhle, whose argument about the backwardness of German American socialists on women's equality is no doubt an inspiration for Messer-Kruse's thesis, reveals her limited understanding of Marx with the embarrassingly erroneous claim that he "mourned" industrial capitalism's undermining of the traditional family (ibid., p. 9).

35. I am largely drawing on here from my *Marx and Engels*.

36. Edith Thomas, "The Women of the Commune," *The Massachu-setts Review*, 12, no. 3 (1971): 411. Proudhon's own views on women were notorious as exemplified by his "famous dictum that woman is either housewife or courtesan" (Persis Hunt, "Feminism and Anti-Clericalism under the Commune," ibid., p. 431).

37. Karl Marx and Friedrich Engels *Gesamtausgabe (MEGA)*, New ed., (Berlin: Dietz Verlag, 1975+), Bd. 20, p. 466.

38. For these and the other proposals see **20**, pp. 187–89.

39. **20**, p. 203.

40. For example, see the "Address of the Land and Labour League to the Working Men and Women of Great Britain and Ireland" and "The Lock-Out of the Building Trades at Geneva: The General Council of the International Working Men's Association to the Working Men and Women of Europe and the United States," both in 1870, respectively in **21**, p. 138 and p. 405. The only exception was the 1869 resolution "The Belgian Massacres: To the Workmen of Europe and the United States."

41. **GC**, 1868–1870, p. 247.

42. **43**, pp. 184–85. Marx's relations with Kugelmann, interestingly, cooled after a visit to his family in 1874. The reason was Marx's objections, as he explained to Engels, to the way that he treated his wife Gertrud: "this arch-pedant, this pettifogging, bourgeois philistine has got the idea that his wife is unable to understand him, to comprehend his Faustian nature with its aspirations to a higher world outlook, and he torments the woman, who is his superior in every respect, in the most repulsive manner. So it led to a quarrel between us " (**45**, p. 46). Evidence for a different interpretation of his earlier-discussed 1868 comment to Kugulmann, this too is conveniently ignored by Buhle and Messer-Kruse.

43. **GC**, 1868–1870, p. 139.

44. Ibid., pp. 170 and 453.

45. **22**, p. 424.

46. What happens when Marx and Engels are not treated as political people is the enormous mountain of misrepresentations which claim to be explications of their views on women—a practice long in progress before Messer-Kruse's book. The most representative collection of this can be found in *Women, Class, and the Feminist Imagination: A Socialist-Feminist Reader*, eds. Karen V. Hansen and Ilene Philipson (Philadelphia: Temple University Press, 1990), particularly part I, "The Past." Almost invariably, the exegesis involves judicious selection of statements from their well-known writings upon which an entire edifice is

erected. There is never any effort to look at their practice, let alone contextualize what they wrote *and* did.

47. Most interestingly, in the United States, where Marx thought the best progress was being made on women in the workers' movement, it had been his supporters and collaborators who, more than a decade earlier, played a vanguard role in this development. "No one worked harder or more effectively to bolster support for women's rights in the immigrant labor movement than Mathilde Giesler Anneke' who had once been part of his political milieu in Cologne during the 1848 revolutions. In 1853 she joined forces with Joseph Weydemeyer to continue her work." For details see Bruce Levine, *The Spirit of 1848: German Immigrants, Labor Conflict, and the Coming of the Civil War* (Urbana: University of Illinois Press, 1992), pp. 124–25.

48. In an otherwise intelligent discussion of the similarities and differences between Tristan and Marx, Máire Cross and Tim Gray, *The Feminism of Flora Tristan* (Oxford: Berg, 1992), fall prey to gratuitous Marx-bashing with the completely unsubstantiated charge that "Marx dismissed women workers as deferential and lacking in political nous, thereby difficult to organise and mobilize" (pp. 135–36)—a claim that flies in the face of the evidence presented here. It's easy to get away with such fables when, as with Cross and Gray, Marx's political activities are ignored. That Marx and Engels were familiar with Tristan's most well-known work, *Union Ouvrière*, is testified to by their reference to her in their first collaborative effort, *The Holy Family* (**4**, pp. 19, 188).

49. *The Hague Congress*, p. 133.

50. Ibid., pp. 134–35.

51. Mary Gabriel, *Notorious Victoria: The Life of Victoria Woodhull, Uncensored* (Chapel Hill, N.C.: Algonquin Books, 1998). See also, Lois Beachy Underhill, *The Woman Who Ran for President: The Many Lives of Victoria Woodhull* (Bridgehampton, N.Y.: Bridge Works Publishing Co., 1995). Another recent biography, Barbara Goldsmith's *Other Powers: The Age of Suffrage, Spiritualism, and the Scandalous Victoria Woodhull* (New York: Alfred A. Knopf, 1998), mentions Woodhull's IWMA activities only in passing.

52. Messer-Kruse, p. 107.

53. **23**, p. 178.

54. I suspect that Margaret Atwood's feminist novel, *The Handmaiden's Tale*, was actually inspired by a comment in the *Manuscripts*. "In the approach to *woman* as the *spoil* and handmaid of communal lust is expressed the infinite degradation in which man exists for himself"**3**, p. 295.

55. **45**, pp. 197–98. Britain's undemocratic voting system, plural voting, privileged property owners like Engels by giving them more than one vote depending on the value of their property.

56. **24**, p. 340.

57. Not only did they part ways with them, but they excluded them from all the official histories of the woman suffrage movement—a practice that continued until recently; see Underhill, pp. 309–10, and Gabriel, p. 169.

58. On his modus operandi in the GC, see my *Marx and Engels*, chapter 7.

59. Messer-Kruse, p. 167.

60. Ibid., pp. 170–71.

61. *The General Council of the First International, Minutes, 1871–1872*, vol. 5 (Moscow: Progress Publishers, 1974), p. 540.

62. **44**, p. 236.

63. **44**, pp. 334, 341–42.

64. The notes, known by the title that Engels gave them, "American Split," are in their original in *The General Council*, pp. 323–32, and in the *MECW*, **23**, pp. 636–43.

65. **23**, p. 125.

66. Messer-Kruse, p. 171.

67. Ibid., p. 281 fn. 33.

68. *The Hague Congress*, p. 731.

69. **23**, p. 126.

70. Again, Hal Draper, *Karl Marx's Theory of Revolution, II* (New York: Monthly Review Press, 1978), pp. 644–53.

71. Messer-Kruse, p. 177.

72. See my *Marx and Engels*, pp. 229–30, and Hal Draper, *Karl Marx's Theory of Revolution, IV* (New York: Monthly Review Press, 1978), pp. 130–75, 270–304.

73. Messer-Kruse, p. 178.

74. Draper, *Karl Marx's Theory of Revolution, IV*, p. 271.

75. **44**, p. 418.

76. Messer-Kruse, p. 179.

77. *The Hague Congress*, p. 133–34.

78. Ibid.

79. Ibid., p. 134–35. In addition to Sorge, Benjamin Le Moussu also took minutes and what he reported, though less detailed, was consistent with Sorge's minutes. See also West's notes regarding the reasons Marx gave for denying his mandate; pp. 47–52, 694 fn. 13.

80. Messer-Kruse, p. 181.

81. **44**, p. 298.

82. **44**, p. 334.

83. **44**, p. 383.

84. Messer-Kruse, p. 164, for example, reads more into Sorge's views about the relationship between the democratic and socialist revolutions in the the United States than is warranted.

85. Philip S. Foner and Brewster Chamberlin, eds., *Friedrich Sorge's Labor Movement in the United States: A History of the American Working Class from Colonial Times to 1890* (Westport, Conn.: Greenwood Press, 1977), p. 37.

86. For the best overview, see Edwin G. Burrows and Mike Wallace, *Gotham: A History of New York City to 1898* (New York: Oxford University Press, 1999), chapter 57.

87. IWAP, August 6, 1871.

88. Noel Ignatiev's most insightful *How the Irish Became White* (New York: Routledge, 1995) underscores this claim.

89. Foner and Chamberlin, p. 37.

90. **47**, pp. 531–33.

91. **47**, p. 541.

92. Irving Barlett, *Wendell Phillips: Brahmin Radical* (Boston: Beacon Press, 1961), p. 339.

93. Ibid., p. 340.

94. Ibid., p. 348.

95. Messer-Kruse, p. 151.

96. An updated version of this line can be found in Michael Hardt and Antonio Negri's, *Empire* (Cambridge, MA: Harvard University Press, 2000). See my critique, "Class Struggle under 'Empire': In Defense of Marx and Engels," *International Socialism*, Fall 2002.

Bibliography

Primary Sources

Beaumont, Gustave de. *Marie or, Slavery in the United States*. Baltimore: The Johns Hopkins Press, 1999.

———. *Marie ou L'esclavage aux États-Unis*, 5th ed. Paris: Charles Gosselin, 1842.

Berlin, Ira, Barbara J. Fields, Thavolia Glymph, Joseph P. Reidy, and Leslie S. Rowland, eds. *Freedom: A Documantary History of Emancipation, 1861–1867: Selected from the Holdings of the National Archives of the United States*. Cambridge: Cambridge University Press, 1985.

Blassingame, John W. ed. *The Frederick Douglass Papers, Series One: Speeches, Debates, and Interviews*. New Haven: Yale University Press, 1985.

Engels, Frederick, and Lafargue, Paul and Laura. *Correspondence, Volumes I–III*. Moscow: Foreign Languages Publishing House, 1960.

Hamilton, Thomas. *Men and Manners in America*, 2 volumes. Edinburgh: William Blackwood, 1833.

Institute of Marxism-Leninism. *The General Council of the First International, Minutes, 1866–1872*, 5 vols. Moscow: Progress Publishers, 1974.

———. *The Hague Congress of the First International, September 2–7, 1872. Minutes and Documents*. Moscow: Progress Publishers, 1976.

International Workingmen's Association Papers, State Historical Society of Wisconsin.

Marx, Karl. *Capital, Volumes I–III*. New York: International Publishers, 1972.

———. *Grundrisse*, trans. Martin Nicolaus. Middlesex, England: Penguin Books, 1973.

Marx, Karl, and Frederick Engels. *Collected Works.* New York: International Publishers, 1975+. This is the primary source for all of Marx and Engels's extant writings and utterances. Of the projected fifty volumes for this series, forty-nine have been published to date. Citations from the *Collected Works*, hereafter *MECW*, will be designated by the volume, as **49**, for example, and then page(s).

———. *Gesamtausgabe (MEGA).* Berlin: Dieta Verlag, 1975+. The major difference between this new *MEGA* series—hereafter, *MEGA*₂—and the *MECW* is that it includes correspondence to Marx and Engels and their notebooks. Of the projected 114 volumes, forty-six have been published to date.

———. *Letters to Americans, 1848–1895: A Selection.* New York: International Publishers, 1969.

———. *Selected Correspondence.* Moscow: Progress Publishers, 1975.

Pierson, George Wilson. *Tocqueville in America.* Baltimore: Johns Hopkins University Press, 1996.

Tocqueville, Alexis de. *Democracy in America,* ed. Phillips Bradley, trans. Henry Reeve, Francis Bowen, and Phillips Bradley, 2 volumes. New York: Vintage Books, 1945.

———. *Oeuvres Complètes.* Paris: Editions Gallimard, 1962.

———. *Selected Letters on Politics and Society,* ed. Roger Boesche. Berkeley: University of California Press, 1985.

Secondary Sources

Applebome, Peter. "What Did We Just Learn?" *New York Times,* 22 December 2002.

Aptheker, Herbert. *American Negro Slave Revolts.* New York: International Publishers, 1987.

Balakrishnan, Gopal. "The Oracle of Post-Democracy." *New Left Review,* no. 13, Second Series (January–February 2002).

Bancroft, Frederic, ed. *Speeches, Correspondence and Political Papers of Carl Schurz.* New York: G.P. Putnam, 1913.

Barlett, Irving. *Wendell Phillips: Brahmin Radical.* Boston: Beacon Press, 1961.

Bergquist, James M. "The Political Attitudes of the German Immigrant in Illinois, 1848–1860," Ph.D. diss., Northwestern University, 1966.

Berlin, Ira. "Who Freed the Slaves? Emancipation and Meaning." In *Major Problems in the Civil War and Reconstruction,* ed. Michael Perman. Boston: Houghton Mifflin, 1998.

Blight, David. *Frederick Douglass' Civil War: Keeping Faith in Jubilee.* Baton Rouge: Louisiana State University Press, 1989.

Boesche, Roger. *The Strange Liberalism of Alexis de Tocqueville.* Ithaca: Cornell University Press, 1987.

Boston, Ray. *British Chartists in America, 1839–1900.* Totowa, N.J.: Rowman, Littlefield, 1971.

Breitman, George. *Malcolm X Speaks.* New York: Grove Press, 1966.

———. ed. *Leon Trotsky on Black Nationalism and Self-Determination.* New York: Pathfinder Press, 1978.

Buhle, Mari Jo. *Women and American Socialism, 1870–1920.* Urbana: University of Illinois Press, 1981.

Burrows, Edwin G., and Mike Wallace. *Gotham: A History of New York City to 1898.* New York: Oxford University Press, 1999.

Castro, Fidel, and Nelson Mandela. *How Far We Shaves Have Come.* New York: Pathfinder Books, 1991.

Chong, Dennis. *Collective Action and the Civil Rights Movement.* Chicago: University of Chicago Press, 1991.

Collins, Henry, and Chimen Abramsky. *Karl Marx and the British Labour Movement: Years of the First International.* London: Macmillan and Co., 1965.

Connolly, William E. "Tocqueville, Territory and Violence." *Theory, Culture & Society* 11 (1994).

Cross, Coy F. *"Go West Young Man!": Horace Greeley's Vision for America.* Albuquerque: University of New Mexico Press, 1995.

Cross, Márie, and Tim Gray. *The Feminism of Flora Tristan.* Oxford: Berg, 1992.

Davis, William C. *An Honorable Defeat: The Last Days of the Confederate Government.* New York: Harcourt Brace, 2001.

Derfler, Leslie. *Paul Lafargue and the Founding of French Marxism, 1842–1882.* Cambridge: Harvard University Press, 1991.

Dobbs, Farrell. *Revolutionary Continuity: The Early Years 1848–1917.* New York: Monad Press, 1980.

Draper, Hal. *Karl Marx's Theory of Revolution, Vols. I–IV.* New York: Monthly Review Press, 1977–1990.

———. *The Annotated Communist Manifesto.* Berkeley: Center for Socialist History, 1984.

———. *The Marx-Engels Chronicle: A Day-by-Day Chronology of Marx and Engels' Life and Activity.* New York: Schocken, 1985.

———. *The Marx-Engels Register: A Complete Bibliography of Marx and Engels' Individual Writings.* New York: Schocken, 1985.

———. *The Marx-Engels Glossary: Glossary to the Chronicle and Register, and Index to the Glossary.* New York: Schocken, 1986.

———. *The Adventures of the Communist Manifesto*. Berkeley: Center for Socialist History, 1994.

Drescher, Seymour. *Dilemmas of Democracy: Tocqueville and Modernization*. Pittsburgh: University of Pittsburgh Press, 1968.

———. *Tocqueville and Beaumont on Social Reform*. New York: Harper Torchbooks, 1968.

———. "Servile Insurection and John Brown's Body in Europe." In *His Soul Goes Marching On: Responses to John Brown and the Harpers Ferry Raid*, ed. Paul Finkelman. Charlottesville: University Press of Virginia, 1995.

DuBois, W. E. B. *John Brown*. New York: International Publishers, 1969.

———. *Black Reconstruction in America*. New York: Athenum, 1962.

Easton, Loyd D. *Hegel's First American Followers: The Ohio Hegelians: John B. Stallo, Peter Kaufman, Moncure Conway, and August Willich, with Key Writings*. Athens: Ohio University Press, 1966.

Fehrenbacher, Don E. "Kansas, Republicanism, and the Crisis of the Union." In *Major Problems in the Civil War and Reconstruction*, ed. Michael Perman. Boston: Houghton Mifflin Co., 1998.

Ferrer, Ada. *Insurgent Cuba: Race, Nation, and Revolution, 1868–1898*. Chapel Hill: University of North Carolina Press, 1999.

Feuer, Lewis. "The North American Origin of Marx's Socialism." *Western Political Quarterly* 16, no. 1 (March 1963).

Fields, Barbara. "Slavery, Race and Ideology in the United States of America." *New Left Review* no. 181 (May–June 1990).

Fitzhugh, George. *Cannibals All! or Slaves without Masters*, ed. C. Vann Woodward. Cambridge: Harvard University Press, 1988.

Fletcher, George P. *Our Secret Constitution: How Lincoln Redefined American Democracy*. New York: Oxford University Press, 2001.

Foner, Eric. *Reconstruction: America's Unfinished Revolution, 1863–1877*. New York: Harper & Row, 1988.

———. *Free Soil, Free Labor, Free Men: The Ideology of the Republican Party before the Civil War*. New York: Oxford University Press, 1995.

———. *The Story of American Freedom*. New York: W. W. Norton, 1998.

Foner, Philip S. *American Socialism and Black Americans: From the Age of Jackson to World War II*. Westport, Conn.: Greenwood Press, 1977.

———. *The Great Labor Uprising of 1877*. New York: Monad Press, 1977.

———. *British Labor and the American Civil War*. New York: Holmes and Meier, 1981.

———. *Organized Labor and the Black Worker, 1619–1981*. New York: International Publishers, 1981.

————. *The Workingmen's Party of the United States: A History of the First Marxist Party in the Americas.* Minneapolis: MEP Publications, 1984.

Foner, Philip S., and Brewster Chamberlin, eds. *Friedrich Sorge's Labor Movement in the United States: A History of the American Working Class from Colonial Times to 1890.* Westport, Conn.: Greenwood Press, 1977.

Foner, Philip S., and Herbert Shapiro, eds. *Northern Labor and Antislavery: A Documentary History.* Westport, Conn.: Greenwood Press, 1994.

Frederickson, George. *White Supremacy: A Comparative Study in American and South African History.* New York: Oxford University Press, 1981.

Fuente, Alejandro de la. *A Nation for All: Race, Inequality, and Politics in Twentieth-Century Cuba.* Chapel Hill: University of North Carolina Press, 2001.

Furet, François. *The Passing of an Illusion: The Idea of Communism in the Twentieth Century.* Chicago: University of Chicago Press, 1999.

Gabriel, Mary. *Notorious Victoria: The Life of Victoria Woodhull, Uncensored.* Chapel Hill, N.C.: Algonquin Books, 1998.

Genovese, Eugene. "Marxian Interpretations of the Slave South." In *Towards a New Past: Dissenting Essays in American History*, ed. Barton J. Bernstein. New York: Pantheon Books, 1968.

Glatthaar, Joseph T. "Black Glory: The African-American Role in Union Victory." In *Why the Confederacy Lost*, ed. Gabor S. Boritt. New York: Oxford University Press, 1992.

Goldfield, Michael. *The Color of Politics: Race and the Mainspring of American Politics.* New York: The New Press, 1997.

Goldsmith, Barbara. *Other Powers: The Age of Suffrage, Spiritualism, and the Scandalous Victoria Woodhull.* New York: Alfred A. Knopf, 1998.

Grégoire, Henri. *An Enquiry Concerning the Intellectual and Moral Facilities, and Literature of Negroes.* New York: M.E. Sharpe, 1997.

Gronowicz, Anthony. *Race and Class Politics in New York City before the Civil War.* Boston: Northeastern University Press, 1998.

Hansen, Karen V., and Ilene Philipson, eds. *Women, Class, and the Feminist Imagination: A Socialist-Feminist Reader*, Philadelphia: Temple University Press, 1990.

Harrison, Royden. "British Labour and American Slavery." In *Before the Socialists: Studies in Labour and Politics, 1861–1881.* London: Routledge and Kegan Paul, 1965.

Hayward, Jack. *After the French Revolution: Six Critics of Democracy and Nationalism.* New York: New York University Press, 1991.

Herreshoff, David. *The Origins of American Marxism: From the Transcendentalists to De Leon.* New York: Pathfinder Press, 1967.

Herriott, F. I. "The Conference in the Deutsches Haus Chicago, May 14–15, 1860." Illinois State Historical Library, *Transactions of the Illinois State Historical Society for the Year 1928*, no. 35, 1928.

Holmes, Steven. "Both Sides Now." *The New Republic*, March 4 & 11, 2002.

Ignatiev, Noel. *How the Irish Became White*. New York: Routledge, 1995.

Jaffa, Harry V. *A New Birth of Freedom: Abraham Lincoln and the Coming of the Civil War*. Lanham, Md.: Rowman & Littlefield, 2000.

Janara, Laura. "After the Mother: Authority, Autonomy and Passion in Tocqueville's Democracy in America." Ph.D. diss., University of Minnesota, 1998.

Jardin, André. *Tocqueville: A Biography*. New York: Farrar, Straus, Giroux, 1988.

Jennings, Lawrence C. *French Anti-Slavery: The Movement for the Abolition of Slavery in France, 1802–1848*. New York: Cambridge University Press, 2000.

Jones, Howard. *Union in Peril: The Crisis over British Intervention in the Civil War*. Chapel Hill: The University of North Carolina Press, 1992.

———. *Abraham Lincoln and a New Birth of Freedom: The Union and Slavery in the Diplomacy of the Civil War*. Lincoln: University of Nebraska Press, 1999.

Kahan, Alan S. *Aristocratic Liberalism: The Social and Political Thought of Jacob Burckhardt, John Stuart Mill, and Alexis de Tocqueville*. New York: Oxford University Press, 1992.

Katz, Philip M. *From Appomattox to Montmartre: Americans and the Paris Commune*. Cambridge: Harvard University Press, 1998.

Keyssar, Alexander. *The Right to Vote: The Contested History of Democracy in the United States*. New York: Basic Books, 2000.

Klingaman, William K. *Abraham Lincoln and the Road to Emancipation, 1861–1865*. New York: Viking Penguin, 2001.

Klinkner, Philip A. with Rogers Smith. *The Unsteady March: The Rise and Decline of Racial Equality in America*. Chicago: The University of Chicago Press, 1999.

Kluger, Richard. *The Paper: The Life and Death of the* New York Herald Tribune. New York: Alfred A. Knopf, 1986.

Lause, Mark A. "The American Radicals & Organized Marxism: The Initial Experience, 1869–1874." *Labor History*, 33, no. 1 (fall 1992).

Lawler, Peter Augustine. "Tocqueville on Slavery, Ancient and Modern." In *Comparative Issues in Slavery*, ed. Paul Finkelman. New York: Garland Publishing, Inc., 1989.

Levin, Michael. *The Spectre of Democracy: The Rise of Modern Democracy As Seen by Its Critics.* New York: New York University Press, 1992.

Levine, Bruce. *The Spirit of 1848: German Immigrants, Labor Conflict and the Coming of the Civil War.* Urbana: University of Illinois Press, 1992.

———. *Half Slave and Half Free: The Roots of Civil War.* New York: Hill and Wang, 1992.

———. *The Migration of Ideology and the Contested Meaning of Freedom: German-Americans in the Mid-Nineteenth Century.* Occasional Paper No. 7. Washington, D.C.: German Historical Institute, 1992.

Lewis, David Levering. *W. E. B. DuBois: The Fight for Equality and the American Century, 1919–1963.* New York: Henry Holt, 2000.

Lipset, Seymour. "Why No Socialism in the United States?" In *Radicalism in the Contemporary Age,* eds. Seweryn Bialer and Sophia Sluzar. Boulder, Colo.: Westview Press, 1977.

———. *American Exceptionalism: A Double-Edged Sword.* New York: W. W. Norton & Co., 1996.

Logan, Kevin. "The *Bee-Hive* Newspaper and British Working Class Attitudes toward the American Civil War." *Civil War History* 22 (December, 1976).

Macpherson, C. B. *The Life and Times of Liberal Democracy.* Oxford: Oxford University Press, 1977.

McPherson, James M. *The Negro's Civil War: How American Negroes Felt and Acted during the War for the Union.* New York: Vintage Books, 1965.

———. *Abraham Lincoln and the Second American Revolution.* New York: Oxford University Press, 1991.

———. *Drawn with the Sword: Reflections on the American Civil War.* New York: Oxford University Press, 1996.

Mandel, Bernard. *Labor: Free and Slave—Workingmen and the Anti-Slavery Movement in the United States.* New York: Associated Authors, 1955.

Messer-Kruse, Thomas. *The Yankee International: Maxism and the American Reform Tradition, 1848–1876.* Chapel Hill and London: University of North Carolina Press, 1998.

Morais, Herbert. "Marx and Engels on America." *Science and Society* 12, no. 1 (winter 1948).

Morrison, Samuel Eliot. *The Oxford History of the American People.* New York: Oxford University Press, 1965.

Nadel, Stanley. *Little Germany: Ethnicity, Religion, and Class in New York City, 1845–80* Chicago: University of Illinois Press, 1990.

Neely, Mark. *The Fate of Liberty: Abraham Lincoln and Civil Liberties.* New York: Oxford University Press, 1991.

Nimtz, August. "Marx and Engels—The Unsung Heroes of the Democratic Breakthrough." *Science and Society* (summer 1999).
———. *Marx and Engels: Their Contribution to the Democratic Breakthrough.* Albany: State University Press of New York, 2000.
———. "Marxism." In *The Oxford Companion to Politics of the World*, ed. Joel Krieger. New York: Oxford University Press, 1993 and 2001.
———. "The Eurocentric Marx and Engels and Other Related Myths." In *Marxism, Modernity, and Postcolonial Studies*, eds. Crystal Bartolovich and Neil Lazarus. Cambridge: Cambridge University Press, 2002.
———. "Class Struggle under 'Empire': In Defense of Marx and Engels." *International Socialism* (fall 2002).
Obermann, Karl. *Joseph Weydemeyer: Pioneer of American Socialism.* New York: International Publishers, 1947.
———. *Joseph Weydemeyer: Ein Lebensbild.* Berlin: Dietz Verlag, 1968.
Osofsky, Gilbert. "Abolitionists, Irish Immigrants, and the Dilemmas of Romantic Nationalism." *American Historical Review* 80, no. 4 (October 1975).
Peled, Y. "From Theology to Sociology: Bruno Bauer and Karl Marx on the Question of Jewish Emancipation." *History of Political Thought* 13, no. 3 (fall 1992): 463–485.
Pessen, Edward. *Riches, Class, and Power before the Civil War.* Lexington, Mass.: D.C. Heath, 1973.
Putnam, Robert. "A Better Society in a Time of War." *New York Times*, 19 October 2001.
Rehmann, Jan. "'Abolition' of Civil Society?: Remarks on a Widespread Misunderstanding in the Interpretation of 'Civil Society.'" *Socialism and Democracy* 13, no. 2 (fall–winter 1999).
Reinhardt, Mark. *The Art of Being Free: Taking Liberties with Tocqueville, Marx, and Arendt.* Ithaca: Cornell University Press, 1997.
Richardson, Heather Cox. *The Death of Reconstruction: Race, Labor, and Politics in the Post–Civil War North, 1865–1901.* Cambridge: Harvard University Press, 2001.
Rios, Ana Maria. "'My Mother Was a Slave, Not Me!' Black Peasantry and Regional Politics in Southeast Brazil: 1870–1940." Ph.D. diss., University of Minnesota, 2001.
Robinson, Donald L. *Slavery in the Structure of American Politics, 1765–1820.* New York: Harcourt Brace Jovanovich, Inc., 1971.
Roediger, David. *The Wages of Whiteness: Race and the Making of the American Working Class.* Rev. ed. New York: Verso, 1999.
Rolle, Andrew. *John Charles Frémont: Character as Destiny.* Norman: University of Oklahoma Press, 1991.

Rubel, Maximilien. "Notes on Marx's Conception of Democracy." *New Politics* 1, no. 2 (winter 1962).

———. "Marx and American Democracy." In *Marx and the Western World*, ed. Nicholas Lobkowicz. London: University of Notre Dame Press, 1967.

Schlüter, Herman. *Lincoln, Labor and Slavery*. New York: Socialist Literature Co., 1913.

Schurz, Carl. *The Reminiscences of Carl Schurz, Vol. 1, 1829–1852*. New York: The McClure Company, 1907.

Sellers, Charles. *The Market Revolution: Jacksonian America, 1815–1846*. New York: Oxford University Press, 1991.

Sifakis, Stewart. *Who Was Who in the Civil War*. New York: Facts on File Publications, 1988.

Smith, Rogers M. *Civic Ideals: Conflicting Visions of Citizenship in U.S. History*. New Haven: Yale University Press, 1997.

Teeple, Gary. *Marx's Critique of Politics: 1842–1847*. Toronto: University of Toronto Press, 1984.

Thomas, Edith. "The Women of the Commune." *The Massachusetts Review* 12, no. 3 (1971).

Trotsky, Leon. *The Revolution Betrayed: What Is the Soviet Union and Where Is It Going?* New York: Pathfinder Press, 1972.

Underhill, Lois Beachy. *The Woman Who Ran for President: The Many Lives of Victoria Woodhull*. Bridgehampton, N.Y.: Bridge Works Publishing Co., 1995.

Vogel, Jeffrey. "The Tragedy of History." *New Left Review*, no. 220 (November–December 1996).

Wacquant, Loïc. "From Slavery to Mass Incarceration." *New Left Review*, no. 13 (January–February 2002).

Weiner, Robert. "Karl Marx's Vision of America: A Bibliographical and Bibliographical Sketch." *The Review of Politics* 42, no. 4 (October 1980).

Welch, Cheryl B. "Colonial Violence and the Rhetoric of Evasion." *Political Theory* 31, no. 2 (April 2003).

Weyl, Nathaniel. *Karl Marxist: Racist*. New Rochelle, N.Y.: Arlington House, 1979.

Wilentz, Sean. *Chants Democratic: New York City and the Rise of the American Working Class, 1788–1850*. New York: Oxford University Press, 1984.

Willich, August. *The Army, Standing Army or National Army?: An Essay*. Cincinnati: A. Frey, 1866.

Wolin, Sheldon. *Tocqueville between Two Worlds: The Making of a Political and Theoretical Life*. Princeton, N.J.: Princeton University Press, 2001.

Zucker, A. E. ed. *The Forty-Eighters: Political Refugees of the German Revolution of 1848*. New York: Columbia University Press, 1950.

Index

Italicized titles indicate that the work is by Marx and/or Engels. Works by other authors have the author's name(s) following the italicized title, in parentheses, or "*See.*" Periodicals are italicized followed by their place of publication in brackets.

About the Author

August H. Nimtz, Jr. came of age in Jim Crow New Orleans and was politically forged by the Civil Rights movement, Black nationalism, the Cuban revolution and other Third World revolutionary upheavals of the 1960s and 1970s. He is Professor of Political Science and African American and African Studies and member of the Academy of Distinguished Teachers at the University of Minnesota in Minneapolis, Minnesota. In addition to *Islam and Politics in East Africa* (1980), he is the author of *Marx and Engels: Their Contribution to the Democratic Breakthrough* (2000) and a number of related articles in edited volumes and journals.